College Admission Essays For Dummies®

Cheat Sheet

Most Commonly Suggested Topics

- A significant experience
- A person who influenced you
- Your views on a current issue in your school, community, country, or in the world
- Important extracurricular activity
- Why this university or college?

Good Ways to Organize Your Essay

- Narrative and interpretation
- Pro/con on an issue
- Argument or assertion and supporting evidence
- Description and interpretation

Grammar Checks

- Verbs — determine tense, match singular or plural verb to the subject
- Pronouns — check singular/plural, be sure that the meaning of the pronoun is clear, choose case (the difference between "who" and "whom" or "he" and "him," for example)
- Sentence completeness — be sure every sentence has a subject and verb and expresses a complete thought
- Punctuation — place an endmark (period, question mark, exclamation point) at the end of each sentence, delete or insert commas, review quotation marks

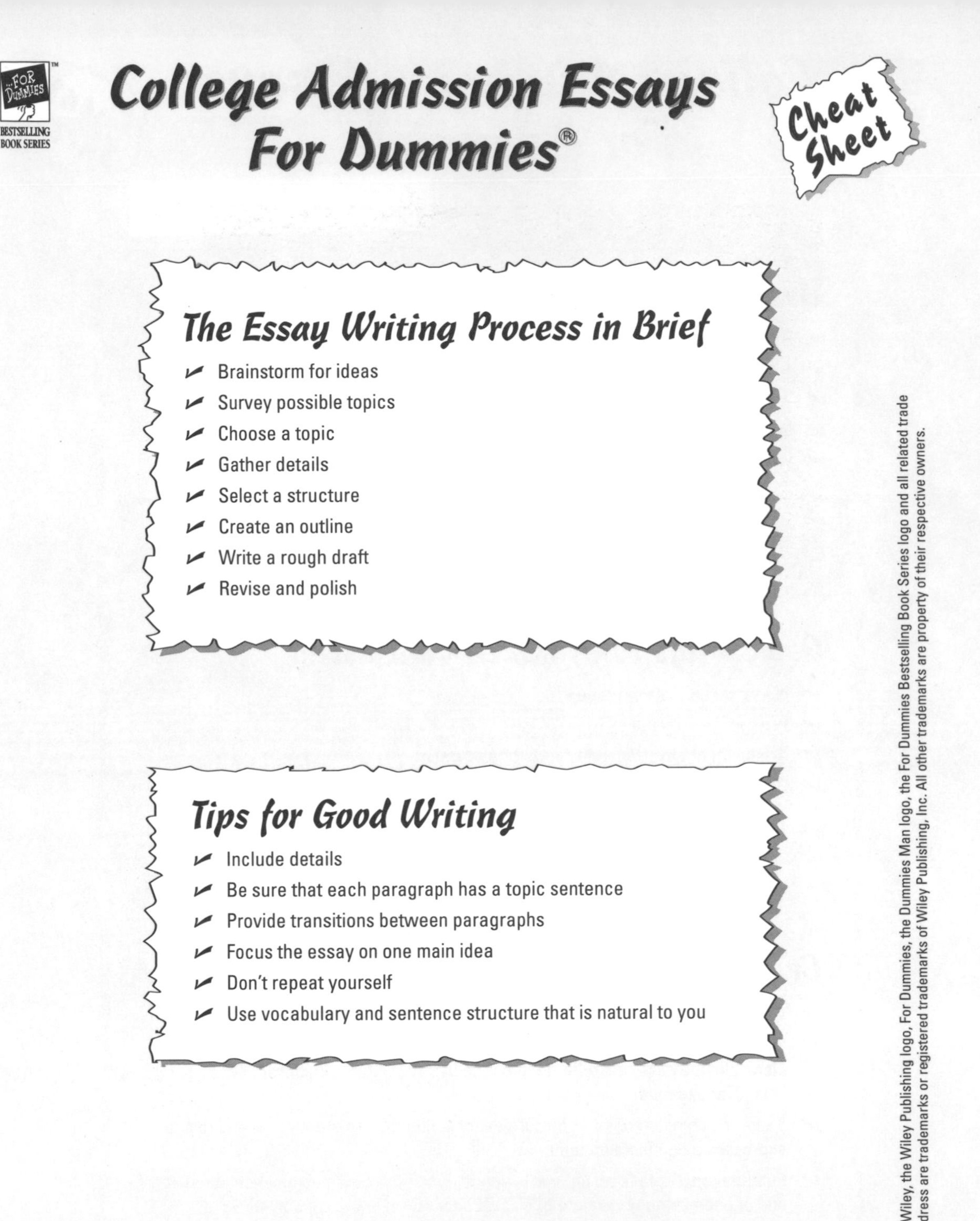

College Admission Essays For Dummies®

Cheat Sheet

The Essay Writing Process in Brief

- Brainstorm for ideas
- Survey possible topics
- Choose a topic
- Gather details
- Select a structure
- Create an outline
- Write a rough draft
- Revise and polish

Tips for Good Writing

- Include details
- Be sure that each paragraph has a topic sentence
- Provide transitions between paragraphs
- Focus the essay on one main idea
- Don't repeat yourself
- Use vocabulary and sentence structure that is natural to you

Item 5482-4.
For more information about Wiley Publishing, call 1-800-762-2974.

by Geraldine Woods

Wiley Publishing, Inc.

College Admission Essays For Dummies®

Published by
Wiley Publishing, Inc.
909 Third Avenue
New York, NY 10022
www.wiley.com

Published by Wiley Publishing, Inc., Indianapolis, Indiana

Published simultaneously in Canada

For general information on our other products and services or to obtain technical support, please contact our Customer Care Department within the U.S. at 800-762-2974, outside the U.S. at 317-572-3993, or fax 317-572-4002.

Wiley also publishes its books in a variety of electronic formats. Some content that appears in print may not be available in electronic books.

Library of Congress Control Number: 2002114847

ISBN: 0-7645-5482-4

Manufactured in the United States of America

10 9 8 7 6 5 4 3 2

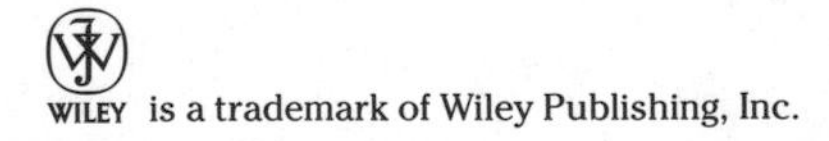

About the Author

Geraldine Woods teaches English and directs the independent study program at a high school for gifted students. Throughout her thirty-year teaching career, she has guided a multitude of harried and anxious seniors through the process of writing successful college admission essays. She has written 40 books, give or take a few, including *English Grammar For Dummies,* and *Research Papers For Dummies*. She loves bookstores and libraries, minor-league baseball, Chinese food, and the novels of Jane Austen. The mother of a grown son (Tom, a lawyer), she lives in New York City with Harry (her husband of 30 years) and parakeets Alice and Archie.

Dedication

For T. and K., beginning their adventure; and for H., continuing ours.

Author's Acknowledgments

My sincere thanks to Stephen Singer, a college counselor whose encyclopedic knowledge of higher education is exceeded only by the generosity with which he shares his time and wisdom. I am also grateful to Tom Katzenbach and Barbara Tischler for their helpful advice, to Linda Brandon for her diligent editing, to Pam Mourouzis for her insight during the outlining stage of this book, to Turner O'Neal for his useful comments, and to Lisa Queen for her support. I am exceedingly grateful to the applicants who cheered me on and allowed me to include their essays in this book: Kristina Bennard, Ruthie Birger, Jordyn Cosme, Lindsay Danas, Shanah Einzig, Marc Philippe Eskinazi, Leonard Fishman, Danielle Ginach, Robert Gould, Horace Andrew Patterson, Justin Pattner, Mark Sanger, and Wontaek Shin.

Publisher's Acknowledgments

We're proud of this book; please send us your comments through our Dummies online registration form located at www.dummies.com/register/.

Some of the people who helped bring this book to market include the following:

Acquisitions, Editorial, and Media Development

Project Editor: Linda Brandon

Acquisitions Editor: Pam Mourouzis

Copy Editor: Linda Brandon

Technical Editor: Turner O'Neal

Editorial Supervisor: Michelle Hacker

Cartoons: Rich Tennant, www.the5thwave.com

Production

Project Coordinator: Kristie Rees

Layout and Graphics: Amanda Carter, Stephanie D. Jumper, Michael Kruzil, Jackie Nicholas, Barry Offringa, Scott Tullis

Proofreaders: John Greenough, TECHBOOKS Production Services

Indexer: TECHBOOKS Production Services

Special Help

Michelle Hacker

Publishing and Editorial for Consumer Dummies

Diane Graves Steele, Vice President and Publisher, Consumer Dummies

Joyce Pepple, Acquisitions Director, Consumer Dummies

Kristin A. Cocks, Product Development Director, Consumer Dummies

Michael Spring, Vice President and Publisher, Travel

Brice Gosnell, Publishing Director, Travel

Suzanne Jannetta, Editorial Director, Travel

Publishing for Technology Dummies

Andy Cummings, Vice President and Publisher, Dummies Technology/General User

Composition Services

Gerry Fahey, Vice President of Production Services

Debbie Stailey, Director of Composition Services

Contents at a Glance

Table of Contents

Part V: Analyzing Questions from Real Applications 219

Chapter 18: Composing Essays Starring You 221

Chapter 19: Describing Significant Strangers and Friends: Essays About Other People 239

Chapter 20: Responding to Essay Questions in the Subject Areas 253

Introduction

"First class?"

"Yes, definitely definitely yes."

The postal clerk prints a label, stamps the thick envelope, and tosses it into a bin. As the envelope lands on its side, one corner folds back. The customer winces, looks away, and then looks again. "Excuse me, you wrinkled my envelope."

No, the postal clerk doesn't describe the many machines the envelope will pass through before it arrives at its destination. Nor does he point out all that can go wrong with this particular letter, including jammed gears and misplaced mailbags. Instead, he glances at the address and smiles sympathetically. "College application?" he asks, gently repositioning the envelope on top of the pile.

When you send that all-important application to a college, grad school, or scholarship committee, you probably won't ask the post office to deliver your envelope without wrinkles, as one of my students did. But I bet you sympathize with her panic! These days more and more applicants vie for the same number of slots at top schools. Yet much of the application process — from the way the post office delivers the mail to the way the application is viewed — is out of your hands. You can't, for instance, predict how your qualifications mesh with the needs of your preferred university. If you're a tuba player and the college orchestra is desperate for bassoonists, you may be out of luck when acceptance letters are sent out. And by the time you're filling in little blanks on the application form with a list of your courses and activities, you can't do much to improve your school record.

Fortunately, one huge element of the admission process *is* completely under your control. Most colleges and graduate schools give you the opportunity or even require you to write a "personal statement," an essay about yourself. Still others ask for several essays on topics ranging from "Why do you want to attend the University of Wherever?" to "Describe a significant failure in your life." Even more fortunately, the college admission essay is open to improvement right up until the filing deadline. Best of all, the essay provides opportunities that no other section of the application allows. Apart from the personal interview, the essay is the only moment in the admission process when your true self shines through, when you become more than a set of statistics.

However, the essay also comes equipped with "sand traps" — phoniness, bad grammar, and vagueness, to name only three — that can sabotage your application. *College Admission Essays For Dummies* gives you a road map around those sand traps. This book helps you decide what to write and then guides you through the process of creating essays that present your best self to the admissions committee. Because many scholarships require personal statements, this book may also pay off in cold, hard cash. Moreover, you'll find *College Admission Essays For Dummies* useful even after you plunk down your last tuition payment. Chances are a few employment-related essays are in your future, especially if you're applying for internships or jobs on the professional level.

How to Use This Book

Twenty-five hours in a day. That's what you need, right? If you're applying for admission or scholarship money, you know that just typing your social security number eight zillion times takes up a month of your life. You don't need another chore, but you do need help. Never fear. *College Admission Essays For Dummies* demystifies the process of writing an application essay — from topic search through final draft, without wasting your time. Of course, I like to imagine you glued to these pages, devouring every syllable I wrote. But I'm a realist. I know you throw this volume into a corner every time your instant messaging beeps or your history professor assigns a paper. No problem. Just gallop through the table of contents to see what's where. Also check out the section in this Introduction entitled "How This Book Is Organized." Then turn to the chapters that deal with the part of the process currently tying your stomach into a knot: getting started (Chapters 2 and 6), creating an outline (Chapter 8), polishing (Chapter 15), and so forth. After you've grasped what you need to do, plop yourself in front of the computer and get to work. Keep a copy of the book nearby, so the next time you're stuck, you can turn to *College Admission Essays* for more assistance.

Two special features of *College Admission Essays For Dummies* ease the writing process. The appendix contains a questionnaire — a personal inventory — that helps you discover the best topics for your essays. Also, throughout the book, I've scattered real admission essays from students who were very happy when the colleges of their choice mailed out decision letters. These essays will help you see what you're aiming for. I've also included excerpts from some fictional clunkers, written by yours truly, so you'll know what to avoid.

Foolish Assumptions

I've got an Imaginary Reader, whom I affectionately call I.R., perched on the edge of my desk. I consult I.R. often when I'm writing. In my fantasy, I.R. is up to the eyeballs in viewbooks and financial aid forms, thinking hard about the future. I assume that my Imaginary Reader is serious about the application process, wanting to choose — and be chosen for — the best possible university, the one that will provide a great educational and life experience. I also see my Imaginary Reader as someone who is a little insecure about writing, maybe not the usual English-report sort of paper, but certainly the "let-me-tell-you-about-myself" type of essay. And who isn't insecure about such a task? After all, summing up a life experience, at the age of 18 or the age of 81, is daunting. I.R. may even be a bit fearful, assuming that one sentence will make or break the entire application. Everything in *College Admission Essays For Dummies* is aimed at this Imaginary Reader — who I assume resembles you, the real reader. I wrote *College Admission Essays For Dummies* to calm your anxieties, improve your writing skills, and help you complete your application essays on time and on target. I also wrote *College Admission Essays For Dummies* to demystify the Authority Figures who will judge your work — the College Admissions Office.

How This Book Is Organized

Part I of *College Admission Essays For Dummies* explains the basics: what you're writing, why, when, and for whom. Part II walks you through the preliminary steps of writing, providing proven techniques for jump-starting your creative process. Part III handles the nuts and bolts of good writing and Part IV shows you how to put the finishing touches on a final draft. Part V concentrates on specifics, alerting you to the best approaches to real, lifted-from-actual-application essay questions. Check out Part VI — the famous *Dummies* Part of Tens — to puncture your myths about the essay, to learn what you *must* include in yours, and to find great sources of inspiration. The appendix is a questionnaire designed to help you explore your own brain for possible essay topics. Now read on for more detail about *College Admission Essays For Dummies.*

Part I: Putting Yourself on Paper

Can't staple a living, breathing, 100-something-pound human onto an application form? Write an essay instead. This part tells you how to capture the crucial stories that reveal who you are. It also explains why "putting yourself on paper" promotes your chances of receiving that fat, lovely acceptance letter.

Part I gets you started on self-discovery, guides you in the creation of a writing timetable, and shows you how to seek help without violating any university, school, parental, or personal code of honesty.

Part II: Getting Your Head Ready for Writing

I'm in the mood for . . . for what? If you answered, "Anything but writing," this part is for you. If you answered, "Writing my college admission essay," this part is also for you. Part II explains how to place yourself in the mental state most suitable for good writing. Part II also shows you how to gather ideas, focus on a topic, and choose the best structure for your essay.

Part III: Writing the Rough Draft

Fire up those electrons. Time to put words on the page (er, screen). This part demystifies the rough draft, explaining why you should "show," not "tell," your story. It gives you the lowdown on topic sentences, use of detail, and strong introductions and conclusions. For those who find themselves alphabetizing the sock drawer when they're supposed to be writing, Part III also explains how to overcome writer's block.

Part IV: I'd Like to Finish before Retirement Age: The Final Draft

This part tackles (gulp) grammar and spelling, but without all those horrible terms that we English teachers love so much. Part IV offers style pointers too — how to choose the best tone, create transitions, and avoid wordiness and repetition. Finally, this part tells you everything you always wanted to know about format, including such exciting topics as fonts and margins.

Part V: Analyzing Questions from Real Applications

Most admission essay questions ask you to write about yourself or about people who have influenced your life. A few resemble school assignments: analysis of a quotation or a current event, for example. Some schools specialize in zingers — really off-the-wall questions that test your creativity. Part V tips you off to the best strategies for the most common questions and provides sample essays. Part V also shows you how to write successful "short answers" — those 200-or-so word queries about your favorite extracurricular activity, career plan, and the like.

Part VI: The Part of Tens

Need inspiration? Check out the list of ten great essays. This part also punctures ten myths about the admission essay and tells you what you absolutely *must* do to write a good one.

The appendix contains a questionnaire to help you take stock of all sorts of personal details. After you complete the inventory, you'll have enough material for all the essays you'll ever need.

Icons Used in This Book

Throughout the book are little signs located in the margins to guide you toward important information. Here's what each sign means:

The material accompanying this icon is more valuable than a message from a jockey about the favorite's chances to win the sixth race. The Tip icon alerts you to shortcuts, ways to improve writing style, and other helpful hints for writing a successful college admission essay.

The Warning icon is like the sturdy fence at the edge of a cliff. This icon tells you how to sidestep the most common errors of admission essays and prevent some seriously nasty falls.

The Winning Strategy icon reveals a series of steps that make the process of writing an admission essay easier, more efficient, and more successful. Think of the Winning Strategy icon as the blueprint for an award-winning building.

"This above all; to thine own self be true," wrote Shakespeare. Good advice! But you can't be true to yourself without truly knowing yourself. This icon accompanies hints on exploring the subject of your essay, you.

Already have a bachelor's degree? Planning to attend law, medical, or business school? This icon's for you. It accompanies material of special interest to those who are applying to graduate or professional school.

Where to Go from Here

If you've got the applications, thumb through them and make a list of essay questions and deadlines. If you haven't yet received the applications, turn to Chapter 1 for a quick overview of the types of questions often asked. Whether or not you have the applications, begin to fill out the "Personal Inventory" in the appendix of this book and spend a few moments thinking about your strengths and weaknesses as a writer. Dip into the sections of *College Admission Essays For Dummies* that address the parts of the writing process most likely to be hard for you. (Don't know what the writing process is? Check out Chapter 5.) And take heart: You *will* write the essay and you *will* survive the application era of your life.

Part I
Putting Yourself on Paper

"I'm just having Mom edit a few lines and then I'm going to add in the music. If my essay is well-written and a chart-topper, surely, they'll have to let me in."

In this part . . .

What is it, why do they want it, who reads it, and how can I possibly write it and still have time for my favorite activities, sleeping and eating? This part answers all those questions about the college admission essay and a few more besides. For definitions, timetables, and tips on questions, check out Chapter 1. Chapter 2 explains how to gather information about the subject of your essay (you) and Chapter 3 describes the people you're writing for (the admissions committee). Chapter 4 tells you how to stay on the right side of the (academic) law and how to keep your parents out of your hair while you write.

Chapter 1

Becoming More Than a Statistic: What the Essay Does for You

In This Chapter

- Taking a look at yourself as the subject
- Knowing your audience
- Creating a timetable for writing
- Discovering how to live your life while writing the essay
- Focusing on the process of essay writing
- Maintaining a sense of perspective during the application process

When's the last time you answered the question "Who are you?" with this response:

> I'm an SAT 600 verbal, 580 math with a B average overall. Pleased to meet you!

Not recently, I bet. Yet for the most part your admissions or scholarship application answers the "Who are you?" question in just that way. But you're *not* a standardized test score or a list of grades. You're a person. The admission essay is your chance to become more than a number to the Authority Figures who judge your candidacy.

In this chapter I explain *why* you're writing an essay and *what* your essay should accomplish. I also tackle *when* — an important issue for those of us who are frantically overworked (in other words, everybody).

Painting a Portrait of You, the Applicant

What does the admissions or scholarship committee learn from a typical application? Name, address, social security number, date and place of birth, family background, academic and career plans, date and place of schooling, courses and grades, extracurricular activities, and standardized test scores. Fine. All that information is important. But what about your struggle to overcome your fear of physics and the 22 consecutive lunch hours you gave up in order to construct the perfect magnetism experiment? And what about the change in your worldview after you read Virginia Woolf's great novel, *To the Lighthouse*? You can't fill in the blanks with a burning desire for social justice or a passion for visual arts. Yet those factors are as much a part of you as your A in English or C in physical education.

Granted, the letters of recommendation submitted with your application may address your personality and experiences. However, you have no control over the content of those letters, and frankly, not all recommendation writers actually know how to write well. Their letters may be vague and limited to statements like "So-and-so is a fine person. Please accept him." The only way you can be sure that the application paints a true portrait of you, the applicant, is to write at length about yourself. Enter the essay.

I say "essay" because in English-teacher terminology, that's what you're writing: a short interpretive or analytical piece of literature with a personal point of view. On applications, the essay is often called a "personal statement" or has no name at all, just a large blank space and instructions to write about "an experience that has shaped you" or "a person who matters to you" and the like. Whatever it's called, this piece of writing is important. All by itself it can't make or break your application's chances, but it's often the deciding factor for close calls.

Specifically, an admission essay can

- show how you react to challenging situations ("When the last lifeboat sprang a leak I. . . .")
- reveal your values and priorities ("Nothing is more important to me than finding the perfect pickle. . . .")
- explain factors in your background that have influenced you ("Growing up on the summit of Mount Everest, I. . . .")
- interpret your academic record ("I got a D in everything but lunch because. . . .")
- discuss how you will contribute to the life of the institution ("I would love to join your chapter of the Pun Society. . . .")
- relate the reasons why you and the institution mesh well ("I am attracted to your unlimited cut policy. . . .")
- display your logic and writing skills

Understanding Your Audience: The Admissions Officers

They're overworked. They're underpaid. (Aren't we all? Except for lawyers and professional athletes, of course.) Fairly often they're also bored. After all, how many hours are *you* willing to stare at test scores and course lists? How many pages of student writing would *you* honestly want to read? Clearly, admissions officers have a tough job. They've got to put together a class of students who will succeed academically and create a lively campus atmosphere. Depending upon the institution, they've also got to supply a backup quarterback, a cellist who can stay in tune, and a reasonably literate staff for the school paper. And if the admissions officers fail, they spend the entire year fielding complaints and listening to inaccurate descriptions from crotchety faculty of "the good old days when we got quality students."

In brief, that's the audience for an admission essay. (Check out Chapter 3 for more information on the admissions office.) If you're applying for a scholarship, your audience is similar, though their workload may be smaller. During the process of writing your essay, you should *at times* keep this audience in mind. Why not all the time? Because if you spend too long worrying about what your reader will think of you, you won't have time to do what has to be done: Write an essay that accurately represents you. Think about the audience *after* you've decided what to write, when you're trying to stay within the word limit (so they'll have time to read the whole thing) and when you're attempting to make your essay interesting (so they won't be bored). No matter what, don't sit around trying to psych them out. Which brings me to my next point.

Forgetting about strategy

"What do they want to read? I'll say anything!" Sound familiar? If so, you're hanging out with the wrong crowd. Too many applicants expend far too much energy attempting to analyze the admissions office, creating myths such as these:

- **Every college has a magic topic that guarantees admission.** "If you want to go to Airhead U, write about hang-gliding. Forget Shakespeare." "*Always* mention sports in your essay for Flatfoot College." Rumors like these spread quickly, but they're a waste of time. Anyone who claims to know tricks that guarantee admission is indulging in wishful thinking.
- **One mistake can sink your application.** "She uses semicolons? Dump her." "This guy spent four years in the debating society. He's gonna argue with everyone. Out he goes." As they say in New York, gimme a

break. Granted, if you write an essay about your admiration for serial killers, you probably won't get into the college of your choice (and a cozy padded room would be a better spot for your next four years anyway). But if you're remotely normal and you write the truth about yourself, you don't have to worry about breaking a rule you only imagine exists. You'll either get in or you won't, but your semicolon habit will have nothing to do with the outcome.

- **Some topics are automatic turn-offs.** Various Authority Figures tell you with great confidence never to write about the Big Game, the death of a relative, or some other particular topic they've labeled taboo. Nonsense. No topic is off limits if you handle it well. (See "Choosing honesty as the best policy," the next section, for *how* to handle it well.)
- **If a particular topic worked for one student, it will work for all.** "Herman wrote about his nail clipper and he got into his first choice, so I'm going with a manicure description." Good idea? No. Okay, reading other people's work may give you valuable tips on style and format. That's why I scattered some real student essays throughout *College Admission Essays For Dummies.* But content is a different story. Herman didn't get in because of his nail clipper. (Actually, Herman probably got in *despite* the fact that he wrote about his nail clipper.) Herman got in because of a host of factors you know nothing about, including his grades and recommendations, his ability to run a four-minute mile, and the fact that his essay contained superb style and format. The moral of the story: Write your own essay and forget about everyone else's.

To correct other misconceptions about the admission essay, read Chapter 22.

Choosing honesty as the best policy

In the previous section ("Forgetting about strategy"), I punctured some myths about the admission essay, especially mistaken ideas about what the admissions officers want from you. Now it's time to state what the admissions officers *do* want to read:

- **Reality.** Why are *Survivor* and other reality shows so popular? Because all of us enjoy peeking into someone else's life. Admissions officers want to hear about the real stuff of *your* life. Like every other human who ever lived, they don't take kindly to liars or exaggerators.
- **A voice.** When you read *College Admission Essays For Dummies,* you hear my voice because my writing sounds like me. You either like me or hate me, but after a chapter or two, you know me. As you write your admission essay, keep in mind that the person reading it wants to meet an actual person, even though the meeting is only on paper. Granted, you should present your best self — the dressed-up-for-company version. But your best self is still *yourself,* not someone else.

- **Thoughtfulness.** I once proctored a philosophy exam with only one question: Design an ideal society. Some students sweated for three hours, explaining the ins and outs of community structure and grappling with the tension between individual rights and group responsibility. Others finished in ten minutes; their papers made statements like "In my ideal community everyone will be happy." Guess which level of complexity is more appealing to the admissions committee? Answer: Door #1 — the thoughtful version.
- **Good writing.** Good writing is vivid; it leaps off the page and takes the reader out of the armchair and into the subject at hand. Good writing is clear; the reader doesn't have to sit around wondering whether you're describing a redwood forest or a brokerage office as the site of your best summer ever. Good writing holds the reader's attention, even if he or she has an almost overwhelming desire for sleep. Write well and rest easy in the knowledge that you've given the application your best shot.

Timing Is Everything

Your second year of nursery school and you still haven't decided on an essay topic? Uh oh. You'd better catch up!

Calm down. I'm only kidding. You should start early, but not too early. Depending upon your other time commitments and your personality type, you can write all the essays you need in six months, three months, or two weeks. Personally, I think the three-month plan makes the most sense: You get the job done, but without leaving yourself too much time to worry. However, I know that lots of people prefer a huge margin for error, so I provide a timetable for the early birds out there. I also acknowledge those people whose motto is "Don't do today what you can put off until tomorrow." (Within limits. If it's New Year's Eve and the essay is due on January 1st, all bets are off.)

I carry a five-year datebook: The long-range plan

If your applications are due in six months, you're on track for a long-range plan. Of course, you don't actually *need* six months to write an admission essay. Three months is just fine for a leisurely pace. However, if you're the kind of person who buys winter clothes in July, here's a workable schedule:

- **Month 1:** Look through some current applications for the schools you're interested in. Note the essay questions, keeping in mind that next year's set may be different. (For a review of the most common essay questions, read Part V. For tips on adapting one essay to several questions, see the section entitled "Writing Admission Essays While Having a Life," later in this chapter.)

Where can you find applications? Check the school's Web site, call their admissions office and ask for a copy, or talk with your college counselor. If any friends are currently applying, ask to see their applications.

- **Months 2 and 3:** Fill out the personal inventory in the appendix of *College Admission Essays For Dummies.* Begin to think about important moments in your life. Start pressing relatives and friends to name "three adjectives that come to mind" when they see you. Flip through your school papers and write "PR" on top of any writing that seems to be "Personally Revealing." (You thought "PR" meant something else, right? Well, the college admission essay *is* a form of public relations, so you were partially correct.) Set aside the "PR" assignments. From time to time look through them to see whether anything is usable for your essay. Begin listing possible essay topics. (For tips on deciding what to write, read Chapter 2. Chapter 6 explains some neat tricks for defining topics.)
- **Month 4:** By now you should have current applications for the schools you're interested in, so you know exactly which questions you're facing. Clump together similar questions that might be answered by one essay. ("Writing Admission Essays While Having a Life," a section in this chapter, tells you how to adapt one essay for several applications.) Check your topic list and write the rough drafts. (Part III tells you how.) Begin to think about the short answers. (Chapter 21 provides everything you need to know about the short-answer section.)
- **Month 5:** Show the essays to a college counselor, English teacher, or adult who knows you well. (Chapter 4 explains what sort of help is acceptable.) Begin to polish your work. (Part IV guides you through the final-draft stage.) Write rough drafts of the short-answer questions.
- **Month 6:** Time to bring it all together. Create the final draft of each essay. Show the short-answer rough drafts to a trusted adult. Polish the short answers, fill in the blanks, and trudge to the post office. You're done!

Surfing for essays: The summer strategy

If you're a high school or college junior applying for admission for the September following your graduation, the autumn term of senior year is likely to be extremely hectic. You've probably chosen a demanding class schedule and arrived at the point of maximum responsibility in your extracurricular activities. You're also facing a battery of standardized tests. So it makes sense to knock off all the chores you can during the summer preceding senior year. Sketch out two essays (or work them through to the final-draft stage if you're confident of the questions you'll be asked). When school begins, you're ahead of the game.

Decisions, early and otherwise

What sort of application are you making? If you're applying for *early decision,* you're telling just one college that it's the university of your dreams. You promise to attend if they admit you, and in return they give you a fairly quick decision. Most early decision applications are due November 1st or 15th of the academic year before enrollment. The results are mailed sometime in December or January. You may be accepted (Hooray for you!), rejected (If they don't want you, they don't deserve you!), or deferred, in which case they look at your application again in the spring. *Early action* applications aren't binding. You send in your application as soon as it's ready, and the college answers within a few weeks or months. Applications for regular admission are usually due in January or February (for September enrollment). You may send as many applications as you wish and then select the lucky winner from among those that admit you. Regular acceptances and rejections are usually sent out in late March or early April.

Three months is plenty for one page of writing: The medium-range plan

Congratulations! If you're reading this section, you've set aside a fine amount of time to craft an admission essay — short enough to avoid boring yourself to death, but long enough to work at a steady pace. Here's a good schedule:

- **Month 1:** Download from the Internet or call/write the admissions offices for applications to all the schools you're interested in. Read the essay questions. If you're applying to several schools, note whether one essay may be adapted for more than one application. (Check out "Writing Admission Essays While Having a Life," in this chapter, for tips on how to reuse essays.) Decide how many and what kind of essays you're stuck with. Check out the appendix of *College Admission Essays For Dummies* and zero in on the items that seem appealing. Look through your old English essays or other school assignments in case anything in them suggests an essay topic. Talk with people who know you well (relatives, teachers, friends, romantic partners) for their views on the important events or qualities of your life. List possible essay topics. (For tips on deciding what to write, read Chapter 2. Chapter 6 shows you how to define topics.)
- **Month 2:** Hit the computer or your favorite notebook and sketch out the rough drafts. Show the drafts to your college counselor or English teacher or to another adult. (Don't go overboard on the help aspect. Why? First, you should trust yourself. Second, too much help is an admissions no-no. The admissions committee will figure out what you've done and send you a very thin envelope when decision time arrives, saying, "Thanks for your interest; hope you got into some other school." How do you keep your work academically legal? Check out Chapter 4 for guidelines.)

- **Month 3:** Smooth out the bumpy spots in your essays (see Part IV for tips) and tackle the short answers, checking your work with at least one adult before signing off on it. (Again, Chapter 4 explains what sort of help is okay and what sort sets off the "automatic reject" button.) Sign, seal, and deliver the application to your favorite mailbox. Now go dancing.

Two weeks ought to do it: The short-range plan

Okay, you're a bit behind on writing your essay, but with some efficient planning and a few long nights, you'll be fine. Here's a timetable that works:

- **Week 1:** Call the admissions offices or check the Internet for the applications you need. Make a list of all the essays you have to write. Fill out the personal inventory from the appendix of *College Admission Essays For Dummies.* List two or three possible topics for each essay. Using the techniques described in Chapter 6, focus on the best topics and gather details.
- **Week 2:** Cancel every single bit of your social life and put on hold all the school assignments you can postpone without severe penalties. (Beg your teachers for extra time, if you think they'll listen.) Write the rough drafts of both the major essays and the short answer questions. Ask a sympathetic teacher/counselor/relative to review your work. (Chapter 4 explains what kind of help they can and cannot give, in terms of ethics.) Edit the drafts and insert them into the applications. Make friends with the express-mail clerk or, if time permits, visit the post office. After the applications are on their way, take a moment to formulate a New Year's Resolution (even it it's not January): "In the future, I will plan ahead." Now get some sleep.

Writing Admission Essays While Having a Life

When I was writing my own admission essays (not quite during the rock-and-chisel stage of human communication, but nearly), my friends and I each applied to two or three colleges, maximum. Now, most of my students apply to eight or nine universities or even more. They also take more difficult courses and cram more activities into their days than my generation did. So the task has become harder and the time to complete it more limited. Efficiency is definitely the name of the game. If you want to come up with a great admission essay and still fit in sleep, schoolwork, and trips to the mall/nightclub/nature preserve (pick one), this section's for you.

The common application

Approximately 230 colleges have agreed to accept the same application form, photocopied as often as you like. The common application, affectionately known as "the common app" asks you to write a personal statement of 250 to 500 words on a topic of your own choice or on one of the following topics:

- a significant experience, achievement, or risk you've taken or an ethical dilemma you've faced
- an issue of personal, local, national, or international concern
- a person who has influenced you
- a character in fiction or a historical figure or a creative work
- a topic of your choice

The common app also includes a short-answer question on the extracurricular activity that you found most meaningful. The common app may save you tons of time, although some colleges require extra essays in a "supplemental" application.

Taking advantage of spare time

Some words to live by as you apply to college or grad school: Every minute counts. I mean this statement literally. If you take advantage of five minutes here and ten minutes there, you'll find that a great deal of the work of writing an admission essay evaporates. Of course, you need a block of uninterrupted time at some point, but not as much as you would if you hadn't grabbed every second. Here are a few ways to squeeze essay-writing into your day:

- **Family gatherings:** Sit next to the relative who knows you the best and talks the most. (If those qualities are in two separate people, sit between them or divide your time.) Explain that you're writing about key aspects of your personality and experience. Ask for suggestions. Pretty soon you'll have some topics lined up.
- **Boring classes:** As a teacher, I'm supposed to advocate that you spend every minute of every class paying maximum attention to every bit of the material you're studying. But as a human being, I understand that you're human too, and you're going to fade at least once during the Holy Roman Empire or the Pythagorean Theorem. So space out with a purpose, gathering essay ideas or details. Keep an "essay sheet" of paper on your desk at all times. As soon as you have an idea, take note of it. Just don't get caught. And don't daydream in *my* class, every moment of which *is* unforgettable and unmissable.
- **Trips:** On the bus to a soccer meet? Stare out the window and daydream. (No, not about *that.* We're talking essay, here, not romance.) Spend a few minutes imagining that the admissions committee can time-travel to one

moment in your life. Which moment should it be? Before you leave the bus, jot down your thoughts. Later, those thoughts may form the basis of an essay.

Use this method only on public transportation or in a car with another driver. Don't daydream if you're the driver. No essay is worth a collision!

By now you get the idea. During the topic-search period, jot down ideas whenever they occur to you. As you write the rough draft, use spare minutes to record great details or phrases. When you have one complete draft, keep a printout in your backpack. Glance at it whenever you can, fixing grammar errors, correcting spelling, and so on.

Adapting one essay to several questions

Crossword Institute of Scolding asks you to "name the most important influence on your life." The University of Smashed Melons requires a personal statement "on a topic of your choice." Agonia College says, "Use this space to tell us about the best summer of your life." All these questions are different, but the answers may not be. An essay you write for one may do the trick for all three. For example, suppose you write an essay for the Crossword Institute about your summer as a mascot for a minor-league baseball team. Your essay talks about the freedom you discovered the minute you covered your head with a giant plastic baseball. The anonymity, you explained, allowed you to discover your inner child and made you realize that mascots are "almost spiritual in that they draw people out of everyday reality." Okay, I'm being slightly ridiculous, but you get the idea. You've got an essay that reflects on an unusual July and August. Assuming it's a good essay, why not send it to Smashed Melons and Agonia as well? All three questions allow the same answer.

Essays written to answer more specific questions may also do double duty at times. Suppose Hopscotch College of Chalk and Design asks for an essay about the meaning of art. The core of your essay about your summer as a baseball-headed mascot discusses self-expression. You add a new opening paragraph explaining that the meaning of art, in your view, is self-expression. Bingo. The mascot essay does the job.

The example I gave in the previous paragraph is valid only if you really believe that the meaning of art is self-expression. If you think that the meaning of art is smearing gooey finger paints, you'll have to write something different. Don't lie just to save time.

Part V of *College Admission Essays For Dummies* is devoted to specific questions from real applications. In each chapter of Part V, I go into more detail about adapting one essay to suit several different questions. Just turn to the chapter that most closely resembles the questions that you're facing.

One particular question should *never* be adapted for more than one application: the "Why us?" essay, as in "Why do you want to attend the College of Sign Painting?" If you answer the question honestly (as you should), you'll include details about the College of Sign Painting that are not relevant to another institution. And if your essay is so general that it applies to several schools, it isn't good enough for any of them.

One more warning: Computer word processing has given rise to the very worst mistake, the closest you can get to an automatic rejection. No matter what, don't copy and paste an answer from one application into another, leaving the name of the first institution. Writing "I want to attend the College of Sign Painting" when you're applying to Posterboard University is a giant no-no.

Deciding whether the optional essay is really optional

Usually, the optional essay *isn't* optional. Unless you're a shoe-in for admission (your grandparents donated a new media center) or unless the deadline is five minutes away, you should take the time to write a good, additional essay whenever the application allows you to do so. The more they get to know you, the more they'll love you, right? And the essay is the prime spot to introduce yourself in all your complex glory.

One rather large pitfall sits in front of the optional essay: repetition. If you've already written about the time you saved the world, don't write another essay telling the same story in slightly different words. Your audience is too busy to deal with duplicates. You can, however, write about two different aspects of the same experience. Essay number one may deal with the actual world-saving and essay number two with the media attention that followed your feat.

Concentrating on Process, Not Product

On campus tours, do you glance at perfect strangers, imagining that *they* never struggled with their admission essays? Has every lunch-table conversation for the past month revolved around how many hours you spent staring at a blank computer screen or sheet of paper? In other words, are you running around in circles, stalling as you try to create "The Perfect Essay"? Relax. "The Perfect Essay" does not exist, but many wonderful, effective essays do. They're all in your brain, waiting to emerge.

I can hear you declaring, "Fine. All the essays I need are in my brain. But they won't do me any good if I can't get them out." Too true. However, "getting them out" is actually easier than you think. All you have to do is focus on the *process* of writing, not the product. If you handle the process well, a good product pops out automatically.

Here's a brief overview of the writing process — in six easy steps — so you know what to expect:

1. Gather ideas, pondering what to write about.
2. After you have a focus, list yards of details about your topic.
3. Punch the material into shape, choosing a structure and creating an outline.
4. Put those words on the page and write a rough draft.
5. Revise, check, and insert the final product into that little blank space on the application. (Don't worry; most colleges allow you to staple a computer printout to the application.)
6. Mail the application and sigh with relief.

The key to the whole process is simple: Concentrate on whatever step you're on and ignore everything else. (As they say in Zen, stay in the moment.) You can do one step, can't you? Piece of cake. And when all the steps are done, so are you . . . and you have an essay to be proud of.

Keeping Perspective

It's not the last spaceship off an exploding planet. Nor is it a cure for a deadly disease or a formula for world peace. It's an essay. Yes, what you write will have an impact on your chances for admission, and certainly you want to do a good job. But how good a job can you do if you see the admission essay as the only possible path to everything you ever wanted out of life? "My entire future depends upon this sentence" is *not* an attitude likely to bring out your best performance.

Remember that writing a college admission essay is not as hard as most of the other things you've already done, such as learning to tie your shoelaces and passing phys ed. You're telling "the truth, the whole truth, and nothing but the truth" about a subject you know very well — your own life. How hard can that be?

Chapter 2

Exploring the Subject of the Essay — Yourself

In This Chapter

- Searching for key moments or influences
- Understanding how all essays reflect your personality and values
- Identifying themes in your autobiography
- Overcoming the taboo against bragging

Typical Applicant trudges one more time to his desk and stares at the blank page still awaiting the first words of an essay. "I'm only 18," he thinks. "Nothing has happened to me yet. I've got nothing to write about!" With a wail, he jumps out of the chair and shakes his fist at the universe. "If only I were abducted by aliens," he screams. "*Then* I'd have a great essay!"

Typical Applicant may be 18 or 21 or 73. Regardless of age, he's on the wrong path if he thinks that only a dramatic, life-altering experience provides fodder for an admission essay. In fact, everyone's life is packed with potential essay material, just waiting to be unearthed. In this chapter I show you how to dig into the subject of your essay — yourself. I also explain why you're the subject of all college admission essays, even if you think you're writing about something completely different.

Mining Your Life

Miners move tons of earth looking for a few precious bits of ore. Their task is dirty, dangerous, and tiring. Fortunately for you, "mining your life" for essay topics carries none of the risks of chopping real minerals out of the earth. You won't get dirty, though you may tire (mentally, at least) after a long trek down memory lane. Plus, mining your life is actually a lot of fun; you get to poke around inside your own head, dredging up all the best moments from your past. True, you may pull up something sad, but if it's inside you, on some level you're dealing with it anyway

Writing an essay is a valuable experience even apart from the admissions context. If you're applying to a new school, you're at a transition point — a good time to take stock of where you've been and where you want to go in life. See the present moment as a pivot between your past and future and give both time periods close attention.

When you "mine your life" for material, you're in search of stories. You're *not* seeking a bunch of general statements like "I am a very strong person. When I face a challenge, I don't give up." General statements are boring. They also give the committee very little information. But stories — everyone loves stories! Tell a story and you'll capture your readers, making them experience your reality for a few moments.

Of course, when you write an admission essay, you present more than the story itself. You must add a few sentences that interpret the story for the reader, explaining why the story matters. The interpretation also presents the theme of the story. In the next section of this chapter, "Collecting the Stories of Your Life," I explain how to uncover the stories you need. In a later section of this chapter, "Identifying Themes in Your Autobiography," I show you how to define the themes of your stories.

Many applications for law, business, or medical schools ask you why you've chosen that particular career. "Mining your life" to answer this question involves thinking about people in the profession you've met, images of the profession on television or in films, or experiences (an illness or a court case, perhaps) that made you appreciate these jobs. See the appendix for additional questions that prod your memory and help you define why you chose your career path.

Collecting the Stories of Your Life

The big moments — the winning touchdown, the award, the opening night of the play — provide good material for an essay. They're also fairly easy to remember. Here's how to collect memories of important events:

- Flip through your family's photo albums or mentally review the milestones you've passed — birthdays, graduations, "firsts," and so on.
- Talk with your parents or other relatives, urging them to tell you stories about your childhood. Establish a nostalgic mood in which each comment begins with "remember when."
- Chat with your best and oldest friends (who are sometimes the same person) about "the good old days." Take note of the stories they seem to remember best.

- Got amnesia? The appendix at the end of this book contains a complete set of questions to spur your recollections.

Take a notebook or open a computer file and name it "Mining" or "Memories." Fill it with a list of all the memories you've gathered. Put a star next to turning points — the times when something changed. Also put a star next to any lunch-table item — the important stuff you tell your classmates the minute you sit down in the cafeteria.

Then turn your attention to the small stuff. Life's little events are important too. The quiet walks with your grandfather around the pond in his backyard. The time you and your friend baked cookies for an elderly neighbor. The first time you sat at the "grown-up table" for a holiday dinner. As you review your past, collect a long list of stories — memories, really — of those times. Work your way through a typical day from the present and then one from a series of intervals: two years ago, five years ago, ten years ago, and so on until you run out of time. The moments you choose to remember from a typical day at each of those ages may provide fine essay material. (The appendix contains a series of questions that will help you remember the "small stuff" of your life.)

After you've got a slew of stories, think about them carefully. Which ones reveal something important about your character? Which ones would you like the admissions office to hear? Do any of your memories relate to the questions on the application? Does any story have a theme that you'd like to communicate to your reader? (For more information on theme, read the section entitled "Identifying Themes in Your Autobiography," later in this chapter.)

Remember that mining your life is *not* writing the essay. At this stage you're just collecting material, not trying to punch it into shape for that large blank spot on the application form. Don't worry about the rest of the process; just dredge up as many memories as you can and list them in a computer file or in a notebook.

Chicago Survivor

The University of Chicago, an intellectual powerhouse, knows how to have fun with the admission essay. In 2001, it began asking admitted students to submit questions for the following year's applicants. Several hundred students complied, sending in essay topics that were, according to the university's Web site, "eloquent" or "downright wacky." Those seeking admission to the class of 2006 had the option of creating a version of "Chicago Survivor," modeled on the popular television show, or describing something that reflects "idiosyncratic beauty." Suggestions for the second essay included "the mutt you adopted at the pound" or the "boa you found in the Wal-Mart parking lot." Applicants for the class of 2007 may respond to "How do you feel about Wednesday?"

Journal-keeping for fun and profit

Have you ever seen those little blank books with colorful covers in stationery stores? They're journals, and they can help you immensely as you tackle the college admission essay. But you don't need a special notebook to keep a journal. A computer file or a pack of index cards also does the job. If you keep a journal, your admission essay will practically write itself. Just dedicate a few minutes each day to jotting down stray ideas, possible essay topics, interesting sentences or analogies, and so forth. Start as early as you can, even a year before you plan to send in your application. If your essay is due in a few weeks, a journal is still useful. You'll have less time to write, but urgency will inspire you to write more. When it's time to write, read over the journal and gather ideas from it.

Getting Personal with Impersonal Questions

The vast majority of admission essay questions relate directly to your experiences ("Tell us something about yourself," "Describe an experience that changed your perspective," and so on). But even questions that seem abstract ("Discuss the role of the printed word in the age of technology," for example) are personal when they're answered in the context of an admission essay. If the admissions officers wanted to read a purely academic, abstract discussion, they'd ask you to submit a report written for one of your classes. Many universities do just that, asking for a graded English or history paper. But an admission essay is supposed to reveal something about your beliefs and values.

Before you answer an abstract question, you should spend some time exploring your reactions to the topic. Memories are still relevant, because your beliefs flow from your experiences. For the question in the previous paragraph, for example, you might reflect on your relationship with books, magazines, newspapers, and other printed material. When do you read? Do you recall the first time you sat down with a book? Think about one experience reading a book and compare it to a session of reading from a computer screen. How do these events differ?

When you write an essay in response to an abstract question, you may use only a tiny portion of a story you uncovered. Nevertheless, the memories will influence your answer and provide the personal slant that the admissions committee needs.

Figure 2-1 is a good example of a personal response to an impersonal question: "Write about a local, national, or international issue that is important to you." Notice that the writer — a real student, by the way — starts out with an actual incident from her life and connects it to the issue of dating violence.

An Awakening

"You played with her like a doll and put her back on the shelf." Written and sung by Eve, Love is Blind, refers to a domestic violence situation in which a woman is murdered by her husband. It is sung from the point of view of the woman's best friend and portrays how neither Eve nor her friend realized what was happening. I thought of this song when I was sitting in a dark room next to my best friend watching a video on dating violence; we were at the "Beat Violence" conference. When the lights came on we turned toward each other. We did not have to use words to express our thoughts; we simultaneously knew what the other was thinking. My best friend, someone whom I admire and respect, had been involved in an abusive relationship with her boyfriend.

Neither my friend nor I had thought that there had been anything significantly abnormal about her 18-month relationship. Sure there had been those times when the typical female/male arguments would take place, but nothing seemed so unusual. As we sat glued to the presentation we knew that her relationship had all the elements of abuse, distrust and harm that were being presented before our very own eyes.

I was shocked. I never thought that someone so close to me would ever have this kind of experience and even more so that we hadn't even known anything had been wrong. How could we have been so blind? I threw myself into finding out as much as I could about dating violence. I researched articles, attended community-based workshops, and volunteered at a domestic violence center for the past three years. I uncovered that dating violence is a societal issue that effects the abused, the abusers, and all those around them.

Teenagers may not believe that dating violence is something they encounter, but in fact they really do; they just may not choose to face it. Actually people of my age can become involved in a harmful relationship; it is so easy to be fooled by a relationship that initially has the elements of admiration but can deteriorate into a harmful physical or emotional relationship which can have traumatic results. Both my enlightened knowledge but more emphatically the haunting reflections of my friend's experience have strengthened my conviction to continue working towards heightening awareness, specifically among teenagers, on the potential brutality of dating violence.

That Sunday morning, I knew that I have been blinded, like so many young people, to the fact that someone I cared about was hurting because of an unhealthy relationship. While my friend's experience was very difficult, we both now see it as a blessing in disguise. I can now talk to others about dating violence with the confidence that what I am saying can help others see their own truth.

Figure 2-1: An essay response to an abstract question.

Identifying Themes in Your Autobiography

The stories of your life are an important ingredient of the admission essay, but they're not the only ingredient. You also need to identify the themes that run through the information you present to the admissions committee. A *theme* is a general category or "big idea" that seems to apply to the most important memories of your past. Creative works have themes too; in English or art class you've probably had to identify the themes of novels or other artworks (poems, plays, musical compositions, paintings, and so on). How do you find the themes that are relevant to your essay? Read on.

Reviewing your life story

Your life has an objective reality: hours worked, food eaten, friends greeted, tasks accomplished, and so forth. But apart from that dry list of details, everyone also makes an internal movie, *The Story of Me.* In *The Story of Me* you are the star, the scriptwriter, and the director. You create the characters (the way you see yourself and others) and select events to film (decide which events are important to you). From time to time you project *The Story of Me* onto the screen of your mind, watching the events (that is, remembering them) and, in the process, weaving a set of random happenings into a plot that makes sense. To identify themes, turn yourself into a movie critic, interpreting and analyzing *The Story of Me.*

For example, your own personal film may revolve around compassion. When you peer into the past, you remember how you helped that little boy in kindergarten who dropped his glob of clay and how you sat for hours with an elderly neighbor as she regaled you with stories of her childhood in Hungary and her career as a cigar roller. Your inner review of *The Story of Me* proclaims, "This film is a moving account of a girl who never met anyone she wouldn't help! The main character is a model of compassion and concern for others." (Sound too boastful? Check out the section entitled "Overcoming the Taboo against Bragging," later in this chapter.)

Revealing significant themes

Identifying themes is crucial because you can't write about your life coherently unless you understand why particular events are significant *to you.* Moreover, if you identify a theme and express it clearly, the reader (that is, the admissions office) will understand how to interpret the information you're providing. And the more deeply the admissions or scholarship committee understands your character, the better off you are.

Here's a selection of themes that may apply to your life:

- **Identity:** How do you define yourself? Think about gender, race, ethnicity, economic level, age, and all the other factors that contribute to your identity. Then think about times when you were particularly aware of those factors. Can you match any memories to these issues? If so, you may have an essay topic.
- **Challenges:** What barriers have you overcome? What difficulties have you gone through? When have you almost lost courage? Think of challenges relating to family, school (both academic and social), and community. What incidents can you relate that illustrate how you have handled tough situations?
- **Curiosity:** What would you like to know about the world? Whom would you like to meet? Where would you like to visit? Have any situations sparked a hunger inside you — not the "I'll faint if I don't get a lunch break" sort of hunger, but the kind that moves you to explore? Check your memory bank (and the appendix). What situations have provoked your curiosity?
- **Future:** When reporters attend your 100th birthday party, what will they hear the speakers say about you? What will you have accomplished in that long life? If your imagination stalls before the century mark, concentrate on something simpler — your life 5, 10, or 15 years from now. What memories would you like to create as you move through your future?
- **Time:** How do you spend your days? When does time fly for you or drag? Are you a planner, a seize-the-moment type, a nostalgia buff? Do any of your memories show how you relate to time?
- **Passion:** No, I'm not talking about physical passion. (This is a family-friendly book!) I'm talking about what moves you intellectually, artistically, emotionally, politically, or spiritually. When you feel with intensity, what are you doing? Or, what do you want to be doing? The issues or situations that get you going are worth writing about.
- **Learning:** How do you learn best? What types of activities or teaching styles match your learning style? Which assignments do you remember? Why those? Can you illustrate your identity as a student with one particular experience?
- **Failure:** I'm not suggesting that you explain to the admissions committee why you're a total loser, because of course you're *not* a loser at all. But if you're human, your reach has occasionally exceeded your grasp, as the poet says, and you've failed. What did you learn from that failure? How did you change your methods or goals as a result? A memory of failure may become a great essay topic.
- **Context:** Where do you fit in? *How* do you fit in — in your family, school, neighborhood, country, world, universe? Or, how *don't* you fit in? See yourself as a small tile in a large mosaic. What is your role?

- **Personality:** What kind of person are you? What qualities or traits are part of your personality? How do you deal with day-to-day life? Collect some descriptive terms, but don't stop there. Look for memories that illustrate those qualities in action. For example, if courage is one of your most important qualities, hunt for moments in which you had to be brave. One of those memories may turn into an essay.

- **Career:** What do you want to be now that you're grown up? Why? How did you start on the path to your chosen job? How do you expect to spend your days? What rewards are you seeking? If you're applying to graduate school, you've probably got a good idea of what your post-school life will be. Your views of the working life provide great essay material.

The preceding list contains only some of the many themes that you may apply to your life as you "mine" it for topics. If others occur to you, jot them down in a computer file or in a notebook.

But Enough about Me: Overcoming the Taboo against Bragging

Remember the old joke in which the bore at the cocktail party says, "But enough about me. Let's talk about you now. What do *you* think about me?" The joke relies on the fact that we've all met someone so self-absorbed that they may as well paste mirrors on the inside of their sunglasses. And nobody wants to be the cocktail party bore who's star-struck with his own magnificence.

However, you *can* talk about yourself without unnecessary bragging. And to write an effective admission essay, you *must* reveal the best aspects of your life and personality to the admissions committee. Why else are you writing? But if you're like most people, you learned early on to play down your accomplishments:

> YOU: Oh, that little medal? It's the (*mumble mumble*) prize.
>
> FRIEND: The what prize?
>
> YOU: The Nobel Prize. So, do you think it's going to rain?

But applying for admission or for a scholarship is *not* a time for humility. It's a time to reveal all the good stuff you usually smile about only when you brush your teeth. However, revealing is not the same as boasting. When you reveal your good points, you speak honestly and specifically, as in the following:

> In my senior science class I was appointed lab technician, responsible for setting out the chemicals or other supplies needed for each day's

> experiment. Last week, for example, I had to place 5 grams of radioactive xylophonium on each table. After the experiment, I was in charge of phoning the National Safety Board so that they could come to school to interview the survivors.

Just kidding about the radioactive stuff. Now read this paragraph, in which the writer qualifies for the "I Love Me" Award:

> In my senior science class the teacher, stunned by my brilliance, gave me the most responsible and important job in the class. No one else could be trusted with the task of putting out the radioactive xylophonium and calling the National Safety Board.

Do you see the difference? In the first example, the writer states exactly what she has done and lets the reader decide to affix labels such as "trustworthy," "mature," "reliable," and so on. In the second example, the writer draws conclusions for the reader — always an annoying habit, but particularly offensive when those conclusions are praise for the writer.

Bottom line: Be clear and specific about your accomplishments and character and leave the admiring comments for the admissions or scholarship committee.

Chapter 3

Writing for the Tired, the Poor (The Admissions Office)

In This Chapter

- Considering the audience for an admission essay
- Writing attention-getting material
- Watching what you write — pitfalls to avoid
- Understanding what the admissions office does want to read

Across a deep, crocodile-infested moat and behind sound-proof titanium doors, they hold top-secret meetings. Each carries an ax. From time to time one of them chops an application into shreds, always with the sort of maniacal laughter you hear on old radio shows. They're the admissions counselors, and they delight in ruining your future.

Does this picture match the one your imagination creates? Be honest now. Okay, maybe a few details are different — perhaps your fantasy admissions office has a high-tech thumb-print lock and no moat — but I bet you think that you're writing the admission essay for trained torturers who are dying to reject you.

Not so. In fact you're writing for a group of overworked, poorly-paid professionals who are dedicated to the institution they serve. In this chapter I discuss how to reach that audience. I also reveal their biggest turn-offs, so you can avoid the ax.

Meeting Your Readers: The Admissions Committee

The Authority Figures deciding your future are a fairly diverse bunch. The typical college admissions office is run by a professional, the director, with a strong commitment to the institution and years of experience evaluating candidates. The director oversees an admissions committee that may include recent graduates of the school, faculty, older alumni, and even current students. The admissions office's tasks are many:

- Attract a bright, varied pool of applicants whose numbers (as in the number of applicants and their standardized test scores) increase each year.
- Present the institution favorably so that those who are admitted choose to attend.
- Respond to the needs of the institution for athletes, writers, musicians, and so forth.
- Administer a financial aid budget for maximum effectiveness.
- Stock the office with brewed-to-sludge-level coffee so that caffeinated counselors have the energy to evaluate mile-high piles of applications.
- Read a zillion essays, some of which are yours.

Also keep in mind that your essay will arrive at one of two times:

- **Early decision applicants:** Autumn, usually by November 1st, when the readers are immersed in football or recovering from the World Series, trying to get some sort of winter wardrobe in order because those summer tee-shirts are so-o-o last season, preparing (if they're faculty or students) for the last assignments of the fall semester, and thinking about whether they're up to cooking or even attending Thanksgiving dinner.
- **Regular applicants:** Late winter or early spring, when the readers are just beginning to realize that those New Year's resolutions were a bad idea, shopping for a bathing suit that erases winter's diet lapses, preparing (if they're faculty or students) for the last assignments of the spring semester, and desperately dreaming of summer vacation.

At most universities, two or more members of the admissions committee read every word of each application, including your essays. At the very least, one counselor will review your work. Though admissions counselors in general want to give you a fair shake, they plow through far too many essays every day. One of your goals in writing an admission essay is to grab their attention and keep it. Another is to make the experience of reading your essay worth their investment of time and energy.

If you're applying to law, medical, or business school, the admissions committee probably consists of professionals in the field. They'd like to see applicants who have thought deeply about what it means to pursue their career of choice, not applicants who say, "Doctors wear white coats. Cool!" Do your homework before you write an essay for a post-graduate institution. Who knows? You may discover that you'd prefer a different career after all, saving yourself essay-writing time and about $200,000 in tuition.

Keeping Their Attention When Yours Is the 9000th Essay They've Read Today

As an English teacher I collect 30 or 40 essays a week. When my energy gauge is stuck on "empty" and I still have ten student papers left to correct, I play a little game with myself. I thumb through the remaining work until I find one that catches my eye with an interesting fact or a great first sentence. Needless to say, I'm grateful at that moment to have anything spark my interest, and I tend to look more favorably on that particular paper than on the one that makes me mutter, "Wake me up when it's over."

I'm not terribly different from the admissions counselors who will read your essay. Consider these imaginary essay sentences and some possible reactions:

Blah Essay Sentence: I was born almost 19 years ago.

Reader Reaction: Yeah, you and just about everybody applying for the freshman class. Yawn.

Better Essay Sentence: Nixon was resigning just as my mother was being wheeled into the delivery room to give birth to me.

Reader Reaction: I remember that day! I was at Yankee Stadium when some guy with a portable radio started screaming about Watergate.

Another Blah Essay Sentence: I have many varied hobbies.

Reader Reaction: I really have to get my resume together. I hear they're hiring at the cement factory.

Better Essay Sentence: Building the world's largest collection of fabric softener bottles is only one of my hobbies.

Reader Reaction: Fabric softener? I'd like to take a look at this guy's garage.

One More Blah Essay Sentence: My friend is always there for me.

Reader Reaction: Congratulations. Everyone else's friends are totally absent.

Better Essay Sentence: When Godzilla ate my little toe, my first thought was to call Emily.

Reader Reaction: Toe? Godzilla? What can Emily do?

Got the idea? Good essay sentences *connect* to the reader, making the reader comment, speculate, or question. The "blah" essay sentences sound, well, blah. They're so general they could apply to just about anyone, and they give the reader no incentive to continue slogging through your paragraphs.

Don't think that you have to encounter Godzilla or do something as weird as collect fabric softener in order to write an interesting essay. Even the most boring life (and yours isn't boring at all, I'm sure) can become good reading material. It's all in the presentation! Check out Chapter 9 to find out how to add vivid detail to your essay. I show you how to write a strong first sentence in Chapter 11.

Avoiding Writing Traits Guaranteed to Annoy the Admissions Committee

In Chapter 1 I explain that you shouldn't try to "psych out" the admissions committee by writing what you think "they" want to read. I'm not contradicting myself here because I'm not talking about subject matter. Instead, in this section I discuss style and tone and reveal the most common turn-offs of the college admission essay.

I studied the word list and by golly I'm going to use it: Unnatural vocabulary

"As I ambulated through the fronds of semi-tropical vegetation, I. . . ." You what? Memorized the word list at the back of your SAT or ACT review book? I know that you want to impress the admissions committee with your scholarly preparedness, but sounding like a talking dictionary is not helpful. Not to minimize the benefits of a good vocabulary, but come on now, do you really have to squeeze every word from an SAT list into the same sentence? To make the point another way: Would you want to continue reading the first sentence of this paragraph? Probably not.

Here's a secret about vocabulary: New words worm their way into your understanding *gradually.* First, you learn the meaning of the word from a list or from a dictionary. At this stage you know how to define the word on a test, but it's still a stranger. Next, you begin to hear the word in conversation or notice it as you read. The word is becoming an acquaintance now, more familiar each time you meet it, but it's not yet ready for an invitation into everyday expression. Lastly, when the word is a true friend, you feel comfortable inserting it into your speaking and writing, where it meshes smoothly with other old friends, the words you've been using for years.

Here's another secret about vocabulary: Words have meanings (denotations, in dictionary terms) and associations (connotations). If you understand only the denotation of an expression but not the connotation, you may end up making some embarrassing mistakes. For example, both "proud" and "haughty" have similar denotations; they describe the attitude of people who are fairly pleased with their own accomplishments. But "haughty" is an insult, and "proud" is more neutral. You can safely write that winning the contest made you "proud," but if you say that the gold medal made you "haughty," you're criticizing yourself. Moral of the story: When you write the college admission essay, don't plop words from a list into your sentences. Chances are you'll use the words improperly. Even if the words are in the right spot, you'll come across unnaturally.

At the sound of the tone my essay will self-destruct: Machine language

Machine language (not the stuff that computer programmers learn, but the words that voice-mail systems spit out) is as stiff as your back after 15 sets of tennis. Don't write your essay in machine language, unless you want the admissions committee to appreciate your robotic qualities. Some examples, with corrections:

Stiff Sentence: It is now my understanding that the event that took place in my early childhood — the rattlesnake's entrance into my crib — played a formidable role in shaping my eventual character.

Better Sentence: The rattlesnake slithered into my crib and changed my entire life.

Another Stiff Sentence: Any 300-word essay that could be written by me must inevitably fail to communicate the entire nature of my character, but I will endeavor to comply with your request anyway.

Better Sentence: I can't possibly communicate my true self in 300 words, but I will try.

Last stiff sentence: It was the best of times, it was the worst of times, it was the age of victory, it was the era of defeat. . . .

Better Sentence: Forget about it! No better sentence exists. The passage above comes from Charles Dickens' *A Tale of Two Cities.* He was a genius, so he could break all the rules and create an unforgettable piece of writing.

If you think you can pull off Dickensian style, go for it. (But be warned: The higher you aim, the farther you may fall if you don't hit the target.) For all non-geniuses out there, the rule is simple: Write naturally, not like a machine.

Having trouble achieving a natural style? Try "writing" your essay by speaking it into a tape recorder. Then transcribe the tape. You may have to clean up the grammar a bit and rearrange a few things to achieve a logical flow, but chances are the tone will be realistic.

I wrote a gooder essay after I read them grammar books: Incorrect language

Okay, I admit that grammar isn't crucial to the fate of the world. Knowing where to put a comma and how to choose the correct verb tense is not as valuable as discovering the formula for cold fusion or negotiating an agreement with the teamsters union. But grammar *does* have its moments, and writing the college admission essay is one of them. Think of the issue this way: Not everyone reading your admission essay is an English teacher, but all are involved in the academic world in some way. And in academia, correct expression is prized. Good spelling is also a plus. You may not be accepted if you write in standard English and spell everything perfectly, but you'll probably be rejected if you don't. See Chapter 14 for tips on writing like an English teacher who swallowed the rulebook. Or (she said as she read her royalty statement) check out *English Grammar For Dummies*, written by yours truly (published by Wiley Publishing, Inc.), for a complete guide.

Computer grammar and spelling checkers may help you, but don't rely on them completely. The programs are still fairly crude; a lot of errors slip by, and those squiggly lines and suggested corrections are often wrong. Your best bet is to learn the rules and apply them with your very own brain.

When the rowboat sank in two feet of water, I was lucky to escape with my life: Untruths and exaggerations

Your essay may be beautifully vivid and relate a compelling story. Great! But your essay must also be true, or you're in big trouble. Choose your topic (see Chapter 2 for help with this task) and write it accurately. Anything else is simply unacceptable. For example, if you won the math medal, say so. Just don't claim that you won the medal against insurmountable odds when your opponents were still struggling with pesky little problems like 2 + 2. Just "tell it like it is," as we used to say in the sixties. Why? Because lying or exaggerating is wrong. Moreover, you probably won't be able to pull off a convincing lie anyway. And did I mention that not telling the truth is wrong?

I am a people person: Clichés

Every so often I point out a cliché — an old, worn out expression such as "raining cats and dogs" or "so hungry I could eat a horse" — to a student and then struggle to answer this question: "What's wrong with using a cliché? It made my point perfectly. Besides, I didn't know it was a cliché." Sigh. The student has a point. Clichés became clichés because they once filled a need; they expressed a common idea in easily understood terms. The problem is that each time a cliché is used it loses a bit of its meaning. The expression has become so comfortable that people hearing or reading it press the automatic-pilot button and switch off their brains. They're not considering your ideas because they've fallen asleep or put your paper aside, convinced that they already know what's in it.

If you're fairly young, you may not recognize every cliché. So how can you avoid using clichés if you don't know what they are? Your best bet is to show your essay to a trusted adult, perhaps your parents or your English teacher, and ask the reader to point out any trite phrases. Then put on your creativity cap and try again.

The main idea of your essay, not just individual phrases, may also be clichéd. You don't want to present the admissions committee with the admission-essay equivalent of the car chase that's in every Hollywood movie. Fortunately, you can easily avoid this problem by writing about your own experiences in a very specific way. The experience you describe may be a common one, but if you throw in enough detail, your story will be unique because the details of your story do not match the specifics of anyone else's story.

My essay's on soccer so I wrote it on a soccer ball: Gimmicks

They've seen it all: soccer essays printed on actual soccer balls, essays baked into cakes or spoken into tape recorders, and essays written on (or in) balloons. They've seen every color of the rainbow, most of the fonts, and all sorts of paper (including wax, parchment, and shelf). So do you really think that you'll get the attention of the admissions committee with a gimmick? Not likely. The more probable reaction is that the admissions counselor will place your essay (soccer ball, balloon, whatever) aside to be read "when I have time," which may be never. Your best bet is to write the thing normally and present it rationally. (Chapter 17 discusses format.) Your words should make the case, not your presentation style.

Writing What They Do Want to Read

No, I'm not talking topic here, because no topic is a guaranteed "proceed-directly-to-orientation-do-not-pass-Go" card. But one type of college admission essay is as near as you can get to a sure thing: a well-written one. The admissions committee wants a sense of who you are and what you've been through. They are interested in your ideas and in the way you think. If you give the committee an honest piece of writing, specific enough to take them into your brain and your life for a "you are there" moment, you're on the right track. (Read Part III for tons of tips on writing well.)

Chapter 4

Keeping It Legal

In This Chapter

- Avoiding illegal pitfalls
- Getting help without breaking the rules
- Dealing with parental over-involvement
- Watching plagiarism
- Finding help when you don't have any

They may be everywhere — pacing the room as you gather ideas and leaning over the computer screen to follow every keystroke. Bugging you for "just a glimpse, we promise" of the first draft. Patiently explaining, for the 15th evening in a row, the topic chosen by "that nice boy down the block, the one who got into all the Ivies." They may be your parents, your teachers, your friends, or any of the people who are trying to help with your college admission essay. They mean well, and they can in fact be worth their weight in acceptance letters. But not all potential helpers know the rules for "legal" help with the essay.

Or they may be nowhere. You may be sitting alone in your room facing a blank screen, ready to scream, "HELP! Will somebody please talk to me about this essay!"

Whatever your situation, this chapter has information for you. It explains how to ask for and manage legitimate assistance with your college admission essays. In this chapter I also provide some strategies for dealing with over-eager helpers. And if you're one of the rare applicants with no helpers at all, I tell you where to look for assistance.

Buying an Essay on the Internet and Other Things to Avoid

As a literate applicant, you've probably taken a spin or two around the Internet. So you know that essays on just about any topic abound, and some of them are for sale. But you've already rejected that option. After all, you bought *College Admission Essays For Dummies* and you're reading it at this very moment. Good for you! The Internet-purchase route is a bad idea for a couple of thousand reasons. The essays there are canned, generic pieces of writing — not about you at all! (How could they be, when you didn't write them?) Also, while not every college admissions counselor is Net-savvy, every college admissions *office* employs at least one person who *does* know how and where to find essays-for-hire. You may get caught if you try to cheat, and frankly, you should. Dishonesty is *not* an attractive quality, as former executives of Enron now know.

So congratulations on choosing the (academically) legal route. But that route doesn't come with the world's clearest road signs. College admissions committees know that at some point in the process someone is likely to help you a bit, and they made peace with that fact a long time ago. But the fact that the institution you hope to attend understands that you'll have *some* help does not mean that *all* help is okay. And even if in some alternate universe (the one in which ice cream is a health food) the university didn't mind parents or teachers more or less writing the essay for you, such involvement would still be a bad idea. Why? Because *you* are going to college or grad school, not your essay-helpers. For the sake of your self-esteem and to insure a good fit between you and the institution, you should do your own work. Also, you should write your own essay for the sake of honesty, a quality that can't be over-rated. (Once again, remember the Enron executives!)

The general principle of legitimate help has two simple rules:

Rule #1: They can help.

Rule #2: They can't write the essay for you.

If at any point in the process you're not sure what assistance is acceptable, check with the college counselor at your school. (If your school has no separate college counselor, the guidance office is a good bet.) College counselors are used to dealing with the issue of help from parents and teachers. They've thought fairly deeply about the line between honesty and dishonesty. Also, their credibility as a college office depends partly upon the students they send along to the universities. So college counselors have a strong interest in maintaining the integrity of the application process.

Some colleges come right out and ask you whether you received any help writing the essay, and if so, what kind. Once again, honesty rules. You *must* answer this question truthfully. If you have qualms about accepting any sort of help, talk with your college or guidance counselor *before* you work on the essay.

Finding the Right Sort of Help

Others can help you, but not over-help you, in writing an admission essay. That's a good rule, but it's not specific enough to keep you out of trouble. In the next few sections, I take you through each part of the process and explain what help is ethical and what's unethical for the college admission essay.

Trolling for topics

One of the most difficult aspects of writing an admission essay is deciding on a topic. (Chapter 2 and the appendix give you pointers.) People who know you well — your immediate family, teachers who've spent a lot of time with you, your college counselor — can provoke a ton of good ideas just by asking the right questions. And as you generate two or three possible topics, the Helper Units in your life (parental or otherwise) may legitimately give you their opinion about the topic most likely to succeed.

No one can define a topic that is *guaranteed* to succeed. The college or graduate school application process has too many variables, many of which are out of your control. (You studied Tae Kwon Do and they need a Tai Chi master, for example.)

Other people are good at suggesting topics because they have an outsider's perspective on your life that you can't achieve. And because the admissions committee will read your essay from exactly that viewpoint — the outsider's — it's worthwhile to hear about that viewpoint before, not after, you mail your application.

Although helpers can comment on the topics you're considering and even suggest some to you, they can't make the final decision, as in "Write about the day the dog ran off with the roast beef." You must remain in control of the choice.

Dialing for details

After you've got a topic, you may certainly ask those who were involved to help you remember the details that will make your story come to life. For example, suppose you're writing about the inspiration you've received from your ancestors, focusing on your grandmother's immigration to the United States. Your mom may remember why Grandma left, how she traveled, where she lived, and so on. Interview your mom or phone Grandma herself and take notes. Or perhaps you're writing about the science fair that you and your best friend entered. Call Best Friend for the lowdown on stuff that has completely slipped out of your mind, such as the comments the judge made as she examined your entry or the way that gooey stuff looked on her face just after the project exploded.

In the search for details, one tall temptation stands before you: fiction, also known as lies. If you can't remember a detail, skip it. Don't make it up! You can, however, speculate or imagine, as long as you make the reader understand where you've wandered off the reality path into novel territory, as in "I always imagine that she wore a red dress, a green apron, and a Yankee cap on the day she arrived in America."

The detail-gathering stage is totally open to your helpers, as long as none of them turn those details into sentences to be included in your essay.

Overseeing the outline

When you begin to structure your ideas, putting the details in order, you may want some feedback. No problem, as long as you keep control of the work. Here are a couple examples of imaginary comments made after you've shown an outline to a Helper. In each pair, one comment is okay and one is too intrusive:

Okay comment: I don't understand why you're explaining the party and then suddenly jump to Uncle Willie's jail term.

Why it's okay: The comment makes you think (emphasis on the "you") about why you want to discuss Uncle Willie after the party. If you have a reason, you'll probably keep the order as it is. If you don't, you may change the order. Either way, the control remains in your hands.

Butting-in comment: After you explain the party, dump Uncle Willie and move up that story about the fishing trip. Then you can end with Uncle Willie's attempt to bribe the guard.

Why it's butting in: The Helper is not truly helping; the helper is creating the outline for you.

Okay comment: Are you sure you've mentioned enough about your intellectual experiences? Right now there's only one: your survey report on the philosophy of shampoo.

Why it's okay: Granted, the comment is a thinly disguised criticism of the number of intellectual experiences you describe in the essay. Nevertheless, the comment merely prods you to reconsider your ideas.

Butting-in comment: The shampoo's fine, but add something here about that term paper on conditioner and the experiment you did on split ends.

Why it's butting in: The helper has made two decisions for you about content (adding the term paper and the experiment) and one about structure (where to place the additions). Out of bounds! Hit the penalty box.

The general principle I stated earlier in this section applies here as well: Helping you write the essay or create the outline is fine; doing these tasks for you is *not* fine.

Roughing it

Now you're in dangerous territory. If you sit down to write and your Helpers intrude, you're in trouble. You need, to paraphrase Virginia Woolf's famous statement, "a room of your own," preferably one with a lock on the door. As you string the sentences together, you have to go it alone. Any help at this stage is pretty much guaranteed to be a no-no. Okay, they can cook you a special dinner, do the laundry (so you don't have to), and pick up the dry-cleaning. They can shout the correct spelling through the door or summarize a grammar rule you're stumped on. But as you spill the whole essay onto the page or screen, by and large you'd better be working by yourself. After the rough draft is complete, the Helpers can read it and make suggestions. (See the next section, "Checking and revising," for details.)

Checking and revising

Time to unlock the door and invite your dedicated Helpers to read your masterpiece. *But* — and this is an emphatic *but* — make it clear that you're asking for feedback, not rewrites. Your Helper may point out grammar and spelling

Too many editors spoil the essay

If you show your essay to too many people, you're asking for trouble, even if each reader gives you only academically "legal" help. The most likely scenario is that all the readers will identify the same problem in the essay, but each will choose a different way to correct it. One reader will say, "I think the section on your first root canal is too long" while another will comment that he'd like to read more about the root canal and less about your visit to the dental school. Both are reacting to a lack of focus in the piece. But faced with contradictory advice, you won't know whom to follow. Choose one primary helper and stay with him or her. If others insist on reading the essay, take their advice with a grain of salt.

errors, but you should correct them. Your Helper may tell you which sections of the essay are unclear and ask you questions about the puzzling parts. Also okay are comments like these:

> You started to lose me right around paragraph 3. Then I got bored. (I didn't say these comments were good for your ego, just for your integrity and the ultimate quality of your essay.)
>
> You move from one idea to another very quickly. How about some transitions?
>
> I like the story, but I'm not sure what point you're trying to make. Maybe you should clarify the last paragraph.
>
> I don't think you actually answered the question.
>
> Clearly ready for publication in *The New Yorker.*

One more time: Your Helper can point you in the right direction but not pilot the boat. *You* have to do the rewrites.

Typing or filling in the blanks

You ought to do your own typing, I believe, just on general principles, because you're going to have to type your own papers in college. But I don't see anything wrong with letting your parents or your parent's secretary help you out with the purely mechanical tasks of the essay, at least in terms of academic honesty. A couple of colleges require you to handwrite the essay directly on the application. I suppose they think that the resulting product will be more authentic, but they're ignoring the fact that you can get all the help you need before you're ready for the final copy. For those colleges, be sure the handwriting on the application is your own.

If you're stuck with the requirement to handwrite the essay, practice on scrap paper first, trying to remember all those penmanship lessons you slept through in elementary school. Buy a big bottle of correction fluid before you get to work.

Dealing with Parental ~~Interference~~ Assistance

They love you. They worry about your future. They also pay the bills. Is it any wonder that your parents want to help you concoct the perfect college application? But . . . it's your application, your future, and your essay. So is it any wonder that dealing with excess parental "help" is a real pain in the neck?

I say "they" and "their" in this section out of nostalgia for the traditional pair of parents living with 2.3 children in a little house with a picket fence. But those of you with non-traditional families (one parent, five parents, step-parents, hippie commune, whatever) may still have to cope with interference (sorry, *assistance*) from those who love you. Don't ignore this section just because your family does not resemble the families on black-and-white television reruns. If too much help is a problem, simply plug in the pronouns that suit your particular situation. Also replace the word "parents" and substitute whatever term applies to your living arrangement. Then read on!

In this section I outline strategies for removing parents from the parts of the application process that should be yours and yours alone. (See the section entitled "Finding the Right Sort of Help," earlier in this chapter, for specific guidelines.) But before I explain how to dissolve the superglue currently attaching them to your back, you should give some thought to *why* they're so hyper about your college applications.

I've come to see the process of raising children as an extremely gradual transfer of power from parents to their offspring. The parents' ultimate goal, of course, is to raise a mature adult who will manage life with maturity. The process begins at the other end of the power spectrum, with the totally helpless newborn baby. At this stage, the parents are in total control. They make every decision for the baby, and all the kid can do is protest loudly and wordlessly when he or she dislikes a decision. During early childhood, the child has a bit more power ("I want the *yellow* crayon, not the blue one"). By adolescence, most teens have a great deal more say in their everyday lives ("I think I'll play my MP3 during study hall today and do the math homework later"), but living arrangements, daily schedules, and a lot of important issues are still in the parents' hands.

Then comes college. Most parents sense at this point that they're about to lose control, big time. Assuming you sign up for a boarding situation, your parents won't know your friends, your social routine, your study habits, or little details like what time you come home after a party. Faced with the reality that you're about to leave both the family home and the family power sphere, some parents freak out. They attempt to micromanage the application process, I believe, because they cherish the last bit of power they've got over your life. Also, I think some parents hold on to the illusion that controlling where you go to college will allow them to control what you do when you get there. Fat chance.

If your parents have inserted themselves inappropriately into the essay you're writing, your best bet is to show them that you're mature enough to handle the application process on your own. Some useful strategies include the following:

- **Time management:** Show them that you're in control of the timing by starting early and working at a manageable pace. Frantic all-nighters do not breed parental confidence. (See Chapter 1 for tips on time management.)

- **Requests for appropriate help:** Be specific in what you ask. Don't say, "I can't figure out what to write." Instead say, "Tell me what you think are the most significant moments in my childhood" or "I'm thinking of writing about Grandpa Bob's work at the nature center. Do you think that would explain why I want to be a marine biologist?"
- **Politeness:** "Back off!" is not exactly the most courteous response to parental pressure. Try "Thanks for offering to help, but I think I should tackle this essay on my own. I'll show you the rough draft in a couple of days." After they recover from their fainting spell, they should leave you alone.
- **Alternatives:** Give them some other way to help. If they're poking into your draft, try the comment in the preceding paragraph and add something like "Could we sit down and discuss Grandpa's work at the nature center? I'd like to use some good details, but I'm not sure what his duties were."
- **Authority figures:** If you're dealing with hardcore interferers, you may have to bring in some hired guns. Make an appointment with the guidance counselor or college advisor and explain your problem. Then you can confidently (and courteously) state, "Mom, I appreciate your wanting to help me with the essay, but Mr. Getin told me that I should do this part by myself." When you show the finished product to your parents, try this statement: "Here's the essay, Mom. Mr. Getin read it and he thinks it's ready to go."

Bottom line: If they're being immature, counter with maturity. If maturity doesn't cut it, bring in a higher authority such as your college counselor. If *that* doesn't work, leave this book where they'll see it, conveniently open to the section in this chapter entitled "Finding the Right Sort of Help." If they won't listen to you, perhaps they'll listen to me!

Noting a Few Words about Plagiarism

Plagiarism is intellectual theft — swiping someone else's brainchild and claiming it as your own. Most frequently found in research papers and homework assignments, plagiarism may still rear its ugly head in an admission essay, particularly one that asks you to comment on a social issue. Because plagiarism is a serious academic crime, calling for the school equivalent of capital punishment (expulsion, or suspension if you're lucky), you need to recognize and avoid it. In the following sections I explain the two forms of plagiarism most likely to appear in your essay.

Quoting without giving credit

If you place the exact words of another writer or speaker into your essay without enclosing the words in quotation marks and citing the author, you're plagiarizing. The solution is simple; give credit where credit is due. Here's an example:

> **Plagiarized passage:** Whenever my grades slip a notch, I immediately buckle down and review all my notes until I'm sure that the problem has been remedied. Good grades are money in the bank, the capital I will spend on my future.
>
> **Corrected version:** Whenever my grades slip a notch, I immediately buckle down and review all my notes until I'm sure that the problem has been remedied. As multibillionaire Ariadne Weaver once said, "Good grades are money in the bank, the capital I will spend on my future."

As you see in the preceding correction, only six words and two punctuation marks divide the ethical from the unethical.

Swiping ideas

If you snatch someone else's thoughts and claim them as your own, you've signed up for a stretch in the plagiarism penitentiary. Swiping ideas is a no-no even if you change the wording of the original source. For example, suppose you're reading about the Powderpuff Revolt in history class. (Don't look for it in your schoolbooks, or anywhere else, for that matter. The Powderpuff Revolt is a product of my very strange fantasy life.) Here are a passage from the book and a plagiarized essay paragraph, along with a possible correction:

> **Original passage:** The Powderpuff Revolt teaches us that human rights, in this case the right to powder one's nose without governmental interference, are an extraordinary motive for social change. The human spirit tends towards freedom, and any government that forgets this truth must arm itself and prepare to use force to subdue its own people.
>
> **Plagiarized passage:** The issue that most concerns me is human rights. Throughout history we see that human rights act as a strong force, motivating people to work for social change. If a government ignores this fact, the government will eventually have to use weapons to control its subjects.
>
> **Corrected version:** The issue that most concerns me is human rights. I recently read an account of the Powderpuff Revolt by historian A.J. Tomato. Tomato makes the point that human rights act as a strong force, motivating people to work for social change. If a government ignores this fact, Tomato says, the government will eventually have to use weapons to control its subjects.

The example clearly shows that staying on the right side of the academic law is quite easy. The addition of a word or two crediting the source is enough to take care of the problem.

Some ideas — the economy matters during an election year, ancient Egyptian culture emphasized the afterlife, boy bands are dumb — are very common and likely to be found in many sources. You don't have to worry about crediting a source for this sort of idea.

Locating Help When You're On Your Own

I have assumed in writing this chapter that your problem is too much help, but some applicants have the opposite problem — no help at all. You may be the first in your family to apply to college or the only one with a command of the English language. You may attend a large, scandalously understaffed high school where the guidance counselor's first open appointment is six months after the application is due. Not to worry! A few avenues of assistance are still available to you.

You've already gotten some help by reading *College Admission Essays For Dummies.* Good for you! (Also good for me.) Here are some other possibilities for assistance:

- **A sympathetic teacher:** Most teachers are willing to spare you a few minutes, even if they have to chomp down a sandwich while reading a rough draft. Your English teacher is the logical choice, but teachers of other disciplines can help as well. Check out "Finding the Right Sort of Help," earlier in this chapter, for tips on appropriate and inappropriate help.
- **Relatives:** Assuming they don't go overboard (see the section, "Dealing with Parental Interference Assistance," if they do), relatives have a lot to offer. Fluency in English or experience in higher education is not necessary because your relatives know the most important subject — you. They can discuss your upbringing with you, tell you family stories, and help you remember or define important aspects of your life and character.
- **Your friends:** Your friends can help you in the same tasks and for the same reasons as your relatives. Apply the strategy explained in the preceding bullet ("Relatives") to your peers.

Part II
Getting Your Head Ready for Writing

In this part . . .

When you're repainting the dining room, you've got to do a lot of chores before you put the brush on the wall: select the color, buy the paint, cover the furniture, and tie up the dog. Skip one of those steps and you'll be sorry, especially if the step you skip involves Rover. You'll have lilac paw prints all over the couch.

When you're writing an essay, you also have several chores to complete before you put the first word on the page. In this part I give you a bird's eye view of the process and show you how to get your head ready for writing. I explain how to settle on a topic, gather details, choose a structure, and create an outline.

Chapter 5

Writing as Process, Not Product

In This Chapter

- Focusing on the process
- Keeping your inner creator and editor separate
- Gathering ideas: Pre-writing
- Putting your words on paper — the drafting stage
- Finalizing your essay

As you tackle the college or grad school admission essay, you may think that every light you glimpse at the end of the tunnel is the headlight of the train, rushing to mow you down. Take heart! This chapter provides a set of powerful fluorescent lights, illuminating an efficient and painless route through the writing process. By the time you finish this chapter, you'll know exactly where you're going and how to get there fast.

Writing with Process, Not Product, in Mind

You sit down, type as rapidly as you can, and then stand up. Does this sound like your writing process? If so, you're focused on the product — the finished paper or essay. Bad idea. Naturally, you can't ignore the product completely when you write. After all, that's why you're writing! You want to end up holding a piece of paper with words on it, preferably words that actually make sense and, as a bonus, sound good. But if you focus on the product, you'll waste time and energy. Moreover, your product won't be half as good as the one that emerges from a well-planned writing process.

Not convinced? You have a lot of company. People who practice product-oriented writing often tell me that they don't have time "to worry about all those steps" in the writing process. They just want to "get going and get done," as a student once said to me. They believe that writing without preparation is the way to go.

I see this belief in action whenever I assign a timed, in-class essay. Before the essay begins, I explain the ideal schedule to the students, given a total writing period of 40 minutes: 5 minutes of idea gathering and outlining, 30 minutes of writing, and 5 minutes of revision. Yet when I hand out the question (which has not been announced in advance), half of the students open their bluebooks and immediately start stringing words together. They're still at it 40 minutes later when I rip the booklets off their desks, mid-word. These students are sure that writing furiously (both in speed and in mood) for the entire time gives them a better result than writing for 30 minutes, with before and after steps.

Unfortunately, they're wrong. Here's what happens when you see the essay as a 100-yard dash: You start out with the first idea that pops into your head. If you get a better idea later, too bad. You're committed to one direction and can't change course mid-essay. As you work, you omit some terrific points because you're too busy writing to think much about the content. You're concentrating on mechanics (the English teachers' term for grammar and spelling, not automobile specialists), so you can't spare any brain cells for creative flourishes. Nor can you expend any energy creating a logical structure for the essay. Result: a weak, disorganized, spotty product, probably filled with mechanical errors you would have caught had you gone back for a second reading.

Granted, you have more than 40 minutes to write a college admission essay, and you will (please, please, say you will) recheck your work for grammar and spelling mistakes. But if you write your essay in a product-oriented way, you're cheating yourself. You're leaving your best writing buried inside.

In this chapter I describe the *process* of writing — the way in which you should go about preparing to write, drafting, and finally revising your work. The best part about process-oriented writing is that it's incredibly easy. No matter who taught you to write — an old-time, memorize-every-rule-in-the-book English teacher or a New Age, groove-with-the-universe type — you can improve your technique by taking the task of writing your admission essay one step at a time.

Separating Your Inner Creator and Editor

The writing process divides into three parts:

- **Pre-writing:** The stage during which you gather your thoughts, consider focus and theme, choose a structure, and outline the essay.
- **Drafting:** The first couple of rounds of slinging words onto the page until you have one complete version of the essay.
- **Revising:** The stage during which you function as a stern critic, reading over the essay, correcting and polishing until it's perfect.

About half of the process — from pre-writing through the first rough draft, minus the structuring and outlining stage — depends upon free-flowing creativity. The other half — from the second draft through the final product — depends more upon a critical eye. (Structuring and outlining also fall into the critic's corner.) To come up with the best possible essay, you've got to keep both halves of the writing process completely separate.

Here's what I mean. Two little workers inhabit your brain, a left-brain editor and a right-brain creator. No kidding, sort of. Scientists who have studied brain function have determined that most of the creative impulses come from the right side of the brain. The left brain is in charge of critical, logical, and analytical thinking. So the right brain gives you great ideas, and the left brain puts those ideas in order and inserts commas and capital letters. Both your inner editor and creator are useful — even essential — to your essay.

The problem is that they fight. Like co-workers who can't share an office without shooting paper clips at each other, the editor and the creator battle for dominance. Your mission, and you must choose to accept it, is to make sure that neither side wins. What you do is fool them. Send the editor out for coffee while the creator produces ideas (the pre-writing stage of gathering thoughts and mulling over focus and theme). After you've got a lot of ideas, invite the editor back in to select a structure and outline the essay. While the editor is busy, give the creator a rest. After a quick coffee break, muzzle the editor and let the creator crank out a draft. Then sit on the creator while the editor revises the essay.

Which half of your head is stronger? No, I'm not talking about the muscles that wiggle your ears and raise your eyebrows. I'm talking about the two halves of your brain — the creative right side and the logical left side. (Read the preceding paragraphs for more information on the right/left divide.) To phrase this question another way: Is your inner creator dominant, or your inner editor?

Not sure? Take this completely unscientific but fun test:

1. I read the last page of a mystery novel first so I can find out the name of the murderer.
2. I *loved* proving theorems in geometry class.
3. I *hated* art class when the teacher told us to play around with the paint and just "let it happen."
4. I always link one idea to another with words such as "consequently," "after," "therefore," and "on the other hand."
5. I hate it when people hop around in conversation with no understandable order.

Do you have more "yes" answers? You like order and logic, so your left brain is probably the one that tends to take over. More "no" answers? Your creator calls the shots. Regardless of the results of this test, remember that you need *both* sides of your brain to write a good essay. Just be aware that one part of the process will probably be easier for you than the other. Don't give in when you hit the difficult bit; try harder!

In Chapter 6 I explain and demonstrate some nifty techniques for freeing your inner creator. Chapters 7 and 8 show you how to build a sturdy structure for your writing and form a logical outline. Part III of *College Admission Essays For Dummies* tackles the rough draft, and Part IV brings it all back home with tips on polishing the final draft.

Now for a more complete overview of the process.

Pre-Writing: The First Steps

Before you put a single finger on a single key (or a single word on the page) of the actual college admission essay, you should be exercising your brain cells. The following sections cover the pre-writing steps.

Idea gathering

While you're idea gathering, you write down any and every possible essay topic without worrying about what your final focus will be. Helpful methods for idea gathering include:

- journal-keeping (jotting down ideas and observations)
- chatting with friends and relatives about possible topics
- taping recollections and random thoughts
- exploring your memories (Chapter 2 and the appendix explain how to do so)
- visual brainstorming, listing, and free writing — three idea-gathering techniques explained in Chapter 6

After you have a good number of ideas — at least five or six possible topics — you're ready to move to the next stage.

Narrowing down

Now you thumb through your idea list, separating topics into "possibles" and "What *was* I thinking?" Eventually *the* topic surfaces, or at least a topic you can live with. If no topic appeals to you, go back to "idea gathering" as described in the preceding section and try again. If all the topics look great, you have two choices. Throw a dart at the list and pick the one you've hit. Or, move on to the next stage and gather details about all the topics on your list. Soon one topic will emerge as best.

Detail gathering

As in the first gathering stage ("Idea gathering," described earlier in this chapter), in the detail-gathering stage you list everything you can think of that relates to your chosen topic. Once again, you shouldn't worry about whether or not you'll use the details in your final product. Just write them down. If you're writing about a memory, take care to include sensory details — the sights, sounds, smells, tastes (if appropriate), and tactile or touch sensations associated with the memory. Depending upon your topic, you may not use any of these sensory details in the finished essay, but recalling them helps to make the memory more vivid.

I discuss three techniques in Chapter 6 — visual brainstorming, listing, and free writing — that work well for gathering details.

Structuring and outlining

In the structuring and outlining stage, you look at all the ideas you've gathered and choose a specific focus and theme to unify the essay. You sort the details, choosing which to include and which to omit. Next, you select a structure that complements the ideas you're trying to express. Finally, you put everything in order. By the time you're done, you should have a complete recipe for the essay.

Chapter 6 shows you how to identify focus and theme. Chapter 7 describes several useful structures and explains how to choose the best one for your essay. Chapter 8 tells you everything you need to know about outlining.

When you've climbed all these steps, you're halfway up the stairs, and the completed essay is within sight. Time to move to the writing stage.

Drafting: Not Just for the Army Anymore

In the essay world, a *draft* isn't an unwelcome set of letters informing the nation's 18-year-olds that their next couple of years will feature really bad haircuts. A draft is one complete version of the essay, from the first word to the last. As you work on your essay, you'll write at least two drafts and perhaps even more.

A *rough draft* is a kind of trial version of your essay, not your best possible writing, but something to work with. To create your first rough draft you spill everything on the page, following your outline but not worrying overly much about the quality of your final product. During this stage you just chug along, placing one word next to another, knowing that later you'll have a chance to improve the work.

After everything is on the page, you start punching it into shape, creating still another rough draft. You turn vague statements into concrete, specific sentences (see Chapter 9 for more information) and liven up your verbs (also covered in Chapter 9). You construct each paragraph with a strong topic sentence and smooth out transitions. (Check out Chapter 10 for the lowdown on topic sentences and transitions.) Each time you go over your work, you create another draft.

Don't throw away any drafts. You never know when you might need them! You may delete a sentence from the first draft that seems perfect for a later version of the essay. But if you've shredded the earlier draft, set fire to it, or poured leftover spaghetti sauce all over it, you're out of luck. That perfect sentence is gone forever.

If you're working on a computer, the difference between one draft and another blurs because you write over previous versions of your work every time you save the file. Keeping drafts on a computer involves changing the name of the file with the "save as" command. For example, suppose the file containing your essay is called (How did I think of this one?) "essay." Every time you save, add a number. Soon you have "essay1," "essay2," and so on. If you need some phrase or section from an earlier draft, you can simply look at the file.

After you've got a complete rough draft, you may want to show it to a college counselor, a helpful teacher, or to your parents. They can tell you whether you're on the right track or not. (Chapter 4 explains in detail what sort of help is "legal" and what is out of bounds.) Bring the rough drafts with you. Your helpers may see value in something you discarded.

Taking the Final Steps

When you've got a good rough draft, most of the battle is over. Only a couple of small — but crucial — tasks remain.

Revising

"To revise" is literally to "re-see" your work. Revision is actually a tough skill to master. If you're like most people, you tend to fall in love with your own words. It's hard to dump a really great phrase or idea just because it doesn't mesh with the final version of your essay. Or, you've read your essay so often that you truly can't see it anymore. Your eye skips over missing letters or awkward phrases because you're on automatic pilot. So before you revise, take a break. Eat a peanut butter sandwich, walk around the block, or study for the next chemistry test. Later, return to the essay with fresh eyes. Bring everything you know about grammar, spelling, and style to the front of your mind. As you ruthlessly read your essay again, sandpaper the rough, clarify the vague, and correct the missteps.

Filling in the form

These days most universities have bowed to reality and accepted word-processed essays. (In the old days you had to hunt for a typewriter and try to hit the printed lines on the application with the typewriter keys.) As you ready your final draft for submission, remember to place your name and social security number at the top of each page. Choose a readable font, good quality paper, and normal margins. Print out, staple, and bingo, you're done.

If you don't have a word processor, check your school's computer room or library or take a trip to the public library to see whether computer time is available to you. Some photocopy outlets also rent computer time; the telephone directory for your town may have a list. Typing is acceptable, but a huge hassle compared to word processing.

A couple of colleges require handwritten essays or impose other rules about paper size, margins, color of ink, and so on. Read the application instructions carefully.

Sighing with relief

Just kidding. (Sort of.) Now you're done. All you have to do now is make a photocopy and send in the application, complete with masterpiece (the essay!).

Chapter 6

Storming Your Brain: Idea Gathering Techniques

In This Chapter

- Allowing your creativity to surface
- Choosing an idea-gathering technique that matches your personality
- Putting idea-gathering techniques to use
- Gathering ideas for specific questions

You've collected a mountain of memories (No? Chapter 2 and the appendix will help), but you can't seem to turn any of them into an essay. Every time you sit down to write, your thoughts logjam. Sound familiar? A lot of writers find themselves facing this dilemma, especially when they're in a high-stakes situation such as college admissions. In this chapter I provide three great techniques to unclog the jam. I explain how to select the technique that fits your personality and guide you as you narrow your focus, moving from random memories to topic and theme and then to details that make your essay come alive. (If you're seriously blocked and this chapter doesn't do the trick, check out Chapter 13 for more ways to get the creative juices flowing.)

You Can't Build a Castle Until You Dump the Blocks

Say you're five years old, sitting next to a can of blocks that is almost as tall as you are. You decide to make a castle. You reach into the can and take out the first block. Perfect! Just what you need to start off. Then you reach in and grab the ideal second block. The third block is the one you intended all along to place on top of the other two. In fact, every block you take out is *exactly the one you need.* Each fits into the right spot in the castle, and you never have to move a block after it's already in place.

As we say in New York City, yeah right. You can't build a castle or anything else that way. The best you can come up with is something resembling one of those melted watch paintings your art teacher raved about so much. At worst you get a pile of multicolored confusion, a mess even your dog doesn't want to look at. Even when you were five, you knew that.

So why are you trying to *write* that way?

Here's how you really build a castle when you're five years old: You dump the can of blocks onto the floor — or onto your brother, the dog, and maybe the peanut butter sandwich your mom made for lunch. You look at all those gorgeous colors and shapes spread out before you. Then you grab a snazzy red block, that little purple guy over in the corner, and maybe the green one that skittered under the couch. You move them around a bit, experimenting, and pretty soon you have a little tower. Only then do you say, "Hey! This is a castle!" Soon you see a pink block that becomes the basis for the drawbridge, and you're on your way. Every once in a while you sweep the whole thing away and start again. Eventually you end up with a castle Lancelot would be proud of. (And then the dog or your brother knocks it over, but that's another story.)

You have to write the same way you build a castle. First, *dump the blocks.* Instead of saying, "My essay is about my camping trip and my first sentence is . . . followed by my second sentence . . . and so on through the 34th and last sentence," you need to throw all the possibilities onto the paper. Then you take a look. You find a red block (memory of the time your mom took you to see the whale at the aquarium) and a green one (the 10th grade kick-off party for a community clean-up project) and maybe a yellow one (the first homerun you hit in little league). You sort through, move a few things around, and occasionally sweep the whole thing away. But finally you end up with an idea you can use. The idea sprouts details, themes, and images. You're on your way. No logjams for you!

Matching Personality and Technique

Three strategies — visual brainstorming, listing, and free-writing — help you gather ideas for your college admission essay. Each technique works best with a particular personality type, so before you try one, take a moment to consider which category you fall into:

The artist: Do you love visual arts — films, paintings, drawings? Do you understand everything better when you draw a little diagram? Are your school notebooks filled with little arrows, circles, squares, and other symbols? When you think, do pictures fill your head? Do you see things that your friends miss?

The logician: Do you love order, method, reason? Is your refrigerator door covered with magnets holding scraps of paper, each with a list? Do you carry a planner or a handheld computer and consult the "to-do" list often? In your school notebooks, is everything written neatly on the lines?

The free spirit: Are your monthly phone bills humongous? Do you love to daydream, to float around in a fantasy world? When you chat with your friends, do you hop from topic to topic seemingly at random? When you studied poetry, did you love digging into levels of meaning, decoding similes and metaphors? Does your school notebook contain stories or bits of writing that have nothing to do with the subject?

If you're an artist, visual thinking is one of your strong points. Try the technique I call "Visual brainstorming." Logical types (I'm one myself) usually have success with "Listing." For the free spirits, naturally, "Free-writing" is best. The following section shows you how to utilize each technique.

Human beings are complicated creatures, so some of the categories overlap. No problem. Try a couple of techniques until you discover which one is right for you.

Gathering Ideas: The Techniques

In this section I take you through the big three — proven techniques for "dumping the blocks" and gathering the ideas that are rattling around in your head. (See the section "You Can't Build a Castle Until You Dump the Blocks," earlier in this chapter, for more information.) Each technique meshes best with a particular personality type. (Check out the preceding section, "Matching Personality and Technique," for details.) But don't feel that you have to limit yourself to one technique only. If you're in the mood, try all three!

Visual brainstorming

Variations of visual brainstorming have been around for years, each with a different name. Visual brainstorming never goes out of style because it is such an effective way to tap into your creative brain cells. In visual brainstorming, you create a picture of your thought process. You also trick the critical portion of your mind into taking a coffee break so that your creativity can take center stage. Finally, visual brainstorming forces you to step away from your usual habits of writing so that truly new ideas may emerge.

You can use visual brainstorming to select a topic for your essay or to amass detail after you've settled on a topic. It's also a great way to discover the theme of your essay (see Chapter 2 for more information on theme) and to uncover the metaphors (creative comparisons) that light up your writing.

For this technique you need old-fashioned pen and paper. So turn the computer off for a while, get ready to have some fun, and do the following:

- Take a clean sheet of paper, preferably one without lines. (If it does have lines, ignore them.) Don't hold the paper the usual way. Turn it on a diagonal or upside down — something to make it look different. You want to break down the habitual categories in your brain.
- If you usually write with a pen, use a pencil. If pencil is your medium of choice, try a pen. Again, the point is to do something to change your pattern.
- Now write a word or phrase in the middle of the paper. Which word? Any will do, but a promising idea from the "Personal Inventory" in the appendix or from the self-discovery exercises in Chapter 2 is a good choice. If you can't find any good candidates, write your name or an abstract word like "loyalty," "friendship," or "challenge."

  Don't obsess over which word to write in the middle of the page. I'm not a psychologist, but I do believe that a part of your mind is active while you're not consciously aware. Whatever you write down has some significance, even if you can't figure out exactly why you chose that particular word.
- For about ten minutes, look at the word or phrase in the middle of the page and write down everything that comes to mind. Don't try to control the direction of your thoughts. Just jot down the ideas.
- Some ideas will flow as a group. Write them near each other on the paper.
- Sometimes you'll sense that you're starting a new set of ideas. Put these thoughts in a new area of the paper.
- A picture may emerge as you write. Fine. Don't spend forever drawing in the details, but go ahead a sketch whatever you like.
- When the flow dries up, stop. Look at what you've written. Circle the ideas that go together or connect them with lines.

Check out the visual brainstorm example in Figure 6-1. The key word is "change." "High school to college" led to "leaving home," which led to "going to camp." Then the idea of camp shifted to "afraid of water," "swimming lessons," "first race," and "medal." Now a new idea surfaced: "living away from home," then "year in Madrid," which drifted to "new language" and "dinner at 10 p.m." Somewhere during this process "snake" slithered in, with "shed skin" and "open to injury" and "danger" following.

Don't edit while you're brainstorming. Whatever you're thinking, don't allow yourself to say, "That's ridiculous. I'll never use it." Just write it. You're not committing to a 30-year mortgage. You're just jotting down ideas! (See Chapter 5 for a complete explanation of why editing and brainstorming don't mix.)

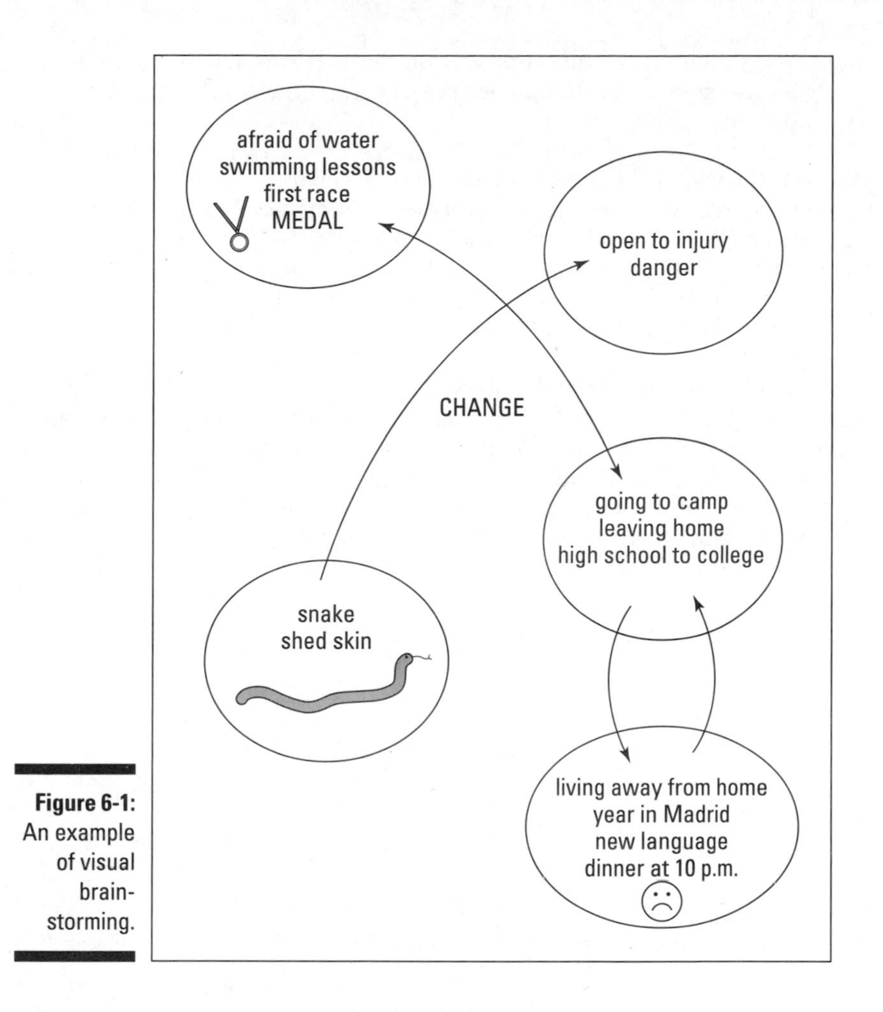

Figure 6-1: An example of visual brainstorming.

After you've completed one round of visual brainstorming, it's time to take out a second sheet of paper and do the following:

- Again, twist the paper around a bit. Change writing implements, if you like.
- Examine your first visual brainstorm. Does any part look interesting? Do you see any possible topics? If not, put a different word in the center of the new sheet of paper and try again. Repeat as often as necessary until something appeals to you.
- When one part of a brainstorm has possibilities, explore it further. Put a word or phrase from the possible topic in the center of a new sheet of paper. For ten more minutes, jot down the ideas that come to you as you think of the centered word or phrase. Again, place thoughts that seem to belong together in a bunch. Whenever your mind skips to a new track,

put those thoughts in a different section of the paper. When you're done, draw lines between ideas that connect to each other and/or circle related thoughts.

In Figure 6-1, the visual brainstorm centered on the word "change." Two possible topics emerge. One has to do with "How I Overcame My Fear of Water and Became an Olympic Medallist" (or something like that) and the second concerns "My Adjustment to Madrid." For the second round of visual brainstorming, you can choose either one of these topics and place either "swimming" or "Spain" in the middle of the page.

Figure 6-2 displays a visual brainstorm centered on "swimming." Notice that the details all relate to competitive swimming. The brainstorm includes some of the hardships ("frizzies," "permanent head cold," "5 a.m. practices," and "green hair"). Some of the advantages came to mind also ("independence," "team spirit," and "body image"). With this visual brainstorm, the writer is in good shape to write about the joys and sorrows of going for an Olympic medal in the backstroke.

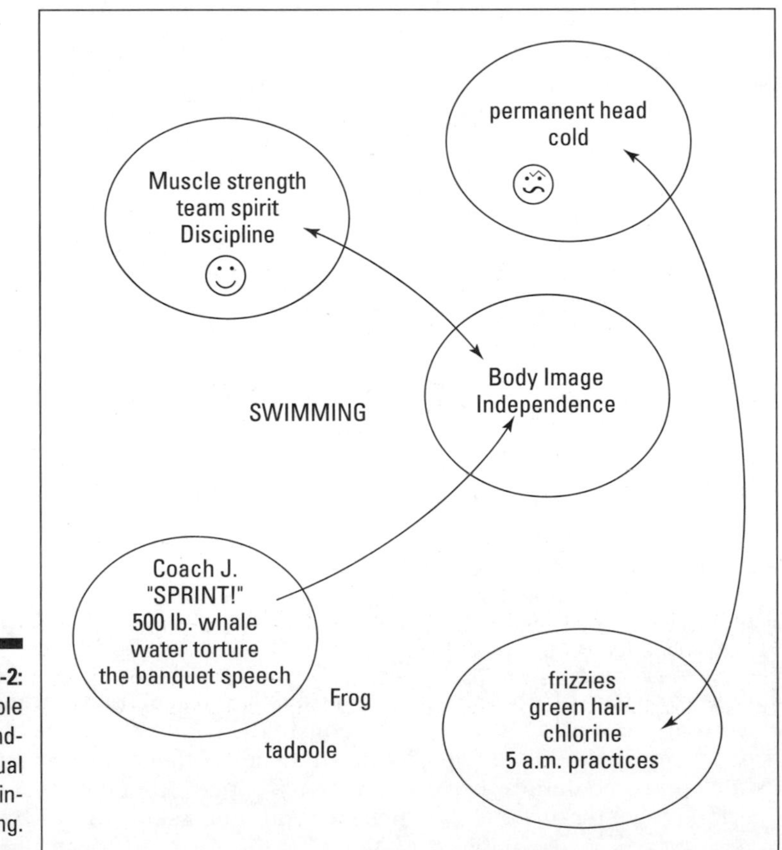

Figure 6-2: An example of second-round visual brainstorming.

If the writer needs more, it's time for another visual brainstorm. In Figure 6-3, for example, the writer brainstormed around "team spirit." She wanted to include a paragraph in her essay about the joy of working with 20 other permanently wet people, but she couldn't figure out how to say so. After brainstorming, she uncovered several relevant memories, including "homework on bus with teammates," "help Marjorie when injured," and "set coach's shoe on fire" — a cooperative and extremely unwise activity the team indulged in after the last meet of the season. Now the writer has enough ideas for a fine essay showing what she learned about cooperation and team spirit from her experience on the swim team.

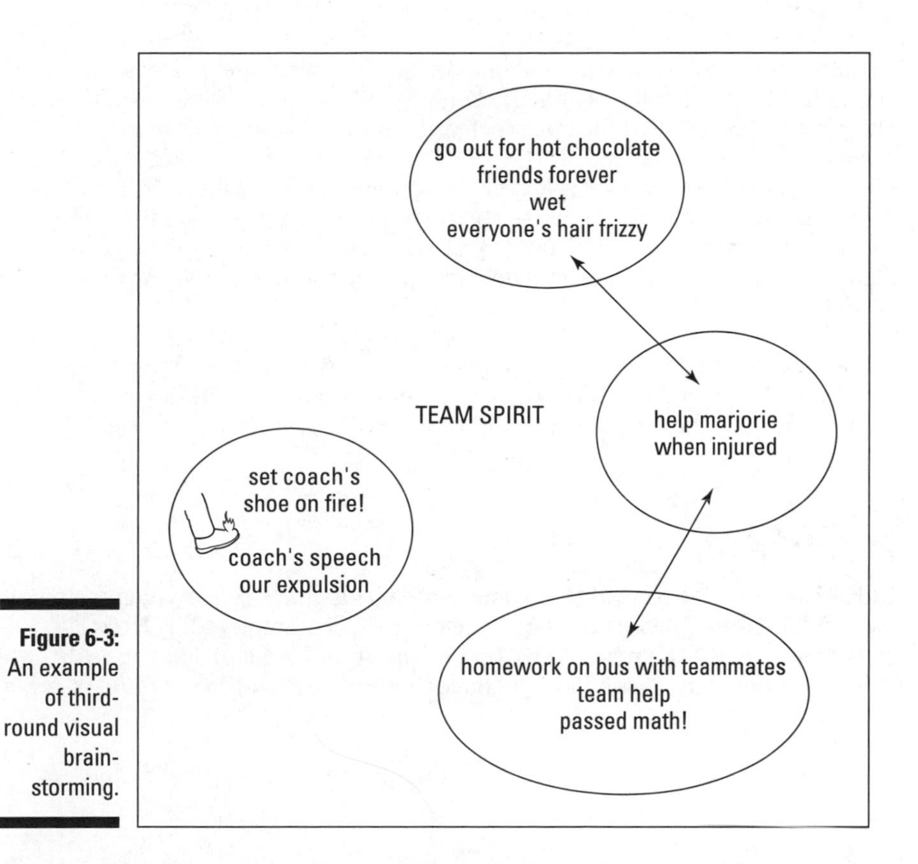

Figure 6-3: An example of third-round visual brainstorming.

While you're visual brainstorming, you'll probably come up with a couple of X-rated details. (You may want to invest in a shredder.) You will also come up with some G-rated ideas or details you don't need. Don't worry about unneeded details, X- or G-rated. Just leave them out when you write the essay.

Sometimes a really strange idea will keep popping into your mind while you're in the midst of visual brainstorming. You might be brainstorming about your first day of band practice, noting things like "clarinet," "out of tune," and "saliva." But the word butterfly floats again and again into your consciousness. *Write it down.* Later, look at all the weird items in your brainstorm. Ask yourself if any of them are metaphors (poetic comparisons) for the meaning of your experience. Maybe your first band practice, when no two notes in a row were correct, was your musical self as a caterpillar. About 5,000 band practices later, when you and your fellow musicians sounded great (okay, at least tolerable), your musical self was a butterfly. Now you've got a working metaphor for your essay.

In Figure 6-1, the "snake shedding its skin" may have slithered in as a metaphor for the feeling of change. You've got a shiny new self, even though the process of getting it hurt as much as peeling off your epidermis.

After a couple of rounds of visual brainstorming, you should have a pretty good idea what you want to write about (the topic). You should have some details you want to include. You may also have an idea for a theme (see Chapter 2 for more on themes) and perhaps a metaphor or two. You're ready to write!

If you need more details or an idea for a theme, or if you have your heart set on finding the perfect metaphor, simply center a word and brainstorm again. Keep centering and brainstorming until you have everything you need.

Listing

I love lists. I makes tons of to-do lists, just so I can have the joy of crossing off (scratching into oblivion, actually) the chores I've completed. I also make lists when I'm getting ready to write. The order and logic of a list appeals to me. (But I don't get carried away; I haven't alphabetized the contents of my freezer for years.)

You can list alone, but listing is even more fun with a friend. Here's the method:

- Pick a word at random, perhaps something from the "Personal Inventory" in the appendix or a memory that you uncovered after reading Chapter 2. If you can't decide on a word, try "car" or "challenge." (I've had a lot of luck with those two.)
- Take a sheet of paper or set up a new file on the computer.
- List titles for ten stories you could tell about yourself in relation to the word at the top of your list. For example, if you chose "car" as the keyword, you should have ten titles for stories you could tell about you and cars.

In Figure 6-4, the writer lists ten possible titles flowing from the keyword "challenge," including "physics labs," "waiting past Wednesday for Lover to call," "learning to parasail," "writing with a broken arm," and so forth.

- If you absolutely positively can't come up with ten titles, stop. But don't let yourself off the hook if you have fewer than five. Try again with a different keyword.
- Chances are one of the stories will grab hold of your imagination. Bingo! You're ready for the second set of lists.
- Write the title of the chosen story at the top of a new sheet of paper or on a blank computer screen (a new file, or just scroll down until you've got a clean slate).
- Now list details about the story. Write everything you remember, one item after another, until you can't think of anything else. Concentrate on sense memories: what you saw, what you heard, what you smelled, what you felt (sensations from your sense of touch, as well as emotions), and, if appropriate, what you tasted. Check out Figure 6-5. The writer decided to list details about "physics labs" from the first list.
- If you remember any conversation, write the words.

CHALLENGE

Physics labs
Waiting past Wednesday for Lover to call
Learning to parasail
Writing with a broken arm
Washing hair in desert
Avoiding dessert when on a diet
Getting the little tab into the slot when assembling furniture
Writing an essay
Speaking out about the new grading policy
Throwing out old shoes

Figure 6-4: An example of listing technique.

WARNING!

Don't censor yourself. As you write the list, don't stop to worry about whether a detail is worth including or not. Just list it. Later you can always decide to leave the detail out of the essay.

How long should your detail list be? The longer the better. If you have 20 to 30 details, you're probably fine.

PHYSICS LABS

Working every lunch hour for the entire winter
Sneaking out of study hall when the lab was closed
Picking the lock on the equipment cabinet
Rival group working in the corner of the room
Band practice outside
Very noisy
Broken tuba – sounded terrible
Band leader: "And a one and a two and a three…" all day long
Dusty smell of old chalk
Dirty floor – ruined two pairs of pants
Mr. O'Conner really proud of our results
Lab report was 20 pages long for some experiments
The balance we made to weigh a feather
The momentum experiment
At least 10 kids didn't finish, but we did
Demonstrating the momentum experiment to the other class
Submitting our experiments to the science fair
Lots of blocks, like kindergarten, and some motors
None of the motors worked
Shocks from the batteries
The water trough

Figure 6-5: Creating list of details.

If you're working with a partner, retell your chosen stories to each other, using as many details as possible. After hearing each story, ask questions: "What did your mother say when you signed up for the bowling team?" "What color was the horse you fell off?" "Did you hear any noise when the president pinned the medal on your shirt?" The more you ask, the more detail you get, and the more you have to work with.

If you're working alone, consider calling a relative or asking a teacher to play the role of partner, quizzing you about your story until you truly can't remember anything else.

If any part of the story is still unclear, write the new keyword at the top of a new page or on another blank computer screen and make another list. In Figure 6-5, the writer listed details about the chosen story, "physics labs." But when he tried to write about the physics labs, he got stuck on "momentum experiment." He couldn't figure out what to say. Check out Figure 6-6: that's the list he made about the momentum experiment. After that list was done, he had a lot more to work with!

MOMENTUM EXPERIMENT

A little car, like a child's toy
Green car
No motor, headed down an incline
Need to stop car at the bottom
Glued a plastic ruler in place – my little red ruler that I had used in geometry
Timing crucial to speed
Used my watch – digital
Then we bought stop watch
Sent the car down the incline
Timer went off
A huge crash when the ruler broke
Nothing stopping the car
Right through the window
Glass everywhere
We got into such trouble
The glass cost $40 and we had to replace it
The other lab group used a pillow to stop their car
Why didn't we think of that

Figure 6-6: Creating a new list of details.

By the time you finish listing, you should have a topic, all the details your little heart desires, and perhaps even a metaphor or two. (Metaphors are poetic comparisons: "Happiness is a hot fudge sundae," and the like.) If you're desperate for a metaphor and nothing pops up on a list, make a (you guessed it) metaphor list.

Free-writing

Free-writing is the pen-and-paper or computer screen version of non-stop chatter. For a set period of time, you write everything that pops into your mind, hoping that something in the stream of ideas will turn out to be an idea you can use. Free-writing, like visual brainstorming (described earlier in this chapter), reaches deep into your mind by tricking the conscious, critical portion of your brain into nodding off for a few minutes. Free-writing also relies on strong finger muscles; guaranteed, halfway through your knuckles will cramp up. Here's the technique in detail:

- Remove yourself from the hordes of friends or family members you usually hang with, if at all possible. If not, tell everyone to leave you alone for a while.

- If you wish, put some music on — not music you usually listen to, but something different. Or, work in silence.
- Set a timer for 10 or 15 minutes. If you don't have a timer, put a clock where you can see it easily.
- Boot up the computer and start a new file. Or, take a pen or pencil and turn to a clean notebook page. Be sure that you're comfortable physically.
- Concentrate for a few seconds on a memory or idea that you've been considering as a possible essay topic. If you've got no ideas at all, turn to the "Personal Inventory" in the appendix or read Chapter 2. If nothing surfaces, no problem. Just sit quietly for a few moments thinking about nothing in particular.
- Now begin to type or write every thought that comes into your mind. Don't stop even for a moment until time is up.

Two nano-seconds after starting to free write, you'll realize that your mind hurtles along at supersonic speed while your fingers resemble a car in a traffic jam. You simply can't write as quickly as you can think. Don't worry! Just write everything you can.

- As you free-write, don't attempt to make complete sentences, spell words correctly, or punctuate your work. If those things happen naturally, fine. If not, just keep writing.
- During free-writing, the mind hops from topic to topic with no clear links. That's good! Go with the flow, however illogical it appears at the time. The randomness is what makes this technique work.
- If you can't think of anything to write, don't stop writing. Just type or write, "I can't think of anything" until the thoughts flow again.
- When your time is up, rub your fingers and take a short break. Then reread what you wrote. Do you see why I told you to send everyone away? If you've done this exercise correctly, some of the thoughts you've recorded will be extremely private. (At some point you should consider shredding all the papers from this exercise. If you're up for appointment to the Supreme Court one day, you don't want this stuff entered into the Senate confirmation hearings.)
- As you reread, underline anything that looks interesting. You're consciously looking for essay material, of course, but if you like something on the paper, underline it, even if you can't quite figure out how you might use it.

Check out Figure 6-7, a free-write that starts with a vague idea about a library job. Notice that some of the material relates to the library job, but some doesn't, like the remark about the fire engine spurred by the sirens the writer heard. That remark, by the way, led the writer to a memory about a child in the library who wanted books about fire engines. Also notice that some words are spelled wrong and the grammar is far from perfect. After rereading this passage, the writer underlined some items, including how hard it was to work on Thursday nights with a chem test every Friday, learning how to do research, story hour, and Ferdinand the Bull. Anyone of those could grow into an essay topic.

After you've underlined a couple of items, it's time for round two:

- Set yourself up as before with a blank screen or page and a timer. Look at one of the items you underlined and think about it for a moment or two.
- Now write the underlined idea at the top of a new sheet of paper (or at the top of a new, blank screen). Begin free writing again. Every once in a while pull your mind towards the underlined idea you chose. Don't stop writing while you do so; in fact, don't stop for anything! All the same rules apply to this round: ignore punctuation, don't censor yourself, write "I don't know what to write" if you're stuck, and so on.
- As you reread the second round, again underline the sections that appeal to you. Do you have an essay topic yet? Repeat for as many rounds as necessary until you have settled upon the main idea of your essay.

started on my 16th birthday couldn't wait to have a real job worked after school for three hours and six on Thursday with a full day on Saturday. Alway had a chem test on fri so the Thursday night gig was hard, but still the money was nice - spending money for stuff I couldn't get before, but still saving for college what is that noise outside? a fire engine? and then the little kids in the children's room were so cute I liked that little red-headed kid who always wanted a book about fire engivnes I bet he thought I was so grown up. He should have seen me playing leapfrog in the aisle with Mary when the boss was on a break. And then there was the advantage of learning how to do research which I still use today and which I would not have known otherwise. I think I could have been flipping burgers for more money but I liked th library the people were mostly nice there was one guy who always took out the "dirty" books and then complained when he returned them that the library shouldn't have books like that but he always took out some more I guess he thought that he could have his cake and eat it too. I can't figure out what to write now I can't figure...okay now I'm thiking about story hour when I read picture books "under the pink umbrella" under the tree in the bakyard to all those little guys that was fun I also discovered all these great authors that I wouldn't know about otherwise and stories I loved like Ferdinand the Bull what a great charcter he is I think that Curious George is a good role model too, though I'm not sure about the man with the yellow hat what's that about?

Figure 6-7: An example of free-writing.

Take a look at Figure 6-8, the second round of free writing about the library job. This time the writer concentrated on working Thursday evenings with chemistry tests on Friday mornings. Notice the underlined material. Do you see an essay topic emerging? The job led the writer to become a more responsible student.

Alway had a chem test on fri so the Thursday night gig was hard

why did we have a chem test every week? I guess he wanted a lot of grades, but boy did those tests take up a lot of time and boy were they boring. All I remember about chem is those tests and the occasional cloud of purple checmicals that my lab partner unleashed he was always adding a little more stuff to the experiment, tryiung to see what happened when he did so and usually we had to evacuate the chem lab when he was done. but working on Thursday nights was good - a good long time, not too busy, and a little overtime too it made me organize the week very carefully I had to start studying for chem on Monday nights and do a little at a time each day once I had the job I definitely got more organized and more focused . I didn't want my grades to go down, so I had to be careful to study when I had the time, not when I used to, at the last minute before the test. So when I got the job I actually became a better student. Imagine that. I guess I never realized that before. Mr. Bernstein, the chem teacher, we called him Bunsen Bernie, he told me that I was always well prepared I remember he quoted poetry all the time in class, and he always tripped over one spot on the floor near the door we could never figure out what he tripped over because the floor looked even to us there goes a garbage truck outside now there always seems to be a truck on the street when I'm freewriting the lab smelled bad - lots of things like rotten eggs. Do chemists become chemists because they like making a mess? Is there an appeal to stinkiness?

Figure 6-8: A second round of free-writing.

The technique of free-writing can be used over and over again until the writer is satisfied with the topic and the number of details gathered. Each round starts with a moment of concentration on the main idea.

One last example of free-writing about the library job. Read Figure 6-9, a portion of a free write done after the writer decided upon the main idea: becoming a more responsible person after taking the job. With each round of free-writing, more details emerge. As always with free-writes, lots of the material is clearly useful, and some will probably be left out.

So when I got the job I actually became a better student

when I got the job my notebook was a mess. I always had time to rewrite or to call friends before the test, but after I started to work on Thursdays, I couldn't really call anyone because it would be too late when I got home, so I had to have the notebook in good shape. Some of those note techniques I still use, like looking at the notes after each class and adding stuff I missed and also underlining the main points or diagramming things more clearly in the evening, even though I would rather be watching television. I actually watched a lot less television after the job too. I guess you could say I had too much free time! Then when I didn't have any, I got more done. I also set up a study group with friends from chem class not the guy that poured all those purple checmicals into the mixture we were cooking for lab - he was the smartest one in the class but just too dangerous to hand around with you never knew what would explode when he was there. explode looks like explore i wonder if that was what he was doing he probably is the Bill Gates of the chemistry world, not following the lab book like everyone else...

Figure 6-9: A third round of free-writing.

If you find yourself wandering into a totally new topic during any round of free-writing, you have two choices. You can switch topics, or you can refocus. How do you refocus? Not by saying, "I am going to think about everything but elephants now (assuming that "elephant" is the topic you've been drifting into). If you tell yourself not to think about elephants, those big gray animals will sit in your mind and blot out everything else. You won't be able to think about anything but elephants! Instead, every time you realize that you are drifting away from the main idea, say to yourself, "I am thinking about the time I swam across the Atlantic" or whatever your preferred topic is. Pull yourself back into focus with a positive, not with a negative.

Reacting to a Specific Question

In the previous section I explain three techniques — visual brainstorming, listing, and free-writing — designed to pull an essay topic out of your head. You can use these techniques when you're deciding what to put in your personal statement or when you're answering open-ended questions like "tell us something we should know about you" or "describe a factor that influenced your life."

Happily, these techniques are also helpful if you're reacting to a more specific question. Don't give up on visual brainstorming, listing, or free-writing. You simply need to adapt the method of your choice to the question at hand. (See the section entitled "Matching Personality and Technique" in this chapter for instructions on selecting a method.) Here's what to do:

- **Visual brainstorming:** Extract the core word or phrase from the question and place the word or phrase at the center of the paper. As you brainstorm again and again, keep the question in mind. Be sure that the centered idea relates to the question you're attempting to answer.
- **Listing:** Take the most important word or phrase from the question and place it at the top of your first list. Every time you start a new list, be sure that the word at the top of the list relates to the question.
- **Free writing:** Before each round of free-writing, take a moment to concentrate your mind on the question. Write a key word from the question at the top of the page or screen. As you free-write, gently pull yourself back to the question whenever you realize that you're wandering.

Here's an example of how to adapt the three techniques to a specific question. Suppose you're asked to choose a photo and explain its significance. You unearth a photo of grandfather standing in the backyard of his house. At the center of the first visual brainstorm or at the top of your first list, write "Grandpa's yard." If you're free-writing, look at the photo for a minute before you begin to write. You may also place the photo on the desk or write "Grandpa's yard" at the top of the free-writing page.

Chapter 7

Building a Structure to Support Your Ideas

In This Chapter

- Enhancing the essay's meaning through structure
- Surveying the most common structures
- Taking a look at structures for career essays

I live in New York, the city that never sleeps. I figure the city's insomniacs must spend the wee hours drawing blueprints, because on every block somebody's tearing a building down or putting one up. So I see a lot of steel framework, the structure that supports the city's high-rises. Framework appeals to me because (as I hope you've noticed) I'm a writer. I appreciate the need for a sturdy base to support my creative expression.

Your admission essay needs structure also. The structure of an essay isn't a set of giant metal girders; it's a conceptual framework. You're probably not aware of the structure underlying most of the material you read. Nevertheless it's there, and if it's done correctly, it enhances the meaning of the writer's words.

In this chapter, I explain how structure works with (and when it's done poorly, against) your material. I show you how to match your essay topic with a suitable structure. Finally, I describe several structures and provide real student essay examples of the structures you're most likely to use.

Structuring Your Meaning

Even when you were toddling around in diapers, you grasped the Big Ideas — the basic structures of reality. For example, you compared that noisy little drum your brother was thumping with the measly toy piano in your corner of the room (comparison and contrast). You weighed the merits of crawling over to grab his toy (pro and con). For a few minutes you sucked your thumb and glanced around the room, checking out the lovely selection of toys strewn across the floor (survey). Finally, you crawled over and bopped your brother on the nose, whereupon he gave you the drum (cause and effect).

You've got all those structures plus a few more on a shelf in your mind, ready and waiting to be plucked from the shadows and established as the base for your essay. But take care; the right choice gets your point across forcefully, and the wrong choice weakens your material and confuses your reader.

For example, suppose you're writing about an issue that's important to you, one of the essay questions on the *common application.* (The common application, as its name implies, is a single form accepted by more than 230 universities.) You've picked air pollution because you're totally committed to environmental causes. Furthermore, you want to brag about the fact that you just organized a successful protest against a plant in your town. You managed to get the plant owner to agree to install filters on the smokestacks. You're now pressing for tighter fuel regulations to reduce harmful emissions.

Here are just a few of the structures available for your essay:

- **Pro and con:** You explain all the arguments in favor of tighter emission regulations and then all the arguments against the regulations. In the last paragraph you state your opinion.
- **Survey:** One by one you describe various important issues, including air pollution, nuclear weapons, civil rights, and so on. Then you cut to your reasons for becoming involved with the issue of air pollution, explaining its national and international implications.
- **Chronological order:** In strict chronological order, you explain how you became involved in the air pollution issue and what you have done to fight for cleaner air, beginning with your first cough at age 2 and ending with the petition you mailed two days ago.
- **Interrupted chronological order:** You begin with a description of a protest you organized at the plant. Halfway through the description, you switch to a discussion of your reasons for caring about the issue. You explain several steps you have taken to fight air pollution. The essay ends with an explanation of your future plans.

I could go on, but I think you can see the point already. Each of the essays described in the previous list has the same general topic (the issue of air pollution) and much of the same information. But each is likely to have a different effect on the reader. The first two structures are a poor fit. The pro-and-con essay will make the reader wonder why you're explaining both sides of an issue when you're clearly committed to one position. The survey essay is the weakest of the four. Why mention issues that you don't intend to write about? The chronological order essay could work, but your reader will wonder why you went back as far as your two-year-old coughing fit in order to talk about air pollution now. None of these essays would be as effective as the last one, which is more tightly focused on the issue you care about and highlights your involvement in it. The last essay is likely to be more dramatic too because it includes a quick "you are there" moment (the protest description).

How do you choose the correct structure? Keep these guidelines in mind:

- The essay should be focused on one main idea. Before you choose a structure, be sure that you can identify that point. In the air pollution essay I just discussed, for example, your main idea is "I care about air pollution enough to do something about it." Once you make that statement, you immediately drop the pro-and-con structure because it so obviously clashes with what you're trying to say.
- The essay should emphasize your main idea, not bury it in yards of detail. Turning again to the air pollution example, you can see that the survey structure treats a number of issues with equal emphasis. Not a good choice! The chronological order structure doesn't feature your most successful feat, the protest at the plant.
- The structure should reflect the way you want the reader to think about your material. If you want the reader to debate, go with pro-and-con. If you want the reader to travel through an experience with you, select chronological order or interrupted chronological order. If you want the reader to consider several ideas in turn, go for a survey structure.
- The structure you choose should give a prominent position to the "why" portion of the essay, as in "why I feel strongly about this topic" or "why this topic matters to me." No hard and fast rules define "prominent position," but readers do tend to pay more attention at the beginning or the end of a piece of writing. If you place the "why" paragraph somewhere else, be sure that it is strong enough to capture the reader's interest and that it fits logically with the preceding and following paragraphs.

Now for more detail and examples.

Meeting the Major Players in the Structure Game

In the preceding section I mention and describe a few possible structures; here I give you the large, economy-sized set, on sale now! Instructions included! (Just kidding.) This section guides you towards structures likely to be useful for a college admission essay, matched to suitable questions and often accompanied by real student essays. As you read you'll notice that some of the structures overlap. For example, a chronological order essay may survey some important events in your life. Don't worry about the labels. The point is not to name the structure but to use it.

Chronological order

When you write an admission essay, you naturally look back over your life and think about the events and people that shaped you. So chronological or time order is a good fit for lots of essays — especially for the ones that ask about events or people that shaped you. (Funny how these things go together!) This structure adapts itself to several different patterns:

- **Relevant events:** Thinking of an important aspect of your life — your passion for smelly cheese or your burning desire to climb Mount Everest — trace your involvement or the origin and development of your interest by describing several events very briefly.
- **Single event:** Focusing on one event in your life, perhaps the time you ran the Kentucky Derby on foot because your horse went on strike. (He wanted more oats and less hay.) Recount the event, hour by hour.
- **Typical day:** For the "person who matters to you" question, describe one typical day (or hour or minute, depending on the essay) with him or her.

In each of these essays you should devote a paragraph or two to interpreting the event(s) you're describing. As you write that paragraph, think of the reader. You're asking him or her to accompany you through time, to experience an event or period with you. The reader's logical question is "Why do you want me to be with you during this experience?" Make sure you answer that question!

Figure 7-1 is a chronological essay by a student who would like to be the next Steven Spielberg — and he may very well succeed. The writer concentrates on a single period in his life — summer study at a filmmaking academy — and focuses on the making of a short film. He begins with a brief reference to his lifelong passion for movies, but most of the essay deals with the few weeks of work on his own production. Notice that the writer takes care to explain what he learned from his brief course in movie-making.

Interrupted chronological order

All those movies about time machines reveal how fervently human beings would like to have the ability to interrupt the usual chronological order. You can't do it in real life, but you sure can tinker with time in your essay. Interrupted chronological order is helpful for essays about an event that changed you or an issue you care about, particularly when you want to relate a past event to your present situation or attitude. Interrupted chronological order has a million variations. Here are two of the most useful:

As far back as I can remember, I have always been captivated by movies, and how they are made. My parents have told me that watching movies with me, as a toddler, was almost unbearable because every ten seconds I would shout,"How'd they do that?" This interest in movies became a hobby of mine when my friends and I began making movies with our video cameras. The first films we made in sixth grade were usually simple five-minute stories that were always blatant copies of our favorite movies. Looking back on the movies we made in middle school, I realize they really brought me closer to my friends. Being a part of something like filmmaking was a great way to exercise my creative side, and make and strengthen friendships. And so, after my junior year of high school, I decided to take the next step from video to film.

I thus began this past summer studying filmmaking at the New York Film Academy. I went into the program with a lot of anxiety. I hadn't had to make new friends since my first summer at Camp Equinunk when I was ten years old. The notion of not knowing anyone, wandering the halls alone, and eating lunch alone concerned me; it shouldn't have, but it did. I also felt that I knew little about the technical aspects of film. Outside of my close circle of friends and my love for pointing the camera at things we thought were funny or entertaining, I was really just a beginner at film making.

The learning process of filmmaking was tiring yet rewarding and I did begin to make friends when the teachers divided the class into groups of four. Within each group, each person would direct his or her own film and the other three were to serve as an Assistant Cameraman, Director of Photography, and a Gaffer in charge of lighting. We rotated responsibilities after each Director's film was completed. As each became Director, he would learn to appreciate his dependence on the other three crewmembers for cooperation.

Unfortunately, the atmosphere in my group of young filmmakers was fiercely competitive. This is not to say I haven't endured competition in my life, after all, attending my prep school for fourteen years taught me a thing or two about it. When my turn to direct my final film had come and gone, you can imagine how horrified I was when I got back the film cans at the beginning of the editing process and found one of two and a half rolls had been double exposed.

Despite having received some sympathy from others who were busy working on their own films, it was too late to re-shoot my movie and I was left to work with what I had. The only thing that mattered was getting my clear, existing shots together, edited, and ready for the premiere with the rest of the students' completed films. After many hours in the dark editing room, I emerged a new man with a new film, much different from my originally planned concept. The next day, much to my relief, the film was very well received at the premiere.

Figure 7-1: An example of a chronological order essay.

Despite the headache, heartache, and backache of the process, I came out of that program having achieved exactly what I had set out to do, and made the absolute best of an unfortunate situation. I made new friends, a movie, and learned the basics of the filmmaking process, and most importantly, I had learned a life lesson as well. Corny as it sounds, I learned the true meaning of teamwork and trust, and without these two very important things I might have become even more lost, scared, and frustrated. I am acutely aware of these things now more than ever, and happily, I am eager to make my next film.

Figure 7-1: An example of a chronological order essay.

- **Flashback:** You've seen this technique on television. The character, usually wearing tons of makeup in order to appear decades older than the actor's real age, stares blankly into space. The music swells, the picture fades, and suddenly the young actor is on the screen. In a flashback essay, start with the present and cut to the past event. End with the present or with an interpretation of the flashback.
- **Bookends:** I call this structure "bookends" because you begin and end with two halves of the same event. The middle is usually the interpretation or background of the event. Suppose, for example, you're writing about the time you won a student election. You describe one particular part of the election in detail — your big speech calling upon the administration to abolish grades. You begin the essay with the first sentence or two of the speech and a quick peek at your audience. Then cut to your decision to run, the challenges awaiting candidates, the goals of your candidacy, and so on. End with the last few lines of the speech.

Regardless of what you're recounting in interrupted chronological order, you must still interpret the event for the reader. Here's what happened, you're saying, and this is why it mattered to me.

Check out the structure of the essay about homecoming in Figure 7-2. The student begins with the end of the evening as his friend is being lifted into an ambulance. He cuts to a description of homecoming, explaining the traditions sanctioned by the school and the private dance party held by some seniors. Then, back to the ambulance. Notice that the last paragraph explains why this incident was significant to the writer.

Homecoming Night

As I watched the paramedics measure my friend's blood pressure, I realized that this was the first time I had ever been in an ambulance; I asked myself, "How did I get here?" I apologize, I'm ahead of myself: this was my last Homecoming at my school.

Homecoming was a festival of sports, cotton candy, and fun. Alumni came back and visited their alma mater, lower school students painted their faces, and parents came to watch their children do what they love. As Student Body President, I had planned for several fundraising booths, and as Water Polo team captain, I had motivated myself to give our opponents a good game. Watching friends score touchdowns or serve aces and little kids run around in joy was truly an inspiring experience, and I couldn't have been more pleased with my last Homecoming- except, of course, if we had come back from our 5-4 Water Polo loss in the last quarter!

Often, to celebrate the event, several seniors rent out a space to host a dance party where, as tradition would have it, some kids arrive completely intoxicated, in hopes of fitting in. You might understand why I wasn't too keen on attending. After endless attempts to convince me that as a senior I would regret missing the party, I finally yielded and resolved to have a good time with my closest friends, far removed from the foolish behavior.

After a dinner, over which we shared some laughs, we approached the entrance to the party. A small group was gathering and whispers around me announced "Look, he's unconscious." I witnessed a classmate, with whom I was friendly, his eyes sealed shut, lying on the cold concrete sidewalk.

Out of the way, I waited in horror and watched paramedics hoist his seemingly lifeless silhouette onto a stretcher. "Oh my," I kept repeating. I tried to pray but my mind wouldn't function. Then my friends and I realized that the guys who had been with him all evening were letting him go alone, that they were going back to the party. We instinctively hopped in back of the ambulance so he wouldn't wake up alone and frightened, so his parents wouldn't arrive at the hospital without any answers. Struggling to remember his birthday or his address, all the while being questioned by suspicious police officers, who didn't believe that we hadn't drunk with him, we were strapped in and whisked away to the hospital. We sat, speechless, in our party clothes and combed hair uncertain what to feel. Our friend, a great student and warm-hearted person, had drunk because of peer pressure.

Figure 7-2: An example of an interrupted chronological order essay.

When his parents arrived in worried tears, they thanked us profusely. I'll never forget his distraught father's words, "We knew when we got here that we'd see who the real friends were." Was I a true friend? Where was I to warn him? I knew that these things happen and I wasn't there. But then I remembered those with whom he had come to the party, and how, to them, these events were but intermissions in the celebration. I remembered a theme in my favorite book, The Great Gatsby: carelessness. No one else would be bothered more than was necessary. No one else cared that he didn't regain consciousness until the middle of the night.

Once again I must apologize: I can't write an essay that I'll for certain be a film-maker, musician, Olympic swimmer, or President of the United States; I love participating in the activities I have chosen in high school but my focus may someday change. I can however state with all the confidence in the world that for the rest of my life, I will live with the drive to be a loyal friend, to care for my peers, and to use my best judgment wherever I am. To me, this is what life is about: compassion and thoughtfulness, or perhaps compassion even without thoughtfulness. As for my first ride in an ambulance, well, I think I'd much prefer taking a taxi instead!

Figure 7-2: An example of an interrupted chronological order essay.

Survey

A survey resembles a mosaic, a picture created with tons of tiny, tinted tiles. (I was going to say "multicolored," but I was having too much fun stringing "t" words together.) In writing, you can create a mosaic by briefly describing a number of objects, people, or events, giving equal weight to each. A survey essay, like a mosaic on the wall, should create a larger picture out of the smaller elements. So be sure that your survey essay has a main idea that you communicate clearly to the reader.

The survey structure is useful when you want to discuss something or someone you love passionately. (I am *not* suggesting that you write about your latest romantic partner, by the way. Bad idea. You'll probably break up before graduation anyway.) Perhaps you're nuts about toucans, those birds with the flashy orange beaks. You write an essay filled with lots of little toucan moments — the first meeting of the Toucans Lovers Society, which you founded; the way your pet Tookie used to sit on your lap while you watched cartoons; the Saturday morning walks in the park with Tookie; the time Tookie ate Grandma's ear; and so forth. The main idea is your devotion to a misunderstood but loveable animal.

Figure 7-3 is a fine survey essay written in response to this question: Please enclose a picture of something of importance to you and explain its significance. The writer submitted a photo of a filled toothbrush holder. The main idea is that this writer's friends are important to her. But how cleverly she gets her point across! Each friend is represented by one toothbrush.

Figure 7-4 is a different sort of survey essay, a hybrid of survey and chronological order. I'm including it here because the main point is a set of small events, not the order in which they occurred. The author, who is extremely interested in Asian studies, talks about a summer in Japan. He briefly cites several experiences of that summer, showing their impact on his view of the world. Notice how the author builds a picture of his evolution to an international point of view.

Description and interpretation

What can you describe? Things, places, events, people, ideas . . . just about anything! And after you describe something, you can interpret its meaning by showing how it is relevant to your life. This sort of structure provides a strong base for essays about people or events that have influenced you, qualities that define your personality (describe the quality and then show how it plays out in your day-to-day life), values you cherish, and lots of other topics. This structure is very adaptable!

When writing an essay with a description-and-interpretation structure, take pains with the description. Tuck in lots of sensory details — the sights, sounds, smells, feel, and (if appropriate) taste. Don't stint on the interpretation section either. Allow yourself to grow a bit philosophical, speculating on the meaning — to you and to the larger world — of what you've described.

Figure 7-5 is a terrific description-and-interpretation essay on crying. The author doesn't simply mention tears; she takes you right into the bathroom stall where she's sobbing her heart out. After she's sure that you can see, hear, and feel that experience, she moves to the larger world, even to television, to ponder the way our culture perceives crying. She manages to weave in her thoughts about stereotypes and feminism.

When you look at this picture, you will probably think that I have sent it to you in order to illustrate my love of dental hygiene or color coordination, and while I assure you that dental hygiene is important to me, the picture has more personal significance than that. Each toothbrush in my bathroom belongs to one of my close friends. Whenever they sleep over, they have a toothbrush waiting for them. This is not only a pleasant change from the method of scrubbing toothpaste onto each tooth by finger, which experience has proved ineffective and unpleasant, but also a reminder of the importance of our lasting friendships. I am reminded of my friends each night before I go to sleep and each morning as soon as I wake up.

The friends whom we grow up with invariably shape who we become. Through examining aspects of what we like or admire about someone, we learn about ourselves. My group of friends illustrates my wide range or interests and my multi sided personality.

The red toothbrush represents my academic motivation and dedication, as it belongs to a friend with whom I have become closer with through school. We struggled through an honors physics class together last year, and continue to work together this year. We have spent hours mastering friction on an incline and graphing polynomial functions, and I know that I can always count on her to help me out with a math problem or to discuss more serious topics. Through our academic success together, I have avoided getting caught up in the competitive nature of my school, and learned that studying together is beneficial to both parties.

The turquoise toothbrush belongs to a particularly fun friend. With her, my fun loving side comes out. Together we have taken spur of the moment day trips to the beach, ventured to downtown New York in search of Mexican food with live music, and danced the night away during "80s night" at a club. Academics are important to me, but I have always left some time for fun and relaxation.

The rest of my friends have various qualities that make me enjoy my time spent with them and admire them for. Ranging from loyalty to a sense of humor to a love for the "Harry Potter" Series, each is important to me. I have learned so much from each person and cannot imagine my high school years without my friends. I am extremely lucky to have such a supportive and diverse group. We have done community service together, pulled all nighters studying, thrown each other surprise birthday parties, and most importantly, encouraged each other. Come next autumn, we will all be on our way to different places all over the country. Although I will miss my friends, I look forward to adding new and inspiring people to their numbers. I am excited to find things in common with those who have grown up in different environments, and discover new interests through meeting new people. In the coming year, the toothbrushes in my bathroom will not get much use, but the qualities that have attracted me to their owners will ensure that the friendships will last.

Figure 7-3: An example of a survey essay.

In the summer of 2001 I found myself living halfway around the world. I was finally in Japan. My first challenge was to adapt to another culture. Although this culture was not entirely new to me because of my prior studies and a previous visit in March of the same year, I was visiting it on different terms. My first trip was a nine-day trip in March as a tourist visiting Odaiba, Kyoto, and Yokohama. This time I was in Japan, living in West Tokyo, to experience life in another culture.

I was first exposed to Japanese language and culture in elementary school when a friend introduced me to Animé (Japanese Animation). I fell in love with the culture and language. Now, with years of continued interest and study, I have had invaluable life experiences that I will never forget and which will be there for me to build on.

During the first two weeks I was granted permission to attend a traditional Japanese school. As a native English speaking person, I took on the role of resident English specialist. I spent most periods helping students with pronunciation of English vocabulary. During classes I participated in discussions of American history, government, and current affairs.

Living with my host family, I realized that I had always taken for granted the amount of living space I had to myself. My host family's apartment was comfortable, but it was only about one and a half times the size of my bedroom at home. Suddenly I realized how attached I had been to materialism; bigger and more of something is not always better. My attempts in making Tokyo my own included several trips to Akiharbara - the consumer electronics district - and a personal introduction to the Vice Governor of Tokyo. Going into the city allowed me to meet people who had the same interests in things that I did: the advancement of technology. When I met the Vice Governor I felt like I had a personal welcome extended to me by a high ranking official who in most situations would probably not notice me, but being declared as an ambassador to Japan by the Mitsui Corporations, my visit meant all the difference.

Near the end of my visit my host brother took me to his friend's house on Oshima Island. Our stay was scheduled for five days but was cut short because of an oncoming typhoon. Having only experienced snow and thunderstorms the idea of a typhoon was more than overwhelming. Nevertheless on the last day before our return to Tokyo we climbed Mt. Mihara, a currently inactive volcano. Climbing a volcano was enough to make me nervous, and with a typhoon coming, I was on edge.

While ascending to the its summit, I expected to look outward from the volcano's peak and witness a beautiful view of this island and the its surrounding waters.

Figure 7-4: An example essay that uses survey and chronological order.

However I had not expected was that I would also look inward and see myself from a new perspective. On Mt. Mihara, the importance of setting goals became critically clear to me. With this realization I became conscious that I had accomplished one of my first major goals in life. I had actually lived in Japan. I was not in Japan merely by chance. Although I received a lot of support, I worked very hard. Having accomplished one goal, I realized I could accomplish bigger and better ones. I felt tiny on top of this island with a population of less than 10,000, looking out at water. Although I felt small in a large world, I realized I could do more than I had previously imagined.

In preparation for college, I began to create new goals, such as maintaining good peer relationships and participating in extra curricular activities. But most importantly, I hoped to find a school that would help my growth and maturation within Japanese language and culture. Looking inward atop Mt. Mihara, I came to know that if I have clear goals and work hard, I can clarify my own vision and direct the path of my life.

Figure 7-4: An example essay that uses survey and chronological order.

Comparison and contrast

Less common than the other structures I discuss in this section, a comparison-and-contrast essay may be useful for the "discuss an issue you care about" question that appears on so many applications, including the common app. In this sort of essay you might discuss two possible solutions to a problem, explaining the advantages and disadvantages of each. You can organize this essay in several ways. The first paragraph may explain the problem, and the second discuss one solution. The third paragraph then reviews an alternate response to the situation. In the final paragraph you explain which solution you believe is best. Comparison-and-contrast structure also works when you're writing about people. For example, you could compare and contrast the influence upon you of two relatives. I once read a great student essay comparing the writer's grandmothers. One was very straight-laced and the other a loveable eccentric. After allowing the reader to experience their vastly different child-rearing styles in the first few paragraphs of the essay, the author devoted the last paragraph to his point: Both grandmothers showered him with unconditional love and shaped his personality.

I sat crouched on top of the toilet in the girl's bathroom outside the cafeteria. I concentrated on the little tile patterns. Anything to stop it from coming again. OK, think about happy things. The upcoming weekend, pumpkin Tasti-D-Lite, Temptation Island on tonight at 9. Oh god, not again. Despite my best efforts, it happened for the third time in two days. I cried.

And it wasn't just a little whimper either. It was full fledged, body heaving, tears running, red-nosed, crying session. As I cried, I thought about all of the events that had led up to this pathetic moment in time… and I cried some more. I emerged from the safety of my stall and looked in the mirror. I examined my eyes, which were crimson and glazed over. My nose was swollen and my cheeks were tear stained. I managed to somewhat drape my hair over my face and quickly put on my sunglasses before anyone could see me in this state. I exited the bathroom and headed toward the cafeteria, where I would spend the next half an hour assuring everyone that I was all right.

But was I? Is this normal? On an episode of Sex in the City, the issue of crying in the workplace was raised. Charlotte, the "emotional" one, cried at work one day in front of her whole staff. From that day on, she was mocked and the amount of respect she garnered plummeted. Everyone would comment, "Don't move that picture to the wrong place: you'll make Charlotte cry!" or something of that nature. She shared her experience with strong Samantha, who had been trying her best to control her emotions in front of her new boss. The question then became, Why can't women cry without being labeled, "typical girls"?

As a first trimester senior, I have gained a full understanding of the words, "stress, pressure, and aggravation" and I have crumbled more often than I would like to admit. In addition to the usual college, work, stress combination, the World Trade Center disaster was thrown into the mix, adding a new level of emotionality and anger. It is this overwhelming mixture of variables that has apparently caused my tear ducts to be on permanent active duty. I used to be able to hold in my tears until I reached home, but now, the tiniest things set me off uncontrollably. Bad grade on a math test? How about a nice sob in the bathroom. Can't remember what you did with the "good draft" of your college essay? Try a tear fest by the tennis courts.

Figure 7-5: An example of a description-and-interpretation essay.

When I cry, however, I feel as though I am fulfilling that typical women's role. It's expected for girls to be the emotional ones, the ones who gush over puppies, the ones who bawl when they break a nail. I always think to myself, "I am a strong person." But when I get frustrated or upset or angered, I feel as though I have to cry. I have to get it out. The fact that I am a vocal senior girl sometimes gives people the impression that I don't need to, or even shouldn't, cry so frequently. People have told me to go for a jog, laugh it off, or take relaxing breaths in order to calm myself. I want to do these things and occasionally I try them, but to me, there is nothing that cleanses me like a good cry. I feel confident in the fact that I am intelligent and capable, so why do I feel so insecure about a reaction that my body feels is necessary? The World Trade Center disaster has made crying more acceptable, since the images of strong firefighters and brave policemen shedding tears has been plastered in magazines and on the news. In a society where we conform to standards and fit in and take things "on the chin," the September 11th disaster has made crying an acceptable way to express anger and sadness. Hopefully, after these horrendous incidents, people will understand that crying is natural and should not only be acceptable when something hugely terrifying occurs. Crying as an appropriate response should not be limited to women and should not been seen as a sign of weakness. Both the "Charlottes" and the "Samanthas" need to cry sometime, and it is not because they're women: it's because they're human.

Figure 7-5: An example of a description-and-interpretation essay.

Pro and con

Another structure that helps out occasionally on the "issue you care about" question is pro and con. *Don't* use this structure if your mind is made up and you're totally committed to one side or the other. But perhaps you're on the fence, seeing some worthwhile elements in each position. You may want to explore the two points of view, showing the admissions committee how you've analyzed the situation and where your sympathies presently lie. The best pro-and-con essay I ever read concerned the abortion issue. The writer, clearly torn, saw some merit in both the pro-choice and the anti-abortion positions. Her essay was a truthful, thoughtful presentation of her views. In the first paragraph she explained why the issue mattered so much to her: A close friend became pregnant and asked her for help. The writer freely admitted that she was not sure how to respond. In the second paragraph the writer discussed the reasons why she supported her friend's right to choose. The third paragraph portrayed the deep sense of anguish the writer experienced as she contemplated the termination of her friend's — or anyone's — pregnancy. In the final paragraph she honestly explained her continuing conflicted feelings and her decision to support her friend regardless of the option her friend selected.

Cause and effect

Cause-and-effect admission essays fall into two categories:

- Here's what happened, and here's what I did about it.
- Here's what happened, and here's what it did to me.

In each of these basic cause-and-effect scenarios, the "it" is a situation or event, also known as a cause. The effect is your reaction to that cause. You may build a fine cause-and-effect essay to answer several application questions, including "describe a person or event that influenced you" and "show how you faced a challenge or exercised leadership." For example, suppose you want to write about your aristocratic aunt's influence on you. You describe a visit in which Aunt Brunhilda terrorized the staff of your favorite restaurant and how you finally stood up to her and ordered her to apologize to the waiter she had hit over the head with the wonton plate. Or, you describe the visit and explain how Aunt Brunhilda's behavior awoke your desire to become a labor lawyer specializing in cases concerning hazardous working conditions.

Structuring the Career Essay

Grad school applications often ask you to describe your career 10 or 15 years down the road. Many graduate schools also question why you want to enter a particular field. Here's the lowdown on structure for these essays.

Future career

You've got a nice variety of choices for this type of essay:

- **Chronological order:** Take the admissions committee through the steps you see yourself climbing as you pursue your chosen field.
- **Survey:** Show the reader several aspects of your professional life as you envision it, giving equal weight to each.
- **Description and interpretation:** Describe a moment in your future practice and explain why that moment epitomizes your ideal career.

Why this field?

Here are some structures for this sort of essay:

- **Chronological order:** Review the events in your life that led you to see the field as a perfect fit for your personality and values.
- **Survey:** Explain all the factors that draw you to the career.
- **Description and interpretation:** Similar to the "how do you envision you future career" essay I discuss in the previous section, you might answer this question by imagining yourself as a professional in the field and then explain why that vision appeals to you.

Chapter 8

Putting It All In Order: Creating an Outline

In This Chapter

- Understanding why outlining is important
- Discovering how to place your ideas in logical order
- Making sure there aren't any holes in your outline
- Staying flexible
- Filling out a pre-write checklist

After you've chosen a topic (see Chapter 6) and a structure (Chapter 7 tells you how), you're almost ready to launch yourself — not into space, but into the actual writing of your admission essay. Think of the outline as number 2 or 1 on the classic "10, 9, 8 . . . blast off!" sequence.

In this chapter I explain *how* to outline your admission essay and *why* you should do so before you write. I also direct you in dropping unneeded information from your essay and adding missing links. Finally, I provide a handy form that steers you through the final, pre-flight check before you embark on the writing of a successful essay.

Outlining: The Logical Choice

When I say outline, I know that all sorts of threatening numerals and letters flit through your mind: IV, IX, XVIII, A, 2, a, b, c. . . . I also imagine that you immediately start worrying about how many spaces to indent everything. On behalf of English teachers everywhere, I apologize for freaking you out about the rules of formal outlines. I also want to tell you that a famous New York phrase is the best solution to this outline nightmare: *Fuhgeddaboutit.* (For non-*Law and Order* fans, that's New Yorkese for *Forget about it.*) You don't have to hand this outline to an Authority Figure; no one will see the outline but you. So the formal outline systems, useful as they are for some types of papers, are not essential here.

But the outline itself is essential. Before you begin the rough draft, you must decide what you want to say and the order in which you want to say it. That's the essence of an outline — not the numbers, letters, and fancy margins. Granted, a written outline is not crucial to the success of the finished essay. Because the essay is a rather short piece of writing, you may be able to keep an outline in your mind, just as some cooks are able to throw in a pinch of this and a cup of that without consulting a printed recipe. Nevertheless, most people find that a cookbook leads to less indigestion and a written outline leads to fewer writing headaches.

Furthermore, the whole indentation mania does have a point. In classic outline structure, everything of equal importance is indented the same number of spaces from the left-hand margin. The indentation actually creates a visual display of the logic of your essay. You shouldn't obsess over the number of spaces or the numbering system, but you should think of your outline as a set of categories. As you create an outline, indent every time you divide a category into smaller subdivisions. When you're done, you should be able to see which categories carry the same weight, and which ideas are subordinate to others — in short, how the whole thing is organized.

Check out Figure 8-1, a humorous (and totally untrue) outline of the college admissions process. Notice that the three largest categories (extraction, fabrication, submission) are not indented at all. These three categories are equal in importance. The "fabrication" category is divided into four equal parts: letters of recommendation, test scores, school grades, and essay. These four headings on the outline are indented equally (five spaces from the left-hand margin, for those of you who like details). The smaller categories are themselves subdivided. The "essay" category, for example, is divided into four sub-categories: intensive psychoanalysis, midnight oil burning, soul baring, and total desperation. (Okay, maybe *some* truth crept into this outline!)

College Admissions: The Process

I. Extraction
  A. Application Fee
  B. Information
    1. Social Security number
    2. Biographical data
    3. Educational data
      a. Courses
      b. Grades
      c. Test scores

II. Fabrication
  A. Letters of recommendation
    1. Seeking writers
      a. Expensive gifts
      b. Writing tests
      c. Loyalty oaths
    2. Nagging writers
      a. Midnight phone calls
      b. Threatening letters
      c. Groveling
  B. Test scores
    1. SAT/ACT prep courses
    2. Proctor bribes
  C. School grades
    1. Cramming
    2. Hacking into the school computer
  D. Essay
    1. Intensive psychoanalysis
    2. Midnight oil burning
    3. Soul baring
    4. Total desperation

Figure 8-1: A sample outline.

(continued)

III. Submission
  A. Typing on the form
    1. Erasing
    2. Trying to hit the line
    3. Correction tape
    4. Little jars of white paint
  B. Stuffing the envelopes
    1. Enclosing good-luck charms
    2. Fitting in the 212-page essay
  C. Mailing the envelopes
    1. Placing too many stamps
    2. Good-luck superstitions
    3. Last-minute desperate acts
  D. Calling the admissions committee
    1. Promising a huge donation
    2. Wining and dining
    3. Pleading
      a. In writing
      b. On bended knee

Figure 8-1: A sample outline.

Putting Your Thoughts in Order

Now for the nuts-and-bolts instructions for turning a mass of ideas into a coherent outline:

1. **Reread the notes you took for the essay.** (No notes? Chapter 6 describes some great techniques for gathering ideas.)
2. **Examine the structure you chose for the essay, noting the basic organizational plan.** (No structure? Chapter 7 describes the most common structures.)
3. **Consider the theme of the essay — the big idea you want to communicate.** (Clueless on themes? Check out Chapter 2.)
4. **Imagine a stack of baskets, some large and some small.** Start dividing the ideas into baskets. If you're writing a cause-and-effect essay, imagine a "cause" basket and an "effect" basket. Or perhaps you're writing an essay with a survey structure. Imagine that each item you're including in the survey is sitting inside a basket. On a clean sheet of paper or in a new computer file, create a section for each basket. Give each basket a name. In Figure 8-1, for example, you'd write "extraction," "fabrication," and "submission" in separate areas of the paper or file. Figure 8-1 also shows you one formal numbering system, in case you like such niceties.

5. **Sort through your notes, placing each idea in the appropriate basket.** As you sort your notes, you may find something that just doesn't seem to fit anywhere. No problem! Perhaps that particular idea doesn't belong in the essay. If you really, really, really want to use an idea that doesn't belong to any of the categories you've set up, reconsider your design. A different structure or a different set of "baskets" may accommodate your favorite thought.

6. **Consider each basket in turn after everything is sorted.** Subdivide the contents into smaller categories. (Imagine yourself placing the ideas in a set of smaller baskets.) Then look at the smaller categories. Can those ideas be subdivided as well? Each time you create a new "basket," give it a name.

7. **Decide whether you're a visual thinker or not.** If you are a visual thinker (you think in pictures and love maps), take the time to indent your outline, as described in the previous section, "Outlining: The Logical Choice." (Figure 8-1 is a good example of the proper indentation.) If you don't feel the need for a diagram, don't bother. Just scan the "baskets" you've created and consider which should be first, which should be second, and so forth. Number everything so you know its proper place.

Have you ever heard the old saying, "Don't put all your eggs in one basket"? That proverb applies to outlines as well. You can't divide something into one part; logic won't let you. The whole concept of "divide" involves chopping something into smaller parts. Notice I said "parts," not "part." You can't chop something into a smaller "part." As you create the outline, don't try to divide the contents of one category into only one more category. Take a look at this example:

I. Swimming lessons

  A. Challenging

II. Spanish lessons

  A. Enjoyable

  B. Expensive

In this outline "Swimming lessons" is divided into one sub-category — "Challenging." No good! Penalty box! Do not pass Go or collect $200. You need at least one more sub-category for swimming lessons.

Why am I making such a big deal out of this? Not because I love Roman numerals, which you can bury with your Latin textbook for all I care. The reason your outline should obey the rules of logic is that *your essay* is bound by those rules. A logical flaw in the outline will show up as a flaw in the finished piece of writing.

Checking for Gaps

Outline in order, ready to write, right? Wrong. Only one more minute, I promise! A small investment of your time at this point in the writing process will yield a large payoff — the best essay you can possibly write. So before you crank out the first sentence, check the outline for gaps.

Why do you need this extra step? Because as you write, your head is literally filled with ideas that soon burst onto the paper. Furthermore, during the writing stage you're worried about things like capital letters and whether "since" is a better choice than "because." You're so involved in what you're doing that you can't tell for sure how much you actually got onto the page and how much you left in your head. If you encounter a gap in the finished essay, your mind will simply skip over it, filling the space with material you've only thought — not written — about. In the outline stage, however, you have a little more distance and thus a more accurate eye. You have a better chance of finding and filling gaps now.

Checking for gaps is a fairly simple process:

- Keep in mind that everything in the essay should have a purpose. You should be able to look at each item in your outline and say, "I'm making this point because. . . ." If you can't finish that sentence, you may have a problem.
- The separate parts of your outline should connect in a logical way. When you move from one part of your outline to another, you should be able to identify the logical link between the two parts. For example, suppose this is a section of your outline for an essay on a summer you spent building shelters for the homeless:

  III. Crew

    A. From many areas of the country

    B. Different educational levels

    C. Many conversations about politics, religion, and other issues

  IV. Lessons learned

    A. My viewpoint not the only one

    B. Listen to and respect others

  These two sections are related as cause (section III: you worked with a diverse group) and effect (section IV: you learned tolerance).

As you identify the logical links, you may come up with a transitional word or phrase such as "nevertheless," "therefore," "on the other hand," and so forth. Great! Write it down in the margin of your outline. Later, as you write the rough draft, you may want to incorporate that word or phrase. Check out Chapter 10 for more on transitions.

- If you can't identify the logical connection between two parts of the outline, rethink the order. Are you sure you want to place that section where it is? Do you need an intermediate step? Should you alter one of the sections so that it fits more smoothly with its neighbors?

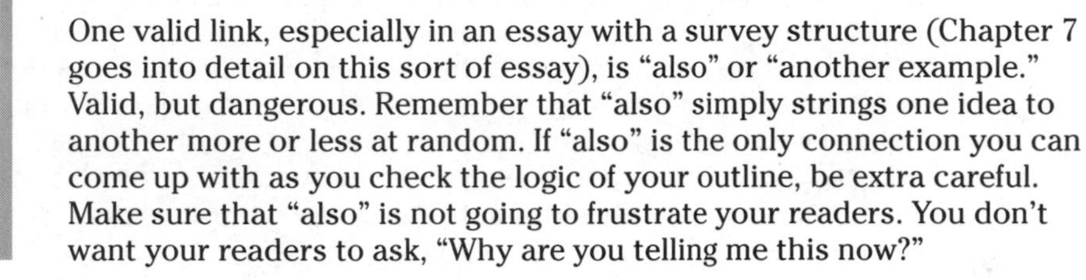

One valid link, especially in an essay with a survey structure (Chapter 7 goes into detail on this sort of essay), is "also" or "another example." Valid, but dangerous. Remember that "also" simply strings one idea to another more or less at random. If "also" is the only connection you can come up with as you check the logic of your outline, be extra careful. Make sure that "also" is not going to frustrate your readers. You don't want your readers to ask, "Why are you telling me this now?"

Staying Flexible

If you've read every word of Part II, you're my favorite reader in the whole wide world. Also, you've laid the foundation for a great essay. However, make sure that you don't plant your feet in that foundation and let the concrete set around them. (I'm into building metaphors again. Sorry.) To make this point another way: No matter how great your preparation, you've got to stay flexible during the writing process.

Suppose that, halfway through the rough draft, you get a terrific idea that's not on your outline. What do you say?

(1) "Too late. Maybe I'll use it when I apply for a job."

(2) "What a shame I didn't think of that earlier. I guess I'll have to throw out everything I've done and start over."

(3) "Hmm. Maybe I can work that idea into paragraph 3, if I just change the focus a little bit."

The answer depends on a couple of factors. If the essay is due in two hours, number 1 is your best choice. If the idea is *really* great and can't be tucked into your existing plan, number 2 makes sense, assuming you have time to write something new. But a lot of times number 3 is an appropriate response. The "new" great idea probably arose from all the other work you've been doing.

Hence, the "new" idea is probably just a variation of what you're already writing. Look at the outline and see where and how the idea fits. Chances are it *does* fit, as long as you are flexible enough to reimagine your plan.

Here I should make a confession: Every *For Dummies* book starts with an extremely detailed outline (12 pages long, for this one). The outline reflects a great deal of thought about content, logic, and structure. But even after the outline was complete, *College Admission Essays For Dummies* changed a bit. Why? Because writing is a form of thinking. As I write, I always think of something new. And so should you! Don't send your brain to Tahiti just because the outline's done. (Unless of course you actually live in Tahiti.) Continually reevaluate your plan for the essay as you write, testing its quality with each new paragraph. Inevitably, here and there a weakness or a gap shows up, or a novel thought appears. When that happens, you have to go with the flow.

Taking the Final, Pre-Write Check

Ready to rumble? Figure 8-2 gives you a final checklist before you hit the rough draft. You should be able to answer all these questions. If you can't, turn back to the drawing board and spend a little more time on preparation — choosing the topic, gathering details, identifying a theme, selecting a structure, and so on.

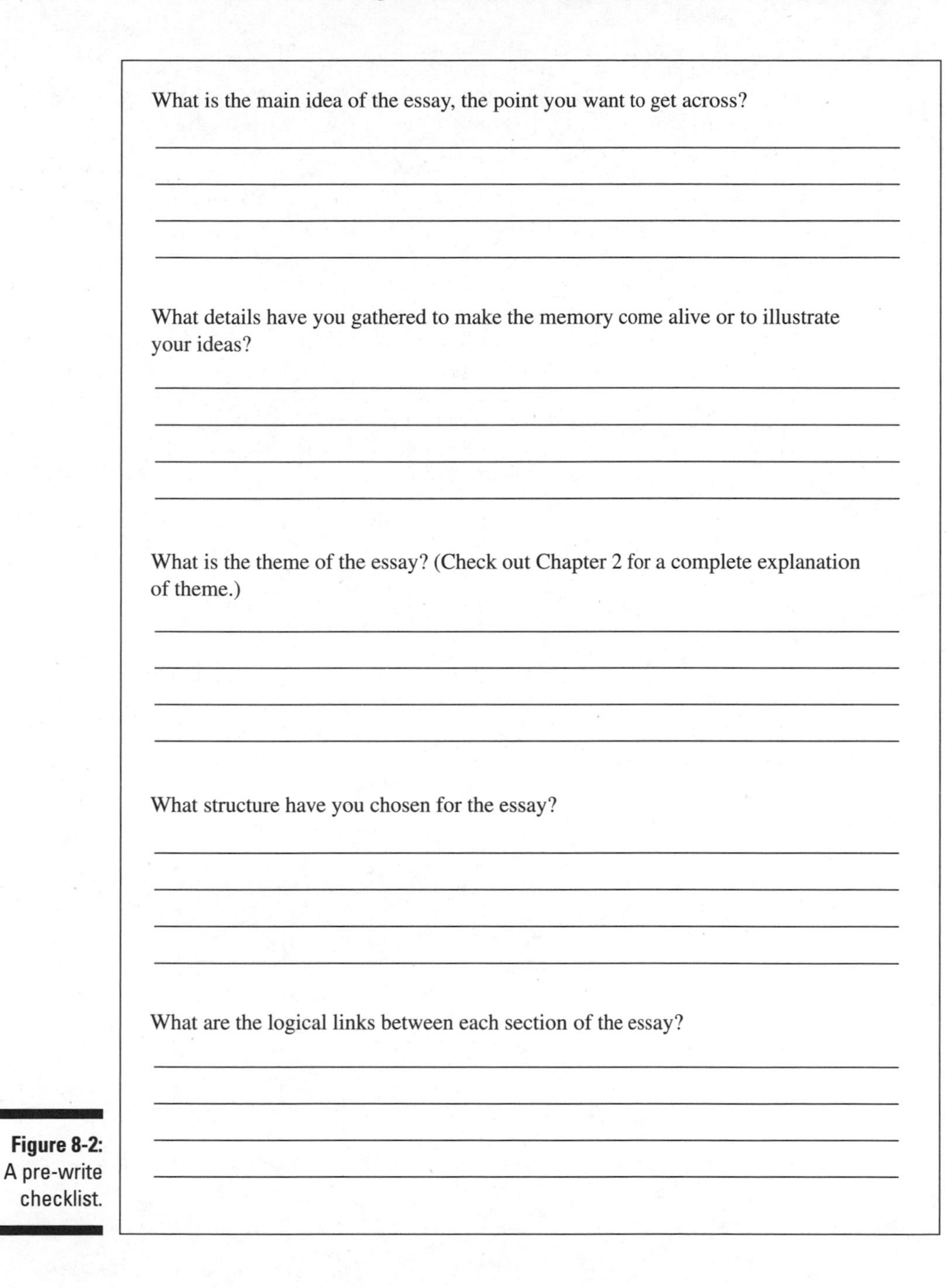

What is the main idea of the essay, the point you want to get across?

What details have you gathered to make the memory come alive or to illustrate your ideas?

What is the theme of the essay? (Check out Chapter 2 for a complete explanation of theme.)

What structure have you chosen for the essay?

What are the logical links between each section of the essay?

Figure 8-2: A pre-write checklist.

Part III
Writing the Rough Draft

"I know it works on late night infomercials, but I still wouldn't separate paragraphs in my essay with, 'But wait, that's not all...', and, 'Act now, and I'll include this impressive list of high school trophies'!"

In this part . . .

In Part III, the rubber meets the road, as they say in all those car commercials I fast-forward through when I'm watching my favorite TV shows on tape. You've got a topic, a structure, and an outline. Time to drive — er, write.

If you're like most people, facing a completely blank page or screen strikes terror in your heart. Words float around in your head, but few settle on the page. Everything you manage to plunk onto the paper looks terrible, at least upon first reading.

But the techniques of good writing are not mysteries. With just a little help, which this part provides, you'll see how to craft a truly fine essay. Check out Chapter 9 for tips on details that make a difference. Chapter 10 demystifies the paragraph. To start off strongly and end with a flourish, read Chapters 11 and 12. Finally, if you're stalled at the starting line, turn to Chapter 13 for a guide to defeating writer's block.

Chapter 9

Showing, Not Telling Your Story

In This Chapter

- Discovering the importance of specifics
- Making use of all your senses to get the point across
- Knowing which details to keep and which to toss
- Choosing strong nouns and verbs
- Finding the perfect metaphor

Standing in the ticket-buyers' line for the first run of *Jaws* some years ago, I found myself behind a young man who had obviously already seen the movie. As the line edged forward, he retold the entire plot. An hour later I was in the theater. Watching the action unfold on the screen was a much more vivid experience than hearing the young man's plot summary. The young man *told* the story of the killer shark, but Spielberg's movie *showed* it.

Regardless of the topic, now that you're ready to write the rough draft of your essay, you should keep this anecdote in mind. If you present the written equivalent of a plot summary, your audience — the college admissions officers — will give you their polite attention. They're dedicated workers, and that's what they're paid to do. But if you draw them into your reality, making them experience the sights and sounds and feelings *you* experienced, you'll get much more than their polite attention. They'll be with you, hanging on every word. And the message you're trying to convey will come across clearly.

In this chapter I explain the best writing techniques that allow you to *show,* not *tell,* your story. I illustrate why specifics are better than generalities and display the power of sensory details. Throughout, I pick apart some sample paragraphs to point out what works and what doesn't. When you've mastered these techniques, you're well on the road to a great rough draft.

Getting Down to Specifics

How hard do you work?

(1) Very hard

(2) Somewhat hard

(3) Not hard at all

Whatever your answer, I've learned almost nothing about you, because those three categories are meaningless. They're just too general. What you define as "very hard" may be someone else's definition of "not hard at all." (You may have noticed this sort of discrepancy when discussing the homework issue with parents or teachers.) Try again. How hard do you work?

> (1) I spend 19 hours a day glued to my books, and another 2 hours typing homework assignments on the computer. I've learned to sleep with my eyes open and my brain on "full speed ahead." About ten years ago I took a three-minute vacation, but that's about it for goofing-off time.
>
> (2) Two hours a night during the week is enough for me to finish all my assignments, except of course for the long-range stuff like term papers and art projects. I study a little on Sunday afternoons when the rest of the family is bowling, but when I'm really pressed with work, I hit the books on Saturday too. Friday night is my time, and unless you're wearing a flak jacket, don't ask me to do anything but party.
>
> (3) I get all my assignments done in one concentrated burst of effort, usually the last three minutes of the bus ride to school. I find that a minute or so of the interval between classes goes a long way; I can usually whip out a science lab or an English paper after I hit my locker and before the bell rings to start class. When I go home, I download a couple of tracks from the bands that interest me, send instant messages to my best buds, and call it a day.

Now your answer means something. I may not agree with your schoolwork schedule (especially if your answer is #1 or #3), but at least I understand your work habits. The details make the difference between a clueless and a clued-in reader.

When you're writing the admission essay — or anything else, for that matter — one rule is vitally important:

> In general, avoid generalities. To be more specific: Be specific!

Thus, you're driving a Jaguar, not a car. You're eating a ham/apple/chocolate quiche (yuck), not a snack. You didn't get hurt; you split your knee open and had to have 28 stitches. Got the idea? Here are a few short examples:

Bad, general statement: My mother had a huge influence on my life.

Better, specific statement: Because my mother super-glued a pencil to my hand, I became a fluent writer.

Another bad, general statement: I enjoyed the science experiment I did in the fourth grade.

The better, specific version: When I blindfolded my guinea pig Porkchop and put him on a leash (not an easy task, given the fact that the average guinea pig has no neck whatsoever), I sent him through 12 different mazes. He found the lettuce much more quickly when the proper route through the maze was rubbed with a lettuce leaf first. Doing this science experiment added to my determination to become a laboratory researcher. Plus, I bonded with Porkchop and had a great time.

One last bad general statement: In my future career I hope to work for world peace, an important quality.

The non-beauty-contestant version: The School of Diplomacy and Really Hard Foreign Languages will prepare me for a career with the Bureau of Incomprehensible Treaties. I hope to learn negotiating skills and apply them in such intractable conflicts as the smelly-cheese dispute that nearly derailed the formation of NATO.

Time to see the principle of specifics in a real admission essay. (Also time to see the consequences of *ignoring* the principle of specifics in a clunker written by yours truly.) Suppose that you have to write about a school assignment. You want to show that you work extremely hard and that you love to learn, two qualities you hope will appeal to the admissions committee. Figure 9-1 contains my too-general version.

What's wrong with the essay in Figure 9-1? Just about everything. Okay, it's not *terrible,* but it's so general that the reader doesn't learn much. The reader, lacking facts, has to take the writer's word for everything. For example, the essay states that "I have read a lot of difficult books in my other courses." What books? How does the reader know they're difficult? Are we talking Dr. Seuss here or Sigmund Freud in the original German? Without a title or two, the reader can only trust the writer.

Now check out Figure 9-2, a real student essay about a school assignment. The writer gets his point across — the fact that he works really hard and enjoys an intellectual challenge more than sleeping — in a very specific way.

When I took European history, I learned a lot about the politics and history of the continent. The teacher often gave us photocopied notes, which were very useful when it came time to write papers. We had to write many long papers, but the hardest thing we had to do was to present our information to the class. On presentation days we had to give out notes that we had prepared and discuss the material with the other students.

The assignments for that class were always hard; I have read a lot of difficult books in my other courses, but in this class we had to talk and write about what we were reading, not just listen to the teacher. When it was my turn to make a presentation, I was too busy to start early. I stayed up all night working on the material. When the class began, I distributed papers about my topic to the class. They read the papers as I explained my main points.

I did a lot of work not only because I care about my grades, but also because I wanted to learn about the topic. I wanted to impress the teacher and my classmates, and I did. The assignment turned out to be one of the best I have ever done because I learned more from it than from anything else I've ever done for school.

Figure 9-1: An example of a very general essay.

Notice some of the details the author of this essay included:

- Tolstoy's *War and Peace*
- Wagner pulsating in the background
- amber light
- 1 1/2 pots of tea
- one-page pamphlet
- clock striking four
- list of 20 most influential people
- five-page pamphlet
- mother's waking him at 6:30
- head face-down on desk
- 8 tea bags
- 100 pieces of paper
- "Good work"

How much more alive is this student's essay than the general one! You're there in his room as he grapples with the material. You see the scene — the tiredness, the dedication, the assignment, his thought processes — because he gave you a wealth of detail.

As the clock struck midnight I grinned. I had completed the Computer Science project, and the rudimentary Spanish, Russian, and Math assignments. It was time to progress to the night's confection: my European History treatise. The project had been assigned four days earlier, on Monday, but I had not yet begun. I had trimester finals throughout the week, and had just returned home from competing in the Ivy League Winter Track Championship. My body yearned for sleep, but I worked hard to overcome my desires. I put on the teakettle and dove into the assignment, for I did not want to disappoint my fellow members of the colloquium.

I was to prepare a presentation on Sir Isaiah Berlin's The Hedgehog and the Fox. After reading Tolstoy's War and Peace for Russian class, I thought it would be interesting to read what the esteemed twentieth century historian had to say about him, so I had volunteered for the task. I read his treatise, with Wagner pulsating in the background and an amber light shining on my desk. As I delved into the book, a surreal sensation emerged of feeling like a twenty-first century Machiavelli, indulging in my texts about the past.

Two hours and one and a half pots of tea later, I had completed Berlin's work. The key concept was that the hedgehog knows just one thing, but knows it well, whereas the fox knows many things but lacks a depth of knowledge. Tolstoy had depth and breadth to his knowledge, fitting both classifications. Plagued with fatigue and sloth, I created a simplistic one-page pamphlet explaining what Berlin had said and its implications.

As I wrote, the theme of hedgehogs and foxes reverberated in my mind, and I started classifying people accordingly. I went through our texts and categorized the major figures. Drifting away from the assignment and into the world of intellectual history, I saw everything through the eyes of Berlin. From the darkness, I heard the grandfather clock strike four, and had little documented work with two and a half hours until I would have to wake up.

Recalling the first day of class when we had discussed who we thought were the twenty most influential people in history, I decided it would be sensible to use this list as my groundwork. Time was a luxury I did not possess, so I used the one tool that could provide me with enough information to make an informed decision: the Internet. As a historian and a bibliophile, I am weary of using the Internet for historical research, but it was the only tenable option.

Once I had categorized the twenty giants and justified my classifications, the time had crept up to five-thirty, and I had built a raw five-page pamphlet for the class. The next thing I can remember was being awakened by my mother at six-thirty, alarmed that my head was face-down on my desk, Wagner was playing on repeat-mode on my computer, eight tea bags were strewn across my desk, and one hundred pieces of paper were resting on the printer's till.

Figure 9-2: An example of a show-not-tell essay.

(continued)

> The colloquium was appreciative of my work, but could not grasp why I would spend most of my night working like a Trojan for a simple presentation. When asked, I could not really answer them. It surely was not to get the 'A' on the assignment as many of my colleagues had suspected. I think it was a mix of my love for academia, my desire to please the class, and the warm feeling I got inside whenever my teacher saw me in the halls and told me "Good work."

Figure 9-2: An example of a show-not-tell essay.

I love this essay, but I am *not* advocating all-nighters. Your health is more important than any grades or admission offer. Go to bed at a reasonable hour! Pour those details in your essays during the daytime!

Aim for specifics regardless of the subject matter of your essay. If you're writing about yourself, as in Figure 9-2, hit the details. Also hit the details if you're writing about another topic. Check out Figure 9-3, another real student essay, which describes "an issue of importance to you."

Notice the wealth of information the writer provides about the greenhouse effect and global warming, including:

- a brief explanation of the Kyoto Treaty
- the European Union's proposal on greenhouse gasses
- the position of the United States government
- the percentage of emissions that would be cut
- the United States per capita production of emissions compared to its population
- Greenpeace's campaign to raise awareness
- the actions of Junior Statesmen of America

By the time you finish reading this essay, you know something about the issue. You are also completely sure that the writer knows a lot about the issue and is willing to back his beliefs with actions. The specifics carry the message loudly and clearly.

In Figure 9-3, notice that the writer makes a personal connection to the issue in the first two paragraphs of his essay. He also discusses his involvement in the last paragraph. Good idea! Members of the admissions committee no doubt care deeply about global matters, but their job is to evaluate *you,* not the Kyoto Treaty and the like. So including something about yourself, even in an essay about current events, is a good idea. (See Chapter 2 for a more complete explanation of this technique.)

Another important reason for including specifics has to do with the nature of college or grad-school admissions. The average admissions committee member has read *thousands* of essays. The literal truth is that you can make no general statement whatsoever that they haven't already read (or heard during interviews). You favor world peace? Think your family is great? Appreciate your friends, want to see justice done, had a great experience with community service projects? Terrific. Join the thundering hordes banging on the admissions door. They all did the same thing. *But* — and this is a really big *but* — they didn't do those things in the same way, because every human being is unique. Your life and ideas — in the details — is different from that of every other person. So if you want to stand out from the crowd, *be specific.*

Using All Your Senses

Every September I give each of my students a raisin and ask for a list of descriptive details. The average student lists five to ten words, such as "brown," "wrinkled," "small," and "sticky." By the time each student has read his or her list, I've usually got 20 items on the board. (Yes, you *can* say 20 different things about a raisin. Try it.) The normal breakdown is as follows:

Visual details: 16

All other senses, including touch, smell, taste, and sound: 4

Before you hit the ceiling, let me explain the category of sound. How does a little piece of fruit make any sounds at all (when it's not dancing in a television commercial)? Easy. When you squish, chew, drop, or shake the raisin, it makes noise. Not a lot of noise, but some faint sounds. Now back to the analysis. You don't have to be an advanced math student to realize that the sense of sight dominates the list of sensory details. And this tally is the result of describing an edible topic, making taste and smell obvious choices. If I ask the class to describe a corner of the classroom, the percentage of visual detail is even higher. In fact, I may get nothing but visual detail for that sort of assignment.

I'm not anti-vision; some of my favorite moments in life arise from my ability to see. But what a barren existence I would have if sight were my only sense! I'd miss out on the cool breezes of summer and the soft nap of velvet (sense of touch). I wouldn't be able to relax with my lilac bath gel or curl up my nose at that five-month-old container of leftovers in the back of my refrigerator (sense of smell, and yes, I know I should clean more often, but housework is *boring*). If I relied only on sight, I would lose the tang of moo shoo pork and the saltiness of street hot dogs (sense of taste). And I'd be sorry to say goodbye to the clang of Levon Helm's drums on my favorite Band song. I'd even miss the FDNY sirens that screech past my apartment (sense of hearing).

As the thermometer rises, my patience falls with the multi-national corporations producing the greenhouse effect. Our changing climate indirectly affects everything inhabiting our planet. When companies pour greenhouse gasses into the air, the stability of our ecosystem is jeopardized. Scientists acknowledge that if we do not curb our profligate greenhouse gasses emissions, we will endanger all living organisms. Although there have been conflicting reports on the matter, there is a consensus that the climate is getting warmer at an alarming rate, and it is not a stretch to attribute this to the discharge of carbon dioxide.

While my friends call me a watered-down conservative and a green Republican, I am concerned for the environment, since there can be no life now or for generations without a healthy planet. As an avid cyclist and hiker, I have developed a love for nature, and consider it immoral to let corporations pollute something that is not theirs. Nature belongs to everyone, and should not be bought or sold. I am not an idealist to the point that we should not burn fossil fuels, but we should expend our natural resources in a conservationist environmentally-friendly manner.

The Kyoto Treaty set down good premises, although I sided with the EU's proposal to cut greenhouse gas emissions by 15% and not America's just to stabilize them. The 5.2% cut was a reasonable compromise; however, if third world nations are not willing to show any initiative in curbing their environmentally devastating habits, little will be gained. The earth knows no boundaries, so if a handful of countries reduce their emissions only minimal gains will be made.

President Bush has taken an unreasonable approach to the Kyoto Protocol, refusing to adopt the legislation because India and China do not have to. On a per-capita basis, America has much higher carbon dioxide emissions than either of those countries, producing 20% of the world's emissions while constituting less than 5% of the population. As a former oil businessman, Bush is favoring special interest groups, using studies they have commissioned to undermine the magnanimity of global warming. It is crucial that Bush changes his stance on the Kyoto Protocol, and sets a good precedent as the leader of the world's superpower for an environmentally stable globe.

An effective way to improve environmental standards is through lobbying. Politicians make legal environmental decisions, not citizens. While politicians represent the goals and ideals of citizens, they also must be aware that the future of our environment is of significant concern in order to protect it. I applaud organizations like Greenpeace, which have raised public awareness over greenhouse gas emissions. This year, as the Director of Lobbying for my division of the Junior Statesmen of America, the largest student-run organization in the nation, reducing greenhouse gas emissions is at the top of my agenda. With well over a thousand students in my division alone, J.S.A. has a moderate lobbying muscle. I work with environmental organizations to get J.S.A. to endorse them and to get student volunteers to actively lobby for the cause. I may be a minute part, but I am a real part of a large movement lobbying politicians to adopt legislation for lowering greenhouse gas emissions.

Figure 9-3: A second example of a show-not-tell essay.

Why am I rhapsodizing about the other four senses? Because those senses, as well as good old, tried-and-true vision, wake up your writing. You don't live in a one-dimensional world, and you shouldn't write as if you did. And unless you take special care to give all your senses a shot, sight will edge out everything else.

You may be asking, right about now, why sensory details are necessary at all in your admission essay. After all, the university is admitting you because you're a good student, not because you can describe the smell of Thanksgiving dinner. True. But in the essay, you're trying to present a piece of your reality to the admissions committee. And reality comes to us through our senses. (Note the plural.) So to convey your reality, you have to use visual, auditory (that's sound, for those of you who haven't swallowed a vocabulary list recently), olfactory (smell), tactile (touch), and taste (there's probably an SAT word for this sense too, but I missed that vocab list myself) senses.

Sensory details are particularly important for two common types of questions: "describe a person who influenced you" and "tell us about an important event in your life." (Part V goes into detail on these two types of questions, as well as all the other common essay questions.) The best way to answer these two questions is to tell the story and then to explain why the story is significant to you. Using a story to answer the event question is obvious. If you're writing about a person, you also need to dig up a memory of one or more incidents in which the person you're describing was a major player. (Chapter 2 and the appendix help you unearth the best stuff from your memory bank.) And when you tell a story, you need sensory details because the sum total of those details created the experience for you.

Discovering sensory details is easy. In Chapter 6 I describe three great methods that may be used to gather topic ideas as well as details — visual brainstorming, listing, and free-writing. Here's one more helpful technique just for details: Spend a few moments concentrating on the memory or the incident you've chosen for your essay. Then mentally load an imaginary videotape of the incident, close your eyes, press "play," and start your sensory list:

1. **With your mind's eye, watch what happens.** Play the "tape" over and over again until you've got the visual details down cold. Make a list of all the visual details you might mention in your essay.

2. **Play the "tape" again, focusing on the sounds.** Note everything that people say. Write down the exact words. Then note the environmental sounds such as the growl of your empty belly, the plunk of the bingo chips on the board, the hum of the paint-stripping machinery, and so on. Make a sound list.

3. **Replay again. What do you smell?** Food smells will be obvious, but most scenes feature other scents too — chalk dust in a classroom, clouds of diesel fumes off the interstate, and so on. Make an odor list.

4. **Pretend that you can play your tape in a futuristic, touchy-feely theater.** (You're pretending to have a tape, so you may as well go all the way to touch, which theaters probably will have some day, at which point I'll stop going to horror movies.) What feelings is your body receiving? (Not emotions, tactile impressions.) Is it warm or cold? Humid or dry? Breezy or calm? Is something rough or smooth touching your skin? What do you feel inside your body? Is your stomach clenching? Do you have little goose bumps on your arms? Make a touch list.

5. **Check out the tape for any taste details.** Taste is not going to be in every story, though it's in more than dinner scenes. Perhaps you're describing a situation in which you were nervous. Did your mouth taste dry, stale, bitter? If any taste sensations are relevant, put them on your list.

As you list all these details, you may realize that the English language has very few words for taste and smell. You may find yourself writing, "The orange tasted and smelled like an orange." You're not going to win a Pulitzer Prize with sentences like that! If you can't think of a good way to describe the detail, consider a metaphor or simile, as in "the orange tasted like the first morning of my vacation in California." If you can't think of any interesting way to describe the orange, just say you ate the orange and leave it at that.

(For more tips on descriptive metaphors and similes, see the section entitled "A Little Metaphor Won't Kill You," later in this chapter.)

Choosing the Best Details and Ignoring the Rest

After you've got a ton of sensory detail (see the preceding section, "Using All Your Senses," for more information on why you need sensory detail), you're faced with a problem. If you tuck all those specifics into the story you're telling, the essay will be 453 pages long. Because your word limit is considerably lower (and because you also have to do a few other things in addition to the essay — pass math, for example), you'll have to winnow the list. In this section I explain how to choose the best details and ignore the rest.

Here's a paragraph about one of my favorite colleagues:

> Mr. B. taught in a room with three chalkboards, ten student desks, and a bunch of bookshelves. The room faced south and east and had two large windows. The teacher's desk was made of gray metal. The sides of his

> classroom were lined with decrepit couches the school's thrift shop couldn't sell. Almost no one sat in the student desks because they all wanted to crash on the rug (another thrift-shop discard). That's where Mr. B.'s dog Rosie slept while he was teaching irregular verbs and the poetry of William Butler Yeats.

The point is fairly obvious, I think. All the details in the preceding paragraph are true. Some details apply to almost any classroom in the world. Most classrooms have student and teacher desks, and a lot of those desks are gray. (Why gray? Would it kill the school board to buy a red or purple desk, just to liven things up?) But a few details show how Mr. B.'s classroom was different from all others. How many times have you heard barking during grammar class? (No fair counting the juvenile delinquent in the back of the room.) When you choose details for your essay, concentrate on those that are unique, that show the special or distinctive aspects of your topic. Don't bother stating the obvious. In the sample paragraph about Mr. B., I'd dump the chalkboards, student desks, bookshelves, and maybe the windows and the teacher's desk. I'd definitely keep the rest.

Try this pop quiz. Which details would you include from this list of observations about the kid eating lunch across from you in the cafeteria?

> likes corn chips dipped in milk
>
> eats sitting down
>
> wears his hair in a two-foot ponytail
>
> says "Touch my chips and die" to the kid next to him
>
> is wearing pants, sneakers, and a T-shirt
>
> cleans up his garbage when he finishes eating

You could probably make a case for most of those details, depending on the situation. The two most general statements — "eats sitting down" and "is wearing, pants, sneakers, and a T-shirt" — might be useful if everyone else in the room you're describing is eating standing up, dressed in pajamas. And in my school cafeteria, the last detail — "cleans up his garbage when he finishes eating" — definitely sets this fellow apart from the crowd. But the most appealing details are likely to be the ponytail, the food preference, and perhaps the challenge to a neighboring diner. Those details are unusual and interesting.

Distinctiveness is not the only quality you're looking for when you choose details. You should also think about the main idea of your essay. If you're writing about cultural differences and how you came to appreciate their value, you might want to emphasize your willingness to consider strange new food combinations. In that case, "likes corn chips dipped in milk" is perfect. If you're talking about bullying, "says, 'Touch my chips and die' to the kid next to him" is the detail you want.

In the pre-writing, gathering detail stage (check out Chapter 6 for more information), don't try to decide whether you need a particular detail. Just make a note of it and keep thinking. Later, when you're writing the rough draft, you'll have time to judge its worthiness. Also, you're in a good spot if you have 50 details and you need to choose 10. If you have 10 and you need 10, you've got to go back to the brainstorming stage.

Selecting Strong Verbs and Nouns

Don't worry; despite the title, this section is short on grammar and heavy on writing tips. I supply only two definitions, one for each section.

Verbs

Verbs are the words in the sentence that express action or state of being, as in the following:

> Carmeline swished the damp mop over Engelbrot's bald head. (*swished* = verb)
>
> Engelbrot has been upset ever since that incident. (*has been* = verb)

Now that the term is clear, I'll get to the point: verbs are the most important words in your vocabulary. You want the souped-up, strong-as-a-weightlifter verbs, not the boring, found-on-every-corner words. Check out this example:

> Tourmaline went to the gem store.

Ho hum. "Went." *There's* a great verb. Haven't seen that one since two whole seconds ago! Plus, "went" is so general that it tells me practically nothing, just that Tourmaline was somewhere other than the gem store, and now she's not. How about these alternatives?

> Tourmaline ambled to the gem store.
>
> Tourmaline strode to the gem store.
>
> Tourmaline slithered to the gem store.
>
> Tourmaline boogied to the gem store.

I don't know which of these sentences is "right," because I don't know how Tourmaline in fact got to the gem store. For all I know, the best possible sentence is "Tourmaline drove to the gem store in her very own Lamborghini." But I can declare confidently that any of the alternate sentences is more specific than the original, and specific is good. General is bad. In general, that is.

Here's another example:

> Tourmaline said that she would go.

"Said," in all its variations ("says," "say," "will say," and so on) is the first runner-up of the All-Time Boring Verb Contest. (Who won? I'll tell you in a minute.) You can get so much more mileage out of other words for verbal self-expression, such as these:

> Tourmaline declared that she would go.
>
> Tourmaline conceded that she would go.
>
> Tourmaline whispered that she would go.
>
> Tourmaline bellowed that she would go.

Now for the winners of the All-Time Boring Verb Contest. Yes, two verbs tie for the trophy: "be" and "have." Okay, I know you need these verbs. They play a part in tons of sentences and often cannot be replaced. But sometimes you can dump them in favor of much more interesting choices. Compare these two passages, in which the verbs are italicized:

> The chair *is* metal and *has* curved legs. The seat *is* wood, and so *is* the back, which *is shaped* to support the spine.
>
> Three-feet tall metal legs *curve* up from the floor. The wooden seat and back *mirror* and *support* the spine.

The verbs in the second passage are more interesting. Also, you saved five words and said the same thing, a real plus in the admission essay, because you're working with a word limit and tired readers.

Bottom line: As you work on the rough draft of your essay, pay special attention to the verbs. Think of the verbs as the tires on a truck that carry your meaning to the reader. Go for the best tires you can afford; in the verb world, best means most specific.

Nouns

Nouns are words that name persons, places, things, or ideas. Read this sentence:

> Carmeline values cleanliness, so she rubbed polish on Engelbrot's bald head. (*Carmeline, cleanliness, polish, Engelbrot's,* and *head* = nouns)

If you're a stickler for terminology, *Engelbrot's* is a possessive noun because it shows that a person — *Engelbrot* — possesses a bald head. (Actually, he's a real chrome dome. If he stands in the sunlight, the glare from his forehead alone will blind you.)

Nouns, like verbs (check out the preceding section on verbs) can be general or specific. As always in writing, go for the specific over the general. Compare these sentence pairs:

> Berylium contemplated the flower as she switched on her computer.
>
> Berylium contemplated the dahlia as she switched on her lilac-tinted iMac.
>
> Nasturtium patted her pet and sustained an injury because the animal was not in a good mood.
>
> Nasturtium patted her pet python and sustained a puncture because the animal was not in a good mood.
>
> Xanthium cooked dinner and fell victim to an illness.
>
> Xanthium cooked Tuna-Strawberry Surprise and fell victim to botulism.

In each pair, the second sentence contains more specific nouns — "dahlia" instead of "flower," "Tuna-Strawberry Surprise" instead of "dinner," and so on. The second sentence packs more meaning into its words. The moral of the story, one more time: Go for the specific over the general!

When you're aiming for specifics, adjectives and adverbs are tempting. (I know, I know. I said only two grammar terms in this section, and here I am using two more. Sorry.) *Adjectives* and *adverbs* are descriptive words. They're great, and you can't express yourself in English without them. But don't get lazy and try to beef up weak nouns and verbs by slathering them with descriptions, as in this sentence:

> He walked slowly.

Simply choose a better verb:

> He strolled.

A Little Metaphor Won't Kill You

Describing everything literally — with the actual facts — gets your point across. Unfortunately, the literal truth may bore your reader to tears (or giggles, depending upon how late they're reading your essay and how loopy they're feeling). Sometimes the best writing veers away from facts and into the realm of metaphors and similes.

Don't let those English teacher terms throw you. A *metaphor* is just a poetic comparison. "Happiness is a warm puppy," as the Peanuts comic strip declares, is a metaphor. A *simile* is also a poetic comparison, this time with the words "like" or "as," as in "as pretty as a picture" and Madonna's "like a virgin."

Metaphors and similes can really liven up your admission essay. I once read a piece about a young man's experience attending a religious service of another faith. The essay was meant to show how this event deepened his appreciation of the many traditions that constitute American life. In the essay he described a partition that separated the male and female worshippers. His description included exact measurements of this wall — length, width, and height. (I have always wondered how he knew. Did he creep in after the service with a tape measure or check the blueprints?) His exciting sentence read something like this:

> The wall is 5'11" high, 21 1/2 feet long, and 2" thick.

Yawn. Next, he changed the sentence this way:

> The wall is just high enough so that men and women can't see each other from anywhere in the sanctuary.

Much better! The description now gives the purpose of the wall as well as a fair idea of its dimensions. Okay, you don't know how thick it is in version two, but do you really, really care about thickness? I don't think so. The final version hit the metaphorical level nicely:

> The wall is a boundary between the world of men and the world of women.

Poetic descriptions are great, but don't overload the reader with your brilliant creations. A little poetry goes a long way, at least when you're writing an admission essay. I've read some essays that make me imagine a writer who declares, "I sat through three months of sonnets last year and by golly I'm going to use that stuff if it kills me." If you have ten details, one might be a good candidate for a metaphor or a simile. Not nine!

Metaphors and similes tend to catch the reader's attention because they change the pace of your writing. The reader is zipping along and suddenly stops to ponder the comparison. Milk the reader's reaction for all it's worth by placing the metaphor or simile at a pivotal point in the essay, a time when you want the reader to pay special attention. Such a point might be a detail that emphasizes the theme of your essay. (For more information on themes, see Chapter 2.)

Lots of metaphors and similes express the most common human emotions and the most universal life experiences. Unfortunately, many of these comparisons have turned into clichés — overused, stale phrases such as "raining cats and dogs" and "as happy as a clam." (Does anyone know where that last one comes from? All the clams I've seen seem fairly neutral in their emotions, not that I'd know how to recognize an annoyed shellfish.) Take care to avoid clichés in your essay. (For more about clichés, check out Chapter 3.)

Chapter 10

Constructing Good Paragraphs

In This Chapter

- Understanding how paragraphs create meaning
- Writing a successful topic sentence
- Discovering where to place topic sentences and details
- Creating transitions

In Martin Scorsese's *The Last Waltz*, one of the best concert movies of all time, Levon Helm creates perfect paragraphs without ever picking up a pen. At one point Scorsese sits at a picnic table as he interviews Levon, the drummer for the band profiled in the film. (The band, by the way, is named "The Band.") As Levon talks, he waves an unlighted cigarette in the air. At one particularly dramatic moment, he stops to light the cigarette. Thereafter deep drags signal a change in topic or a thought to be emphasized. If you transcribe the interview, the paragraph breaks are clearly marked by the cigarette. New topic: puff. Dramatic emphasis: puff.

Levon Helm seems to have a perfect sense of timing. No surprise there; after all, he's a drummer. His interview demonstrates that he knows when to separate an idea from the material surrounding it and when to group related thoughts together. Too bad you can't ask him for help with your college admission essay!

This chapter provides the next best thing to an hour with Levon. In it I explain why, when, and how to place paragraph breaks in your essay. Fortunately for you, I do so without clogging your lungs with smoke.

Punctuating Your Points with Paragraphs

In the introduction to this chapter, I hint at the two most important reasons to create a paragraph break: logic and drama. (I explain the other reason — quotations — in Chapter 14.) Time for more detail on the Big Two.

Logic

Move this book out, slightly beyond the focus range of your eyes. What do you see? Clumps of gray print, also known as paragraphs. Even before you read a word, you have an idea how many ideas are contained in Chapter 10, just by estimating the number of paragraphs. In general, one important idea equals one paragraph.

Move the book back in and start to read. You see immediately that a paragraph break stops the flow of words, not greatly, as a new heading or a new chapter does, but briefly. If you're reading aloud or speaking, a paragraph break comes across as a short pause, longer than a quick breath at the end of a sentence or the even quicker breath of a comma.

The paragraph break shows you that it's time for something new — another example, a change of story line, a shift in location or person, or a further link in a chain of thought. If you're writing the essay based on an outline (and you should be — see Chapter 8 for the reasons why), each new letter or number in the outline turns into a paragraph in your text.

Suppose this is a section of your outline for an essay about your desire to have dinner with George Washington, the first president:

III. Really cool dining room

- A. Kelly green walls
- B. Nice wood table
- C. Fireplace right next to the table
- D. Seven dishes for each person
- E. Five forks each!

IV. Nice view

- A. Potomac River is visible from the porch
- B. Front windows face massive lawn
    1. Sheep on lawn
    2. Drive up to house on carriage path through lawn
    3. Occasional horse or pony on lawn
- C. House on a hill

Your essay will have one paragraph on the dining room description (the walls and woodwork truly are bright green, fashionable in Washington's day but a real eyeball assault now). The next paragraph shifts location, describing the view from the dining room, not the room itself.

If you're writing a long essay, each line of the outline might be a separate paragraph. In the Washington example, you might have a paragraph about the sheep, another paragraph about the driveway, and still another paragraph about horses and ponies. Just be sure that your breaks are logical and consistent. The main ideas of each paragraph should be of roughly the same importance. For more information on main ideas, see the section entitled "Creating a Strong Topic Sentence," later in this chapter.

Drama

When I watch mysteries on television, I always know when a commercial break looms because the story has built to a dramatic moment. The detective gathers the suspects and declares, "The murderer is in this room. . . ." Cut to a dancing tub of "new and improved" marshmallow gunk. (Just once I'd like to hear them say, "It tastes worse but has a longer shelf life!" Ah, honesty.) The break arrives at a dramatic moment because the pause heightens the tension. Same thing for essays.

Say you're writing an essay about how you faced a major life crisis. You discuss your happy, pre-crisis life in the first three paragraphs. The third paragraph follows you into the principal's office, where she states, "I wish I didn't have to tell you this, but. . . ." The reader is all but panting to read the next paragraph. Who can stop there? (I can, actually. I'll let you decide which crisis is detailed in the fourth paragraph.)

Dramatic paragraph breaks work only if you insert them sparingly. If every paragraph ends on a high note, the effect is lost. With too frequent use, dramatic paragraph breaks turn ho hum. The reader gets to the big moment, sighs, and thinks, "Here we go again." Not the reaction you're hoping for! So think of this paragraphing technique as a chili pepper. For the Tex-Mex deprived, chili peppers are *very* spicy — good for an occasional intense sensation, but not acceptable in big bunches.

The most dramatic technique — and here we're talking once per essay, tops, because this technique is definitely not for frequent use — is the one-sentence paragraph. The shortness of the paragraph grabs the reader by the throat and says, "Look at me!" Hence you should place this kind of paragraph break only at a truly crucial point in the essay.

I once read an essay in which a veteran soldier describes some of the terrible things he saw in battle. Near the end of his account he writes of his postwar years, during which he has turned to religious texts for help in understanding the meaning of his experience. One paragraph ends with his statement that the meaning must be in the holy book somewhere. The next paragraph, in its entirety, is "I can't find it." The essay goes on in subsequent paragraphs to describe his work with various veterans' groups. Wow! That one-sentence paragraph blew me away. My eye went back to it over and over again. Also, that tiny paragraph summed up the theme of the essay — the search for meaning in the context of war.

I describe logic and drama as two separate categories of paragraph breaks, but in practice they overlap. Dramatic paragraph breaks must occur at logical spots in your essay — moments when emphasis changes, the speaker or topic shifts, or a new stage in the story arrives.

Creating a Strong Topic Sentence

One way to check the logic of your paragraph breaks is to identify the main idea of each paragraph. The main idea is generally expressed in a single sentence, which we English teachers call the *topic sentence.* The topic sentence is the umbrella that covers all the ideas in the paragraph; just as you want a strong umbrella to protect you from the weather, you want a strong topic sentence in each paragraph of your essay.

The word *topic* also applies to the main idea of the entire essay — what you're writing about. In this section I talk only about the main idea and topic sentence of each paragraph, not about the essay as a whole.

You should be able to underline the topic sentence of each of your paragraphs — *mentally* not physically. (Don't underline any sentences on the final draft.) If you have two candidates for topic sentence and can't decide between them, you may have two paragraphs mistakenly glued together. Consider breaking them apart, with one topic sentence left in each. If you can't find any topic sentence at all, you probably have a disorganized paragraph. Identify the main idea and add a good topic sentence to the paragraph.

But what *is* a good topic sentence? What's the difference between an "I lift weights" topic sentence and one that needs to eat more spinach? A tight fit. A good topic sentence covers all the material in the paragraph, but it doesn't flap around loosely, spreading itself over tons of ideas that aren't in the paragraph. For example, suppose you have a paragraph describing an antique rolling pin that once belonged to your grandmother. (Don't laugh. The rolling pin was the subject of one of the best admission essays I ever read. The author related that rolling pin to the Italian heritage she received from her maternal relatives. I think she became an English major at Harvard. Good for her.) Examine these two paragraphs, neither of which is from her essay. (I made them up.)

> The slender wooden tool resembles a clean, perfectly smooth log. It has no handles. Perhaps Grandma didn't want anything extra separating her from the feel of the dough, or perhaps Grandpa, who fashioned the rolling pin, didn't know how to make a handle. Either way, the pin represents

function at its purest — all you need, and nothing more, to stretch the delicate dough.

The slender wooden tool resembles a clean, perfectly smooth log. It has no handles. Perhaps Grandma didn't want anything extra separating her from the feel of the dough, or perhaps Grandpa, who fashioned the rolling pin, didn't know how to make a handle. All tools should be simple.

In each paragraph the topic sentence comes last. (Topic sentences can be placed anywhere in the paragraph. Check out the next section, "Placing Topic Sentences and Details," for more info.) In the first sample paragraph, the last sentence stays focused on the rolling pin. It sums up the idea in the paragraph: that the rolling pin is simple, but it does the job well. A fine topic sentence! In the second sample paragraph, the topic sentence is far too broad. The writer hasn't been discussing all tools — just the rolling pin. Not a good fit! Granted, later in the essay the writer may go on to make broader, more general points . . . perhaps that the best things in life are simple. But this paragraph isn't about the best things in life; it's about a rolling pin. So the topic sentence should also be about a rolling pin.

Take care not to make a topic sentence that is too narrow. In the sample paragraph about the rolling pin, a too-narrow topic sentence might refer only to Grandpa. Grandpa is in the paragraph, but he's only one half of one sentence. A topic sentence about him would leave out the pin description and the musing about Grandma's preferences in dough-stretching equipment.

Bottom line: Write a topic sentence that fits everything in the paragraph and nothing outside the paragraph. Like Grandma's rolling pin, the topic sentence should be all you need to do the job of summing up the paragraph *and nothing more.*

When you've finished your essay, place it slightly beyond the focal length of your vision and check the paragraphs. Are they all more or less the same length? If so, you may want to consider altering them a bit, for the sake of variety. A longer or shorter paragraph here and there breaks the monotony.

Placing Topic Sentences and Details

In the preceding section, "Creating a Strong Topic Sentence," I wrote two sample paragraphs about a rolling pin. Each paragraph ended with the topic sentence. Your topic sentence may fill the last spot in the paragraph, or it may land somewhere else. Similarly, your details may roam around a bit. Check out the following sections for three sample paragraphs, each of which presents a different alternative. (You can tell by the lunatic ideas they contain that I wrote these paragraphs, not a reasonably sane applicant.) Then run your eyeballs over the section "One more word about details" for tips on organizing the rest of the paragraph.

Topic sentence first

A topic sentence in this position starts the paragraph off with a bang. If you want to orient the reader immediately, clearly revealing the most important point of the paragraph, go for a first-place topic sentence. However, be aware that everything after the topic sentence may feel like a letdown. Also, because a vast majority of paragraphs begin with the topic sentence, your reader may be tempted to jump from Alp to Alp, reading the topic sentences of each and skipping everything else. (Not a bad reading tip, by the way, when you're actually *in* college and facing more reading than you have time for.) Here's the paragraph. I underlined the topic sentence to make it absolutely clear, but don't underline anything in your finished essay.

> <u>Everything I need to know about life I learned from breadcrumbs</u>. Each little morsel of wheat is absolutely unique, both separate from and connected to its fellow crumbs. No breadcrumb is worth wasting, but nothing good comes from only one crumb. To fry a tasty piece of fish, to bake a savory meatloaf, or to pave the way for Eggplant Parmesan, you need a cup or more of breadcrumbs, not one small shred. Furthermore, when the going gets tough (in hot oil or humid weather), the breadcrumb presents a united front and sticks more securely to its fellow bits of wheat.

See the set up? The first sentence tells you what to expect: a series of lame comparisons between life and breadcrumbs, which is exactly what the paragraph delivers.

Topic sentence last

If you're building up to a big payoff, a last-place topic sentence is best. This sort of paragraph brings the reader along slowly and gives the reader a chance to come to the conclusion (the main idea of the paragraph, which is in the topic sentence) at the same time the writer gets there. The reader feels smart, and a smart-feeling reader is a happy reader. Check out this paragraph, in which the last sentence sums everything up. (I underlined the topic sentence for the sake of clarity, but don't do so in your essay.)

> Consider the lowly breadcrumb. Each little morsel of wheat is absolutely unique, both separate from and connected to its fellow crumbs. No breadcrumb is worth wasting, but nothing good comes from only one crumb. To fry a tasty piece of fish, to bake a savory meatloaf, or to pave the way for Eggplant Parmesan, you need a cup or more of breadcrumbs, not one small shred. Furthermore, when the going gets tough (in hot oil or humid weather), the breadcrumb presents a united front and sticks more securely to its fellow bits of wheat. <u>In short, everything I need to know about life may be learned from breadcrumbs.</u>

Not vastly different from the topic-sentence-first variety of paragraph, but an interesting variation. Try one in your writing!

Topic sentence in the middle

Topic sentences may land in the middle of the paragraph, though this position is rarer than the other two. The middle spot is good for variety, for when you'd like to keep the reader alert and hunting for your message. The downside is that the reader may hunt but not actually find the main idea, and you risk losing clarity. Read this paragraph, in which I've underlined the topic sentence. (Note: Don't underline anything in your essay.)

> Each little morsel of wheat is absolutely unique, both separate from and connected to its fellow crumbs. No breadcrumb is worth wasting, but nothing good comes from only one crumb. What a life lesson! <u>In fact, everything I need to know about life I learned from breadcrumbs.</u> To fry a tasty piece of fish, to bake a savory meatloaf, or to pave the way for Eggplant Parmesan, you need a cup or more of breadcrumbs, not one small shred. Furthermore, when the going gets tough (in hot oil or humid weather), the breadcrumb presents a united front and sticks more securely to its fellow bits of wheat.

Would you have found that sentence without the underlining? Maybe yes, maybe no. And now you know why few writers make a habit of placing the topic sentence in the center of the paragraph. But as a change of pace, try the middle position.

One more word about details

As you see in the examples earlier in this section, the details fill up all the space in the paragraph not taken up by the topic sentence. Fine. But what should you put where? Which detail goes first, which second, and so forth? Sometimes the answer to those questions is a simple statement: It doesn't matter. But more often you'll end up with a stronger piece of writing if you consider the internal logic of the paragraph and place the details accordingly. Suppose, for example, you're describing your grandmother. You might follow a kind of geographical order, describing her dyed blue hair first and working your way downward to her gigantic, size 15 feet. Or you may choose to work by the clock, mentioning your earliest memory of Grandma and moving forward in time — or backward to family stories about her life before you were born. A point of view approach also works, as in this paragraph:

> Everyone in my family talked about Grandma at her funeral. My grandpa thought that Grandma was "the finest person I have known," as he said in a voice filled with tears. He didn't smile once for the first year after her

> death. My brother told a story about picking a bouquet of weeds for Grandma, who accepted them as if they were the finest orchids. She didn't even scold him, he said, for trampling the real flowers in her garden during his bouquet-gathering expedition. My mom's comment was the only one to make me cry. She said that she saw my grandmother whenever she looked at me.

Notice that the details are grouped by person: Grandpa, brother, mom. The writer might have chosen a different order — perhaps brother, Grandpa, mom — and still ended up with a fine paragraph. Whatever the order, the groupings give the paragraph a logical structure, allowing the reader to grasp the ideas more easily. By the way, the first sentence of the sample paragraph is the topic sentence, which sets up the main idea of the paragraph. For more about topic sentences, read "Creating a Strong Topic Sentence," earlier in this chapter. Also, if you're having trouble gathering details for your essay, check out Chapter 6 for some nifty detail-discovery techniques.

As you write your admission essay, think for a moment about where you place the details. Random order may be all right, but if you can come up with a structure that makes sense, go for it!

Setting Up a Transition

When you set up the outline for the essay (You didn't? Check out Chapter 8 to see what you missed!), you placed each idea in its spot for a reason. If the design of your essay is effective, the ideas flow logically from one to another. Now that you're writing, you should help the reader "go with the flow" by providing *transitions.* Transitions are like little hands that reach between paragraphs for a good, strong clasp. Sometimes the transitions are repeated ideas — one at the end of a paragraph and the other at the beginning of the next paragraph. Often the transitions are words that illustrate the logical connection, such as "on the other hand," "afterwards," "because," and so on.

Repetitive transitions

Figure 10-1 is a real student essay by a young man who is destined to win the Nobel Prize for Robotics, if such a prize is ever given. His little metallic creations flipped, scuttled, and slithered across my classroom floor one year. This essay about his "disaster bot" provides good examples of repetitive transitions. (To help you identify these transitions, I underlined them. Don't underline anything in your application essay.) Notice that paragraph one ends with the idea of perfection. Paragraph two begins with a statement about perfection. Similarly, paragraph two ends with a statement about disappointment, and the first sentence of paragraph three mentions "disillusioned," "confusion," and "panic" — all ingredients of disappointment. The advantage of a repetitive transition is that the reader can easily grasp the links between paragraphs. However, a repetitive transition does carry one important risk. If you repeat too many words or reuse the same terms, your reader may wander off mentally, sure that the meaning you're trying to impart has already been received. If you use a repetitive transition, take care to keep the repetitions short, and vary the wording as much as you can.

Word or phrase transitions

None of the word or phrase transitions are strange terms that you have to look up in the dictionary. The fact that these terms are so easily identifiable tells you that they're quite common. Indeed, you probably insert them into your writing without a second thought. Here are the word or phrase transitions most likely to be useful in a college admission essay, along with sample sentences.

RELATIONSHIP: additional idea

TRANSITIONS: also, moreover, in addition to, besides, furthermore, likewise, not the only, not only

SAMPLE SENTENCE: *In addition to* my work on the student council, I *also* initiated a coup and took over the school board. (links a section about the student council to a section about becoming czar of the Community Educational Oversight Committee)

SAMPLE SENTENCE: *Besides* getting an A+ in recess, I *also* won the Most Likely to Be Arrested Before Age 30 award given by local merchants. (links two paragraphs about slacker behavior)

RELATIONSHIP: contrasting idea

TRANSITIONS: on the other hand, in contrast to, however, despite, in spite of, nevertheless, nonetheless, otherwise

SAMPLE SENTENCE: *On the other hand,* I am attracted to the opportunity to sue really pompous public officials who oppress powerless high school students. (links two sections about possible legal careers — one in trusts and estates and the other in public interest)

SAMPLE SENTENCE: *However,* my grandmother taught me much more than poker. (links a description of applicant and grandmother at the card table to a description of the same pair playing slot machines)

RELATIONSHIP: comparison

TRANSITIONS: than, equally, as ___ as, similarly, similar to, like

SAMPLE SENTENCE: *Similar* to my interest in gooey chemical compounds is my housecleaning hobby. (links sections about two favorite pastimes)

I have built four completely functional robots to this day. As proud as I am of them, the focus of every one of my conversations dealing with robotics always revolves around the HMW#2, my disaster bot. It was built for my independent study course on robotic locomotion. The purpose of this bot was simply to move with the aid of four legs, but I set out to do much more than that. My intentions were to amaze and astound my mentors and even myself. The completion of the bot was meant to be my big accomplishment. It represented my mastery of motors, sensors, pics (programmable integrated circuits), and miscellaneous electronic components. Unlike the soporific act of memorizing Spanish vocabulary words, which I was never good at, building a robot requires creativity and intuition. I can actually remember drawing diagrams and schematics for the construction of the bot months before I even looked at my soldering iron. I was making sure that there would be absolutely no uncertainty about anything. It was supposed to be perfect.

Everything did, in fact, go *perfectly* according to plan. I completed the robot just a few days before it was due, and it was absolutely beautiful. It was capable of transportation by the method of flipping itself in all directions, responding to voice commands (with the help of Voice Direct by Sensory Inc.) and avoiding all foreign objects with its numerous infrared proximity detectors. For the next couple of days, I reveled in my accomplishment. On the night before my big presentation, I decided to give my creation an exhaustive test run to ensure that there were no bugs. Sure enough, there was one. I found that there are cases where the legs get caught on each other, resisting further movement. After forgetting to turn the robot off, I pulled each leg free from the others. By doing this, I managed to turn the servomotor towards its opposite direction while it was still operating. Apparently, this forced a current back up through the wires from which the motors were receiving their power. This current fried everything in its path and debilitated the pic. When I realized what I had done, I dropped a tear for the first time in a decade. This was the single biggest disappointment in my young engineering career.

After many disillusioned hours of confusion and panic, I was reminded that nothing comes without failure. As a future engineer, I had to comprehend the fact that failure means nothing if I don't learn from it. What I took away from this project was a deeper knowledge of circuit design, servomotors, integrating microphones and speakers, soldering circuits, and the value of failure, all of which only come from hands-on experience. I later salvaged what I could for my presentation. I separated the voice command system to display the outputs to LEDs in place of the pins on the pic and I also implemented a few proximity detectors into circuits that make use of the unharmed motors. But more importantly, I was able to explain exactly what caused the bug and how to fix it. I displayed a new altered design of my robot that was now really perfect. Luckily I was not evaluated purely on the quality of my robot, but on my newly acquired knowledge as well. I am currently in the middle of rebuilding this bot, which I respectfully call the HMW#2-rev.II.

Figure 10-1: An essay example with transitions underlined.

SAMPLE SENTENCE: My interest in gooey chemical compounds is *as* long-standing *as* it is profound. (links a section describing fun with a child-hood chemistry set to a statement of perpetual commitment to gooey compounds)

RELATIONSHIP: cause/effect

TRANSITIONS: therefore, because, hence, thus, so, accordingly, consequently, as a result

SAMPLE SENTENCE: *Because* I plan to practice medicine on Mars, I am attracted by your major in extraterrestrial biology. (links a section describing the applicant's interest in space medicine to a paragraph praising a truly weird biology major)

SAMPLE SENTENCE: *Thus,* I urged the student council to abolish all standardized tests, particularly those which I had failed. (links a section describing problems with certain tests to a paragraph about the legislative response)

RELATIONSHIP: time

TRANSITIONS: previously, after, before, since, still, yet, up until, then, later, before, earlier, finally, in the end

SAMPLE SENTENCE: No community service project was too time-consuming for me *after* I realized how much this sort of activity counts in the college admissions process. (links a paragraph about an early slacker period with a later activist phase)

SAMPLE SENTENCE: *In the end,* I built 461 houses for displaced rodents, providing a clean, safe environment in which they could kick back and chew little food pellets to their heart's content. (links a paragraph describing a bizarre community service project to the heart-warming results of that project)

RELATIONSHIP: example

TRANSITIONS: for example, for instance, illustrating, showing

SAMPLE SENTENCE: My mother, *for example,* insisted that I walk barefoot to school every day. (begins a paragraph illustrating several hardships that the applicant overcame in his academic career)

SAMPLE SENTENCE: *Illustrating* my commitment to your institution, I enclose a snapshot of me kneeling in the campus quadrangle, begging for admission. (begins a paragraph of undignified groveling)

The preceding sample sentences, the products of my strange imagination, are intended to be humorous. Don't try them in a real essay!

Many of the transitional words and phrases I just explained look like *conjunctions* — words that are legally allowed to join sentences. (Legal according to grammar teachers, that is.) But looks can be deceiving. Don't attach one complete sentence to another with any of these words: *however, moreover, also, furthermore, consequently, therefore, then,* and *in addition to.* You may join two complete, equal sentences with these words: *and, or, but, nor, for,* and *yet.* Other "legal" joining words, which attach two ideas and make one more important than another, include *after, before, since, because, although, so, while,* and *when.* For more information on grammar, including a complete list of words that attach one thought to another, check out Chapter 14.

Word and phrase transitions do a fine job marking out the logical path that you want the reader to take. Just be careful not to overuse them in your writing. If the connection between one paragraph and another is already clear because, for example, you've inserted a repetitive transition (see the preceding section for more information on repetitive transitions), don't plop in a word transition also. Overkill is not an attractive quality.

Chapter 11

Leading with Your Best Shot

In This Chapter

- Understanding the role of the lead
- Grabbing the reader's attention
- Establishing the tone of the essay
- Directing the reader to your topic
- Side-stepping pitfalls in your lead

Nothing has done more to ruin the attention span of twenty-first century television viewers than the invention of the remote control. Press the button. Watch for two seconds. Don't like what you see? Blam, new channel. Two seconds later, another decision. Interesting or boring? Stay or go? To blam or not to blam?

The readers of your admission essay are not quite as twitchy as the remote-control operators I just described, but they *are* human, and they're overworked. They will read your essay, regardless of the opening lines, with one of two attitudes: "Hmm, this looks interesting" or "Wake me when this one's over." Which attitude are you hoping for? I thought so. In this chapter I show you how to create a lead (the journalists' term for the opening sentences) that will grab the reader's attention. I also show you how the lead sets the stage by establishing the right tone and orienting the reader to the contents of the essay.

Taking the Right First Step: What the Lead Does for Your Essay

The Queen of England recently put the best of her not-too-shabby art collection on public display in one wing of Buckingham Palace. At the street entrance to the gallery, an architect constructed a small Greek temple containing the ticket counter, souvenirs, and so forth. That temple is the physical "lead" to the gallery experience (the equivalent to the first few sentences of your essay). Like all good leads, the gallery does three things:

- It catches attention. (You don't see many Greek temples on the streets of Athens, let alone London.)
- It sets a tone. (They're not actually saying that the Queen should be worshipped like Zeus, but they *are* hinting.)
- It orients the visitor. (When you enter the temple, you know where you are and what you're going to see.)

The lead of your college admission essay should accomplish those three tasks. How? Read on.

Capturing the Reader's Attention

What attracts you (apart from sex, which attracts everybody but is not appropriate for a college admission essay)? How about these factors:

- **An interesting comment.** I ride the subway to work every morning, and like all sane New Yorkers, I keep to myself. But almost every day I hear a comment that pulls me right out of my doze and into a nearby conversation (at least as a listener — to respond may be risky). For example, my fellow straphangers have caught my attention with the following:

  "He always wanted to sing on Broadway, so he's singing in the Broadway subway, not the theater."

  "I went to school with David Justice." (He's a great baseball player, in case you are so misguided as to ignore America's finest sport.)

  "She never slaps me in the morning." (This one from a 250-pound linebacker type.)

- **An interesting anecdote.** Also part of my New York experience are extensive walks around the city. When I return from one of my walks, I have plenty of stories to tell, including the following:

  my conversation with a man who had a giant snake around his neck

  an encounter with quintuplets dressed identically and completely in purple

  a close call involving a man wearing nothing but those little orange net bags they sell onions in

- **An intriguing moment.** Once more into the city streets. Here are some of the strange only-in-New York glimpses that have made me wonder for *years:*

  a lady shampooing her hair in the pouring rain on a Madison Avenue corner. Did she have no shower? No time for grooming? An urge to experience nature while cleaning herself?

a tourist hopping over a fire hydrant. Was he practicing for the Olympics? Auditioning for a musical comedy with a street scene?

an escape artist having himself buried alive in a city park. (Don't worry — he got out unscathed.) Why would anyone ever do something like that? And how much did they pay him?

- **Coming attractions.** I know they annoy some people, especially given the high price of movie tickets, but almost no one walks out on the coming attractions reel at the local theater. The chance to snatch a glimpse of movies you haven't seen yet is just too tempting. So everybody stays glued to the seat, watching car chases, smooches, and other highlights.

If these factors catch people's attention in real life, think what they'll do for your college admission essay! Furthermore, you don't need a New Yorker's daily quotient of zaniness to create an interesting lead for your essay. Any topic, even those that seem to be the verbal equivalent of a sleeping pill, can be made interesting with the proper approach.

In the following sections I illustrate several techniques based loosely on the four elements I just described. Each super-glues the reader's mind to your essay.

Quoting the notables

Everybody famous, from Julius Caesar ("I came, I saw, I conquered") to Bart Simpson ("Eat my shorts"), has said something interesting at one time or another. Also, the world's bookshelves are filled with the writings of authors who were desperate to sell their books . . . er, to create literature that they hoped would make the reader buy a copy or two. So if you're looking for a quotation, you'll find one for every essay topic you could ever conjure up from the depths of your imagination. If you lead with a quotation, your essay will

- Call upon the wisdom of the one of the world's great thinkers, or at least the wisdom of one of the world's great characters. (Note the reference to Bart Simpson in the preceding paragraph.)
- Force your reader to wonder, "Why is this quotation here?" Assuming that question has an appropriate answer, you're in good shape because you've immediately involved the reader in your essay.
- Show that you've read or at least listened to someone other than your immediate group of friends. The quotation may even exhibit (hooray for you) education and wisdom.

Quotations do have a downside, however. If you're clumsy in placing the quotation, you risk these reactions:

- Why is this writer quoting someone else? Doesn't he/she have anything to say that's original?
- Oh, no, not "a man's reach must exceed his grasp" *again.*
- Does this quotation have anything to do with the essay? Looks tacked on.

If you're committed to leading with a quotation, you have three choices. You can plop the quotation inside the first sentence, make the quotation itself the entire first sentence, or center the quotation on the line above the first sentence of the essay. To illustrate these three methods, I've written three leads, all quoting that famous (actually, non-existent) sage, Lulu Belle. (***Note:*** these leads are a bit nutty, not unlike myself. Model your own leads on these in terms of technique, but *not* in terms of content.)

- **Quotation inside sentence one:** Whenever I fail a math quiz, I think of Lulu Belle's remark to the United Nations General Assembly as Antarctica invaded her country for the fifth straight year: "No penguin is going to make me pay taxes." Well, no math teacher is going to keep me after school for extra help.
- **Quotation as sentence one:** "Never take public transportation without bringing at least five books." Lulu Belle's comment perfectly reflects my own approach to commuting and, indeed, to literature.
- **Quotation on a separate line:**

  A man's reach should not exceed

  his grasp, at least while the surveillance

  cameras are on.

  - Lulu Belle

  Whenever I enter the campus bookstore, I glance stealthily at the ceiling. Is Big Brother watching me? Does he have to do that? It's *so* annoying. And why isn't it Big Sister?

Regardless of where you place the quotation, be sure that it connects to *your* first words. Also be sure to name the author of the quotation. (For instructions on how to connect ideas, read Chapter 10. For everything you need to know about avoiding plagiarism, check out Chapter 4.)

If you're looking for a quotation to set the tone of your essay, the best place to start is on your own bookshelf. If the quotation comes from a piece of literature that you love, you'll have an easier time writing about it. If your own library doesn't help, you can turn to one of the many reference books devoted to quotations. *Bartlett's Familiar Quotations* (published by Little, Brown, & Co.) is probably the most famous, though several others serve the same purpose. You can also access collections of quotations on the Internet at sites providing reference works. One good site is the Internet Public Library at www.ipl.org/ref. Choose a search term that matches your essay topic ("art" if you're writing about the meaning of artistic expression, for example) and see what pops up.

Sharing an anecdote

If your essay is based on a story from your life (*a* story, not *the* story of your life), you'll naturally begin with part of the event. Lead with the first thing that happened (chronological structure), or if you want to play around with time travel, a later part of the story (interrupted chronological order). For more information on structure, check out Chapter 7.

Even if you're not primarily interpreting a memory in your essay, you can still insert a little story — an anecdote — into the lead. This technique is a favorite of after-dinner speakers for very good reason. If the anecdote is interesting, heads immediately rise from the apple pie to listen attentively. A good story or anecdote sends the crowd into five-year-old storytime listening mode.

Regardless of whether the story makes up the bulk of your essay or only one paragraph, it should be interesting. Look for a small detail that will bring your reader into the reality of the story. (Chapter 10 gives pointers on choosing details.) For example, suppose you're writing about your summer project. Check out these two sentences and my imagined reader responses:

> **Bad, boring detail:** The soup kitchen was located on a block in a poor neighborhood. (Yawn.)
>
> **Better, interesting detail:** I'd never seen lentil soup with pickles in it until last summer when I volunteered at a soup kitchen. (Lentils and pickles? Why? Can I order some from the deli for lunch?)

Apart from the interest factor, if you lead with an anecdote, you must also be sure that it relates closely to the ideas you're going to discuss in the essay. I still remember an essay that began with a story about two tigers, a plum, and a kid on a vine trying to escape. To this day I have no idea why the author inserted that particular anecdote into his essay, because the rest of the essay talked about the importance of relaxation in life. Maybe he was trying to say that you should eat the plum before the tigers do? Or that you're going to get eaten by a tiger anyway so you may as well relax and enjoy the time you have? (!) I don't know the meaning of that story, but I do know that if a reasonably intelligent reader can't figure out your meaning, you're in trouble. Remember that your audience is overworked and tired (see Chapter 3). They won't happily turn back three pages in an attempt to make sense of your anecdote.

Intriguing the reader

This sort of lead is the verbal equivalent of a quick glimpse of an unusual or mysterious sight. It's a bit risky, but it can be dynamite if you do it correctly. The lead sets the reader up with a question or a teasing statement. The body of the essay is the pay off — the answer to the question or the meaning of the "tease." Where's the risk? If the pay off is inadequate, the reader will feel let down. (Think of a knock-knock joke with no punch line.)

I like to intrigue the reader with a good question myself, as you may have noticed while reading *College Admission Essays For Dummies.* I think I picked up the habit through my teaching experience. If I begin the class by droning on about one poem or another, the kids may nod off (though they do pick up a little when I say, "This poem will be on the test."). Not wanting to hear them snore, I tend to start my lessons by calling on someone, asking a leading question, and then relating the student's answer to the poem. The advantage of a question lead is the immediate involvement of the reader. Just be sure that your question is answerable and that your essay answers it.

Take care to avoid clichéd questions such as the following:

> What is the meaning of life?
>
> Have you ever wondered about the meaning of life?
>
> Why should you accept me? (a cliché peculiar to the college essay)
>
> How do I love thee? (Just kidding. This one comes from Elizabeth Barrett Browning, one of my favorite poets.)

The teasing statement doesn't have to be a question; it can be anything at all that relates to the topic of your essay. Here are a handful of examples:

> The day that I died was sunny and pleasant. (essay about a near-death experience)
>
> No one ever has to tell me twice that I'm not wanted. (essay about prejudice and discrimination)
>
> Most of the great mathematicians I know walk around in T-shirts, even during snowstorms. (essay about becoming totally involved in one's work)
>
> I met Beethoven last week. (essay about learning to appreciate music)

Previewing the coming attractions

You've been to the movies, so you already know this technique: a swirl of images from the movie, designed to give you an idea of what the movie's about and also to make you want to part with ten bucks for a ticket. (Yes, ten bucks. I live in Manhattan. It's expensive.) In the admission essay, a "preview of coming attractions" lead is a set of quick references to the subject matter, as in the following sentences:

> My high school is so flexible that you can study classical Arabic, fencing, AP Calculus, and the Victorian novel all in the same year. And I did. (essay goes on to describe the courses and the total learning experience)
>
> When I cook up a pot of stew, I think of my family and all they have given me. My parents are the meat that sustains me and helps me grow. My sisters are the potatoes; they're not flashy, but they nourish me daily. My Aunt Theresa is the spice. (essay about the influence of various family members)
>
> I've done three terrible things in my life and learned from all of them: I accidentally cut off all my sister's hair when she was a toddler, I stole a library book on purpose, and I slacked off when we studied genetic engineering. (essay goes on to describe these three events, with the emphasis on the last one and the author's newfound seriousness about science)

Previews work best if the material in the essay itself is interesting. If you've got only boring stuff to work with, who cares about coming attractions? Also, be careful to write a specific, not a general, lead. Nobody wants to read an essay that begins "I am conscientious, kind, and thoughtful." (Okay, maybe your mom does, but unless she's on the admissions committee, her interest is not helpful. And if she is on the admissions committee, you probably don't have to worry about writing a good essay. Just don't drool and you'll get in.) For the "conscientious, kind, and thoughtful" lead, substitute "Even if I'm bleeding from an artery, I do my work, help those less fortunate, and learn from my experiences." Much more eye-catching.

Setting the Right Tone

At the sound of the tone . . . you'll hang up. But first you'll recognize a certain quality in the voice coming through the telephone. *Tone* is the English-teacher word for the mood that the voice reflects. Tone is created by several elements in your writing, including word choice, word order, and content. In the *For Dummies* series, for example, the tone is humorous and informative, a little hip and sarcastic. In most of your schoolbooks, the tone is serious and informative, a little boring (sadly) and carefully neutral.

Chapter 15 goes into a lot of detail on tone. Here I'll just say that the tone of your lead should match the tone of the rest of the essay. The reader has the right to expect that whatever tone you began with will be the tone you continue with in the essay. One exception to this rule is a deliberate switch designed to shock the reader — a tough-to-pull-off but extremely effective tactic.

The tone should also match the seriousness of the topic. If you're writing about the family members who were lost in the Holocaust, you can hardly begin with a humorous anecdote about dropping your suitcase on your toe as you checked into a hotel during your visit to the concentration camp site. Similarly, if you're writing about the time you failed a biology test, don't use a tone that signals a major world tragedy.

Your normal tone of voice should come across in the essay, though it should be your "best behavior for company" tone, not the "I'll get you later, Butthead" tone you employ with friends. Also, if you choose a humorous tone, be careful. Humor is serious business — hard to write (unless you're Jerry Seinfeld) and tough to mix with factual information. Not that I'm ruling out humor. Humor can be great. I love humor! I do write *For Dummies* books, as you know. But if you choose a humorous tone for your essay, run the finished product by a couple of trusted advice-givers. Ask them whether you hit the mark or fell on your nose.

Orienting the Reader

Taking a walk in the woods? Bring a compass and a map so that you can orient yourself to your surroundings. Writing a lead? Place clues about the content and theme of the essay up front, so that readers may orient themselves to the message you're trying to convey. For example, imagine that you're writing a college essay about your brother's senate race and your role in the campaign. Somewhere in the first paragraph, be sure to mention (prepare for a shock) your brother's senate race and your role in the campaign. An indirect reference is great, as in this paragraph:

> "Committee to Re-elect Senator Oscar Woodrow III, how may I help you?" My voice was a little hoarse because I had already answered 159 phone calls. It was only 10:00 a.m., and I had eight more hours to go. But I didn't care at all about my throat. Getting my brother re-elected was my only concern.

This lead communicates not only the topic (the senate campaign) but also several themes to the reader: brotherly love, hard work, and sacrifice. Not bad for a few lines!

The admission essay is not a school assignment; it's a combination magazine article and advertisement for you, the applicant. ("Get the new and improved version of Suzy Q. Scholar. Guaranteed to turn in all her term papers on time! On sale at newsstands this month only!") In school assignments you've probably been told to open with a paragraph containing your *thesis statement* (the point you're proving in the paper) and the supporting points. Nothing wrong with that structure; it certainly orients the reader to the subject matter of the essay. If you're very fond of this sort of writing, go ahead and write an admission essay that way. The problem is that school assignments tend to be very boring. (Trust me; I read thousands of student papers each year. I know what I'm talking about.) A little suspense doesn't hurt.

You can create suspense by holding your big guns, the most important ideas, until later in the essay. For example, in a fine essay by Thomas Merton, the author opens with a statement about the trial of Adolf Eichmann, one of the war criminals of Nazi Germany. Merton states that Eichmann, who was responsible for the death of millions, was judged sane by the examining psychiatrist. He goes on to discuss Eichmann's calm demeanor at his trial and then explores the concept of sanity. He notes that the soldiers responsible for launching nuclear missiles are all certified sane by military doctors. His conclusion: If sanity allows for the killing of huge numbers of people, it's like the muscles of the dinosaurs, an "advantage" that leads to extinction. In Chapter 12 I discuss conclusions at length. But the point I make here is important: You don't need to tip your hand and reveal everything in the lead of your essay, but you do need to include the topic and the first step in your chain of logic so that the reader has some idea of the direction in which the essay is going.

Avoiding Common Pitfalls

Browse through *College Admission Essays For Dummies* and read the first couple of sentences of each student essay that are sprinkled throughout the book. Which leads appeal to you? Why? Your answers may not match mine. No problem. You should be trying to write a lead that matches your own personal taste. Remember, you're trying to sound like yourself in the essay, not like me. You're a unique individual, and your essay should reflect that fact.

I can't tell you what's right for you. However, I can point out a few style elements that are *wrong* for you and everybody else. Avoid these pitfalls as you write your lead:

- **Don't announce.** A lot of teachers instruct their students to "announce" the main idea of a homework essay, as in this lead: "In this essay I will discuss my brother's senate campaign and my role in it." Sigh. I really hate this sort of opening paragraph, even in school assignments. In a college admission essay, it's deadly. Take this as a good general rule: Talk about the topic, *not* about the essay. Also, try for a little subtlety!
- **Don't address the reader directly.** I've seen a number of student essays that attempt to emulate the title character in Charlotte Bronte's *Jane Eyre.* Every chapter or so Jane speaks to "Dear Reader" or just "Reader." Okay, Bronte got away with it, but she was a genius. Don't begin your admission essay with "Dear Reader, please admit me," as one student did.

- **Surprise is okay, but shock isn't.** Don't lead off with gory or gross images. Actually, don't put gory or gross images anywhere in the essay. Stay away from profanity and bathroom humor. (Why? How many adults of admissions-committee age have you seen at teen gross-out movies?)
- **Don't begin with a cliché.** Actually, don't end with a cliché either, and try not to put any in the middle of your essay. The admissions officers have read thousands of essays that begin with these or similar statements:

  My friend _________ is always there for me.

  Nothing is more important than my family (or learning).

  When I ____________, I understood the meaning of life.
- **Don't try to sound older than you are.** If you're applying for admission after a lifetime of learning, you may certainly declare that fact. But if adolescence is still a fairly sharp memory, stay away from blanket statements about the meaning of your whole existence. I once had to dig my fingernails into my palms to avoid laughing at a young man who told me, "I was born in New York, I've lived in New York my whole life, and I'll die in New York." He was ten years old at the time.

Chapter 12

Going Out with a Bang: The Conclusion

In This Chapter

- Eliminating repetitive or irrelevant conclusions
- Leaving a strong last impression
- Creating a conclusion that matches the content and form of your essay

Typing away, you glimpse the light at the end of the tunnel. You're almost finished! The last line . . . just one more line . . . and you can rest easy knowing you have a complete draft of your admission essay. Maybe a couple of sentences. A paragraph. No more than a paragraph, right? How hard could a little paragraph be? Okay, maybe you'll go for a walk and write the conclusion later. After all, you're nearly done.

So near and yet so far. Is that how you feel as you attempt to conjure up a conclusion to your essay? If so, you have a lot of company. Most people find those final couple of sentences quite a challenge. In fact, any number of terrific pieces of writing have crashed nose first into the conclusion barrier. The resulting wreck is seldom a pretty sight.

Fortunately, if you keep a few simple guidelines in mind, the best conclusion for your admission essay will practically write itself. This chapter supplies those guidelines and provides tips for the most common essay questions, along with two real student essays displaying strong conclusions.

Repeating Yourself and Other Non-Answers to the Conclusion Question

More than any other part of the essay, the conclusion attracts mistaken ideas. I don't mean that writers insert false information in their conclusions (though I'm not guaranteeing that every student essay I've read has been totally correct). Rather, I'm referring to the fact that lots of writers *think* they know what should be in the conclusion, but they're mistaken. Indeed, the art of writing a conclusion is surrounded by more myths than ancient Greece. So before I explain what a good conclusion *is,* I must discuss what a conclusion is *not.*

Not a reworded introduction

Contrary to what you may have learned in elementary school, a conclusion isn't a restatement of your introduction, with slightly different wording. For example, suppose you're writing about an issue of importance to you. You chose the New York City law prohibiting pet ferrets. You love your little furry friend Ferry, but you have to board him in the country because inside the city line he's a fugitive. Your first paragraph explains the law and describes in excruciating detail the Million Ferret March on City Hall you organized to protest the no-ferret rule. (By the way, ferrets really are forbidden in New York City, but thus far all the protests have been smaller — a *lot* smaller.) Your last paragraph states the terms of the ferret law and waxes poetic about the patter of four million paws in the protest march, plus the plod of nearly a million human shoes. Good idea? No, bad idea. You made those points already!

Some teachers of young children tell their pupils to rewrite the introduction and tack the new version of paragraph one onto the end of the composition. I imagine that they do so because young kids can't write a true conclusion, and the teachers believe that any ending is better than just stopping short. But when you're out of middle school, you must aim higher. Forget the reworded introduction!

One structure I describe in Chapter 7 relies on bookends — two halves of one story framing the essay. One half of the story begins the essay and the other half ends it. (The middle discusses the issues raised by the story or relates other events.) This structure isn't repetitive because although you are telling the same story in both the introduction and the conclusion, you're relating different parts of the story in each spot. If you apply this structure to the ferret example, you may begin the essay with a description of the Million Ferret March just before the little furry guys take their first steps towards City Hall. In the conclusion, you may concentrate on the council hearing or focus on the tired protestors curling up in their pet carriers for the ride home. The essay focuses on one event, but everything in it is stated only once.

Not a miniature essay

A conclusion is *not* a restatement of all the points you made in the body of your work. I've seen "conclusions" that are nearly as long as the entire preceding essay. Here's a (fictional) restatement ending for the forbidden ferret essay, with extra, not-included-in-the-essay comments from me in parentheses:

> You might think that the Ferret Law protects the public, but in fact it does not. (A point you made in paragraph two.) These little creatures are not dangerous at all. (A point you made in paragraph three.) I've had a ferret for most of my life. (As you explained in detail in paragraph one.) Ferry has never nipped me and has always been a perfect pet. (Ditto — paragraph one goes into Ferry's good qualities.) After the Million Ferret March, the law did not change (paragraph four's main idea), but I am not discouraged. (Check out paragraph five.) I have begun a letter-writing campaign to the president and to several animal rights organizations. (Paragraph five told about these measures as well.) Ferry and I will overcome! (A declaration already made in paragraph one.)

Anything new here? Nothing at all! I know that the writer is very insecure when I read such a restatement ending. (I refuse to dignify that sort of writing with the term "conclusion.") Afraid that the point hasn't come across, the writer goes through the whole thing again, hoping that one last round will make everything clear. But if your essay is reasonably well written, the information in each preceding paragraph *is* already clear. And if the essay is floundering around in complete confusion, a restatement at the end won't solve the problem.

Not an announcement

One truly deadly ending goes something like this: "In this essay I have shown that pets like my ferret Ferry should be allowed in New York City." Yikes! Personally, I hate this kind of ending for any paper, though I know that a few of my colleagues in academia favor a version of the "announcement" conclusion for some research papers. Good for them. But for a college admission essay, this ending is totally inappropriate. Remember that you're showing off your writing skills for the admissions committee. They're hoping to see something a bit more creative. Besides, if you truly have made the point, the admissions committee will know *without* an announcement.

Not a new topic

Some writers avoid repetition, restatement, and announcing by going to the opposite extreme. They plunk down a completely new idea in the conclusion — something brought in from another universe for the sake of novelty. Going back to The Ferret Factor example, you can imagine the reader's confusion if the last paragraph suddenly veered off into a description of the other pets the writer has had through the years or into a general protest against the mistreatment of animals. If you've had a sudden brainstorm, write another essay. But as you conclude the one you've just written, stay on topic.

Concluding the Essay with Class

If you plowed through the preceding section, "Repeating Yourself and Other Non-Answers to the Conclusion Question," you know what you shouldn't put in your conclusion. But what *should* you write? Before you pick the words, keep in mind the tasks the last paragraph of your essay must accomplish. Specifically, a good conclusion:

- ties up all the loose ends
- places the topic of the essay into a larger context
- gives the reader a feeling of completion
- provides the last link in the chain of logic you've forged
- creates a lasting memory for the reader

Not every conclusion performs every single one of these functions, and some of the functions overlap. To help you understand the role of a conclusion, in the following sections I tackle the characteristics of a true conclusion one by one, showing you how to achieve each in your essay.

Tying up loose ends

If the bulk of your essay is a story, the conclusion is the spot to let the reader know how the story ends. Perhaps your essay is about your experiment in novel writing, which occupied countless hours during your sophomore year. In the conclusion you say whether you actually finished the novel, how your writing was received by its intended audience, and what you learned from your year as a budding Dickens. Your conclusion ties up the loose ends and gives the reader a feeling of completion. The reader's reaction is "Ah, so that's how it all worked out! He finished it after all. And he gained confidence in his writing skills. Great!" Or perhaps your essay is a reflection on the meaning of your brother's bout with illness and how his struggle affected you. The conclusion gives the reader an update on your brother's condition and your current thoughts on the experience. Those current thoughts place the event in the wider context of your life. One more example: say you're writing about an issue of importance, perhaps the persistence of homelessness. In the essay you explain your view of the problem and present two or three corrective measures. The conclusion might be your estimation of the possibility that these measures will be carried out. In your view is society willing and able to do the right thing, as you've defined it?

Here's the tying-up-loose-ends technique in action, in skeletal form ("bones" only, no details) in response to the "tell about a significant experience" question:

Introduction: description of family's escape from war-torn area, mother and father in separate refugee camps, children divided, two left behind when soldiers prevented them from crossing the border

Body: details about the family's life before the war, the strong bonds between family members, the values shared by all, their reactions to the early stage of the crisis and increasingly difficult conditions

Conclusion: how the family reunited and resettled, the current status of family members, reflections on the effect of these experiences

For a glimpse of this sort of conclusion in a real student essay, check out Figure 12-1. Notice how the conclusion resolves several issues raised by the body of the essay. By reading the conclusion, the reader learns that

- The older brother resolved the fight with his parents.
- No punishment was given to the author of the essay.
- The parents approved of the author's behavior.

Only a few sentences long, the conclusion nevertheless packs a lot of information into a small space. Moreover, it has a dramatic punch, leaving the reader with a strong, impressive memory that won't soon fade!

Creating a wider context

In a properly focused essay, you zero in on a narrow topic — the time you potty-trained the local zoo's yak herd, perhaps. But what's the meaning of that experience beyond the fact that the zookeepers don't have to shovel all day and the fact that you had to wash your hands a lot last summer? And do universities care?

Yes, they do. Universities, when they're doing a proper job, prepare students for a meaningful role in society. So, by definition, the institution you're applying to needs to think about the meaning of your years on its campus — not just "What will you learn from us?" but "What will you contribute (and I don't mean only money) after you leave us?" Consequently, they're interested in your ability to look beyond your own concerns towards the wider context — your view of the world beyond yourself. One way you can provide this information is by writing a "wider-context" conclusion. A wider-context conclusion, as its name implies, begins where the rest of the essay left off and expands outward. If your essay is about your family, the wider context may be the way families like yours are perceived in the community. In an essay about your learning experience, the wider-context conclusion may broaden outward to a philosophy of education. (***Note:*** Sometimes "tying-up-loose-ends" conclusions also place the issue or event in a wider context. Check out the preceding section for details.)

Here's a summary of an essay responding to a typical med-school question: "How do you envision your future practice in the field of medicine?" (Non-med-school applicants write about different subjects, but the larger-context technique is still valid.)

Introduction: ten years down the road working with a group of pediatricians to offer quality care in a rural area

Body: raised in a city but loved summers in the country, appreciates kids, doesn't want to be on call 24/7 but knows patients need coverage, group practice solves problems and gives population a needed service

Conclusion: understands that rural areas are underserved, health of the poor has not been a national priority, next generation of doctors should do their part to improve health care itself, not just heal individual patients

Completing the experience

You may have heard the expression "coming full circle." The full circle (as opposed, I imagine, to a half or semi-circle) is a complete figure. The beginning and end come together seamlessly, and nothing more is necessary. In an essay, a full-circle conclusion encloses everything you've written in a neat package. The reader has a feeling of fulfillment, an "I know it all now" sensation. This sort of conclusion often resembles or overlaps the "tying-up-loose-ends" conclusion because it brings the topic to a close for the reader. (Check out "Tying up loose ends" earlier in this chapter for more information.)

The easiest way to write a "full-circle" conclusion is to end where you began the essay . . . in time, in ideas, in location. This technique is fairly easy to apply; if you're writing about your room, for example, you may begin and end at the most important feature — your 40-pipe, ultra-loud, antique organ. If you're writing about the neighbors' attempts to have your 40-pipe, ultra-loud, antique organ blown up, you may begin with the visit from the Environmental Protection Agency's Noise Squad, cut to the importance in your life of the instrument (your first lessons, your carving of replacement pipes, your discovery of Bach at high volume, and so on), and then back to the Noise Squad, whose measurements showed that the organ was not as bad as a freight train engine but louder than a heavy metal concert.

Coming full circle does *not* mean repeating yourself. End where you began, but don't overlap. Check out the section entitled "Repeating Yourself and Other Non-Answers to the Conclusion Question," earlier in this chapter, for reasons why repetition is not okay.

"Your approach to schoolwork is simply unacceptable!" yelled my father from the kitchen table. My older brother had gradually slackened in his effort in physics class to the point that his teacher had sent my parents a progress report, alerting them to the problem. The resulting argument became a shouting match, and suddenly I, now in seventh grade, was watching my father chase my brother from the house. I was astounded. Here, two men whom I had always admired for their equanimity, had sworn never to associate with each other again. I heard the garage door slam and saw my brother's Toyota minivan speed away. I sat at my desk and attempted to finish my homework, but I could not; I was paralyzed. I began imagining that I would never see my brother again. That night I went to bed without brushing my teeth, without taking a shower, and without kissing my parents goodnight.

I woke up the next morning, a Saturday, at eleven o'clock. Surprisingly, my parents were not at the kitchen table reading the newspaper, as usual, but instead were still in their bedroom. I went upstairs to find my brother's bed still untouched. The house was painfully silent; that Saturday seemed to last forever. I hurried to the garage several times thinking I had heard it open, but it was always empty. I spent nearly the entire Saturday rearranging my room, trying to forget what I had witnessed. My conversations with my parents were few and terse. Sunday passed with as much tenseness as Saturday had, until I was about to get in bed and the phone rang.

It was my brother. He told me he had been staying at his friend's house and was not sure when he would come home again. He said that our parents had treated him unfairly, and asked me to bring his clothes and calculus textbook to school on Monday. As I was collecting the requested items, my mother caught me and said that if I brought him anything I would be grounded.

That night I could not sleep. I had to choose my allegiance. While I tossed and turned, a courtroom drama unfolded in my mind, and I was the judge. First, my parents' lawyer spoke, arguing that my parents loved me and provided for me. Therefore, he continued, I owed them my loyalty. Then, my brother's lawyer reminded me of what a great brother he had been, and that he and I were best friends. I realized that if I disobeyed my parents I would be grounded, but simultaneously, I knew my brother would feel betrayed if I did not help him. As the night turned to morning, my ruling changed several times.

Monday morning I left for school with the clothes. My decision was less an act of rebellion against my parents than a desire to help my brother, who I felt needed me. Although I knew punishment was certain, I believed that my brother's feelings outweighed whatever castigation I would incur. Upon seeing me, his face lit up in a huge smile as if to say, "Thanks a lot, little brother. I knew I could count on you."

Sitting at the same kitchen table several years later, after the story had become part of the family lore, I asked my father why I had never been grounded. I was surprised to see a grin appear on his face, but I was more shocked by his response, "Punish you? The idea never once crossed our minds. You acted exactly as a true friend does - you stuck with your brother even though you thought there would be repercussions."

Figure 12-1: An example of a tying-up-the-loose-ends conclusion.

Here's the haiku version (short, as in the 17-syllable poem) of a full-circle essay:

> **Introduction:** explanation of your view of beauty — that even the ugliest things, when they fulfill their function without waste, may be beautiful
>
> **Body:** discussion of the classical definition of beauty and its shortcomings, appreciation for function, concerns about waste and the environment, need for new definition
>
> **Conclusion:** description of a solar-powered lemon-squeezer, ugly in terms of conventional aesthetics but beautiful according to your definition

Forging the last link in a chain of logic

By "forging" I don't mean cranking out your very own twenty-dollar bills in the basement. I refer to the hammering the blacksmith does on a piece of hot metal, the turning of a lump of iron into a yard of chain. You don't have to sweat over a hot fire to create links; you just have to think logically. And when you get to the last link, the final step should be a cinch. When have you taken the reader with your reasoning power? The answer to that question is your conclusion.

The essay structure most often taught in school is simple. In paragraph one you make a statement, and in the rest of the essay you back up that statement with proof. The structure I discuss in this section is different. Instead of backing up, you lead the reader forward to a new idea.

A chain-of-logic conclusion flows naturally from the ideas that precede it. You're saying, "If this is true, then that is true. And if that is true, this other idea is also true. . . ." Here's a chain-of-logic conclusion for an essay about penguins, in answer to a request to "write about someone or something that is meaningful to you." (***Note:*** The "information" bears absolutely no resemblance to any actual fact about penguins.)

> **Introduction:** description of the Emperor Penguins' appearance
>
> **Body:** the penguins' appearance resembles a tuxedo, a tuxedo is formal attire, the penguins are always formally dressed, formally dressed people generally exhibit good manners, the penguins follow the rules of etiquette
>
> **Conclusion:** Emperor Penguins' "dress" and manners should serve as a model to all other birds and even to people

Depending on the drama of your subject and the impact of your concluding thought, a chain-of-logic conclusion may make a strong impression on your reader. The next section goes into detail on this function of a conclusion.

Making a strong impression

Composers of Broadway musicals speak of the "eleven o'clock number" — the showstopper at the end of the performance that sends audience members out into the night, humming and tapping their feet. Your admission essay needs an eleven o'clock number too: a strong last paragraph that makes an indelible impression on the reader.

Fortunately, human nature makes the task of writing a memorable conclusion easier. Why? Think about all the speeches (or class lectures and church sermons) you've attended. You probably tuned in on full power at the beginning. Most people are optimists, and unless proven otherwise, they live in hope that the speech will be at least moderately interesting. Sadly, unless you were listening to an exceptionally fine orator, you may have faded a bit in the middle. But everyone perks up towards the end, giving the speaker one last bit of attention. The same phenomenon holds true for essays. Even readers who skim the middle on automatic pilot switch to manual control for the last paragraph. So you've got a good audience for your parting shot.

Take advantage of that increased concentration. As you plan your essay, identify particularly strong points or interesting details and save them for the end, as long as you don't wreck the logical structure by doing so. To be more specific:

- If your essay is primarily a story, interpret the story in the conclusion.
- If your essay contains a lengthy description, choose a great sensory detail or a metaphor for the last paragraph.
- If you're interpreting a quotation, make your strongest point at the end of the essay.
- If you've broadened the focus of the essay to a wider context, consider concluding with an interesting anecdote illustrating that context.
- For an essay with a survey structure (check out Chapter 7 for more on structure), in the last paragraph interpret the overall meaning of the items surveyed.
- If you have one line that's a real zinger, place it at the end.

Figure 12-2 is another real student essay with a great concluding line. The author speaks of two assemblies he organized at his New York City school in the weeks following the September 11th attacks. The very last line — a zinger — communicates the students' reactions and shows that the author's efforts were successful . . . all in six words!

Even before entering the dimly lit auditorium, I had anticipated their reticence. After all, what else could I have expected from my fellow students, who were still walking through the halls quiet as ghosts. Two weeks had passed since my first attempt to foster discussion among the entire student body. As Student Body President (SBP), I had organized a school-wide seminar assembly, concerning different aspects of the September eleventh tragedies. The thirteen workshops and presentations focused on topics ranging from various interpretations of the Koran and the different sects of Islam to the media's role during wartime, and the assembly was a huge success according to my teachers and friends.

But this wasn't a healing process that could be completed in one step. Now here I was in the final minutes of my fifth assembly, and, judging by the silence in the vast room, I felt reluctant to go ahead with my plans to facilitate an open microphone discussion. Something about not thinking the students will respond. Maybe, I thought for a moment, it was too soon to try to make sense of what had happened; maybe I should call it off. Inside, though, I was certain that if we could just share our feelings with one another, begin to understand that each of us was going through something totally unique, and yet somehow similar, we could then begin to re-knit the precious social fabric that existed in the school community: a sort of blanket that had never once failed to give me solace through rough times.

In more ordinary and optimistic periods, this community spirit had inspired me to run for SBP in the first place. It had inspired me to give something back. As I stood there at the podium, I felt as though I were engaged in a staring contest with 600 upper-schoolers, making me realize that no other student body president who came before me had ever had to deal with an issue as difficult as the one we all now faced together. "Come on guys, hasn't anyone got something to say, something to share?" I thought about how, in the course of one tragic September morning, my role as Student Body President had changed radically. I had long since assured myself that if I harnessed what made me unique, my sense of humor, my creativity, the fact that I was approachable, I would then be more likely to influence my community better than any adult could. I would then be able to give that "something" back. I knew I wanted to re-define the role of the Student Body President, but I had never imagined I would encounter a situation such as this one, and have to unite and comfort the student body in the midst of such a horrible tragedy. As uncertain about what to say or think as any one of my peers, I knew that September eleventh had made me re-evaluate what it meant to be creative, honest, and open, what it really meant to be a leader in my community.

"Until September eleventh," I began softly, "we were on track to be a generation- the generation- that wouldn't know war, and now that it's upon us, we're not prepared to face it. Reality, for us, has become something skewed by the evening news, showing us footage that resembles Hollywood movies and bad dreams more than anything we've ever seen in real life." Scanning the audience, I saw a hand go up. I continued. "So we sit here, feeling helpless, because we think no one will even listen to us. But we can listen to each other; this is our chance to be heard. I think it's a chance we shouldn't pass up." There was another hand, and another. With a deep sense of pride and excitement, I took a deep breath and asked once more, "Does anyone have something to say?"

Apparently, quite a few people did.

Figure 12-2: An example of a conclusion that makes a strong impression.

One of the best conclusions I've ever seen was written by John McPhee, a non-fiction writer whose work has appeared frequently in *The New Yorker.* McPhee's essay, "The Search for Marvin Gardens," has an interlocking structure. In a series of short segments he recounts playing the board game Monopoly. As you may know, the properties for sale in the traditional game are named for streets in Atlantic City, New Jersey. McPhee's paragraphs on the game are interwoven with paragraphs describing the actual streets and other locations from the game, including the local jail. One property — Marvin Gardens — proves elusive. The narrator can't find that street, though it appears on the board game. For the second half of the essay the narrator asks everyone he meets in Atlantic City about Marvin Gardens. No one knows where it is. Finally, in the last paragraph, the author discovers that Marvin Gardens is a planned community outside the city limits. The reader shares the narrator's relief that the puzzle is solved. That last paragraph is a good payoff to several pages of rising tension.

Chapter 13

Overcoming Writer's Block

In This Chapter

- Figuring out what's stopping you
- De-stressing the application process
- Tweaking writing techniques to overcome the block

You can write a homework assignment, a grocery list, an e-mail to a friend, and millions of other things. No sweat. So how come you're stuck at the starting line for the admission essay? Or perhaps you've made a fine opening move, but now you're stalled three paragraphs into the best piece of writing you've ever done. No matter what you do, you can't seem to go forward.

Congratulations. You've joined an extremely large club whose membership at one time or another has included some of the best authors on the planet: The Blocked Writers (TBW, for short). Of course, TBW is a club no one wants to be in. Hitting writer's block gives you the same sensation as the tenth month of pregnancy. Enough already! What's inside you just *has* to emerge, and you're willing to do almost anything to get things moving.

Chin up. Writer's block is not fatal, and in this chapter I show you several strategies that help you leap over whatever barrier is confining your ideas.

Understanding Your Block

The key to surmounting the two-story-high, three-foot-thick wall of writer's block is to understand what the bricks are made of. Are you worried about failure, thinking too much about the future, trying to write and edit at the same time? Or have you become mired in details? These are some of the many factors that may bottle up your writing. Each of these factors presents a different problem with a different solution.

In my experience, writer's block in the context of the admission essay stems from one of these two issues:

- the emotions surrounding the application process itself
- faulty approaches to writing

In this chapter I address both types of problems. For the emotional stuff, check out "Confronting Your Application Anxieties." For writing-approach blocks, turn to "Leaping Over Writing-Related Blocks."

Confronting Your Application Anxieties

Before I say anything else, I need to make one thing perfectly clear. I'm not the successor to Sigmund Freud. I'm not any sort of mental health professional at all! I'm an English teacher. But I have gone through the college application process with batch after batch of high school seniors over the course of my 30-year teaching career, and I've observed closely and learned a fair amount about the anxieties of my students as they fill out their applications. I can give you some hints on how to handle your emotions, but if you're feeling down and self-help measures aren't making a difference, talk with a counselor or a trusted friend. You won't be the first person to need some assistance in handling the transition between one level of schooling and another.

If you've hit the wall with your essay, see if any of the following descriptions match your mood. Often the answer arises the moment you recognize the problem. At other times the solution is a change of attitude — easy to prescribe, harder to accomplish. (Harder, but not impossible.) I've placed attitude-adjustment tips in each of the following sections. If you've recognized your problem and taken a stab at fixing it, but you're still stuck, move on to the section "Leaping Over Writing-Related Blocks," later in this chapter. The proven "block-buster" techniques there may smash through emotional blocks as well.

Overcoming a fear of failure

If you don't run the race, you can't lose it. Of course, you can't win the race either, but sometimes that particular truth seems like a side issue. The most important thing, for some people, is not to fail. Adding to the pressure is the tendency of many applicants to see the admissions process as a judgment on their entire lives thus far. Are you a good person? Is the sum total of your years on the planet successful? "The envelope, please," as they say at the Academy Awards. That fat or thin envelope contains the verdict, or at least that's what many students think. Is it any wonder why many opt out of essay writing?

But the admissions process is *not* an Oscar ballot (which, I understand from the gossip columns I hardly ever admit to reading, also has procedural problems). The admissions process is a well-intentioned but flawed attempt to select a small number of applicants — from a pool of *many* totally qualified people — for an incoming class. No more, no less. It doesn't judge *who* you are, and it doesn't even do a very good job of judging *how* you've lived your life or spent your school years thus far. Beyond a certain, basic level of competency for each school, the admissions process is just a matching game between an institution and a set of students. They need a graphic artist and you've excelled in every art course your school offers; fine, you're in. They have 12 violinists and you're a star fiddler; sorry, try somewhere else.

If you fear failure, take a long look in the mirror. Repeat after me, filling in the blanks appropriately:

> The University of ________ will *not* evaluate my worth as a person. Their decision does not reflect what I have accomplished in my ___ years of living. I am more than my application. Regardless of the outcome, I will still be proud of my achievements.

Go through this little ritual each morning until you believe what you're saying. And you *should* believe what you're saying, because every word is true.

Also, keep in mind that the only way to fail the essay question is not to write an essay at all. Every essay, no matter what level of writing skill you've achieved, tells something about you. And that's the job of the essay. So if you write it, you automatically pass.

Reclaiming power

Applying to college or graduate school or seeking a scholarship puts you in an unequal power relationship. The committee deciding your fate holds all the cards, and powerlessness never feels good. In my humble opinion most of the world's wars have begun for exactly that reason: one group or another feels an acute lack of power and challenges those who appear to have all the advantages.

I don't mean to suggest that you're waging war on the admissions or scholarship committee. Such an action would be difficult. (How, exactly, would you go about it? Sabotage a file cabinet? Not very satisfying, I imagine.) Also, waging war on the admissions committee would be silly because you'd never get into the college of your choice if you did turn the admissions process into a battle.

Because that option's a non-starter, perhaps you've decided to turn all those warlike urges on yourself. By blocking your writing talent (and you *do* have writing talent — everyone does), you at least gain power over one aspect of the process. You tell yourself, "Don't write." Then you obey your own command. Bingo! You're not writing, but you *are* in charge!

The solution here is to redraw the battle lines. You will *never* be in control of the admission decision. Too many variables, many of which have more to do with the university's needs than with your background and achievements, influence the committee's choices. Instead of banging your head against that brick wall, move your expectations over a notch or two. The United States has thousands of terrific institutions of higher learning, and the world has many thousands more. If one school doesn't admit you, another will. Instead of narrowing your view to a tiny slice of academia, cast a wider net. In your application list, include universities that are likely to feel honored by your interest. You will undoubtedly enjoy a wonderful career and a great life after graduating from any number of schools!

The scope of *College Admission Essays For Dummies* doesn't include college counseling. Check with your school's college or guidance office for help on choosing schools, or consult one of the reference books devoted to descriptions of schools and their requirements. (If finances are an issue, you can find these texts in the reference section of most libraries.)

Most undergraduate colleges provide an academic advisor for each student; the advisor can help you decide which graduate or professional school is a good match for your interests and abilities. Also speak with professors in your major department; they may suggest the best next step for your education.

Embracing change

She was a straight-A student with leading positions in several major extracurricular activities. She filled out all the applications and completed drafts of all the essays. She put stamps on the envelopes. Then she shoved the envelopes into her sweater drawer. That's where her mother found them months later, far past the application deadline. Everyone asked her the same thing, "Why didn't you send in your applications?"

It took her a long time to come up with the answer, but after some heavy-duty counseling, she identified the issue. She had entered the school's nursery division at age 2½. For the next 15 years she felt cozy, smart, and loved. As college loomed, her self-doubts mounted. Suppose that the next step was harder, suppose that no one liked her, suppose that her family forgot her, suppose that . . . well, you get the idea. She was dreading the move to a new school. So she opted out of the process altogether.

If your essay is bogged down, reflect for a moment on your fantasies about the coming year. If fear of moving on is your problem, you'll immediately see, as did the student with the application-filled drawer, that staying put is *not* an option. No matter what your plans for the next school term, you can't remain in your current school after graduation. Of course if you're out of school and working, thinking of returning to full-time study, you can keep the status quo. But do you really, truly want to do so? Are you willing to let fear govern your actions?

Make no mistake, fear of the unknown is the root of the problem. A completely understandable, everyone's-been-there-at-least-once feeling. However, giving in to this fear solves nothing. How much better to face the challenge and conquer it! How much more life-affirming to embrace change! (I know I'm going all Oprah on you, but I think I'm right.)

If you're terrified of the future, make a "scare" list. Then look for a college or grad school that puts the odds in your favor. For example, if you're worried about getting lost in the crowd, find a small school or a big one with a great orientation program. Along with your scare list, make a "bound to be better" list. Jot down everything about the new stage in your life that you're likely to enjoy. Read that list from time to time, focusing on the positive aspects of your future. After you've worked your way through your "scare" and "better" lists, go back to your essay. You may even write about the experience you've just gone through. It's a great topic!

Overcoming self-doubt

I like humility. It's a good virtue, and if more people chose the humble path, the world would be a better place. At the very least, sports events would be shorter because athletes would forgo that little dance they do every time the ball goes in the right spot. But humility isn't always the best choice for a college admission essay. In fact, writing an essay is a good time to brag a little. Not a lot; you don't want to swell your head so that it's too wide for the doorway. But some degree of self-appreciation is fine.

In Chapter 2 I explain how to write about yourself without sounding overly boastful. Here I want to address the fact that humility is sometimes a mask for another feeling, one that doesn't fall into the virtuous category. That feeling, which everyone has from time to time, is self-doubt. Okay, self-doubt *can* be a fine phenomenon; if someone's got a finger on the nuclear trigger, I'd like him or her to ask, "Am I capable of making this decision?" before pressing anything. But self-doubt at the wrong time becomes a dead end.

Ponder your feelings. Are you reluctant to speak well of yourself because you're afraid you don't deserve the attention of the reader (that is, the admissions committee)? Do you suspect that you're not worthy of admission? If I've described you correctly, it's time for an attitude adjustment. You're writing for the admissions committee of a school, not the guardians of the pearly gates. Regular people, just like you, attend the school. They may be smart, but they're not necessarily smarter than you are. And if they are smarter than you, you'll learn. That's why you want to go to school, right?

Gaining perspective

The best word for sentence three of paragraph two is "the." No. It's "an." "An" is definitely the right choice! Um . . . "the" looks better now. (Sob.) I don't know which to choose! They'll hate me if I pick the wrong one. They'll *reject* me if I pick the wrong one. And then I won't go to college and I won't have a career and no one will love me, ever.

Sound familiar? If so, lighten up. You're writing an essay, not a peace treaty ending 600 years of armed conflict. No one word — or sentence or even paragraph — will make or break your essay. Come to think of it, no essay, all by itself, will make or break your application. But if you get yourself into a make-or-break frame of mind, you won't be able to write anything. The anxiety will fill your mind and force all the words in your head to vanish.

Apply a little logic to the situation. Do you really think the admissions committee cares whether you write "pink" or "rose"? Okay, maybe you do. So just pretend that you don't see the essay as a life-or-death issue. Simply write, assuming that everything that lands on the page represents perfection. Then put the draft away for a while. Take it out when you're calmer. Now edit your work. Make the essay the best writing you're capable of creating. Plunk it in the envelope, take it to the post office, and go watch a baseball game. On the way to the ballpark, hum that old tune, "Que sera, sera, whatever will be, will be."

Leaping Over Writing-Related Blocks

Even if you weren't confronting a college admission essay, you might stub your toe on a writing block somewhere along the way to a finished product. Writing isn't brain surgery, but getting those words onto the page isn't the easiest task in the world either. I once read an interview about an fine author of many non-fiction books and articles. He claimed that he had to tie himself to the desk chair with a belt whenever it was time to begin a new piece!

You (probably) won't have to go that far to overcome blocks that arise from the writing process. Mostly you need to identify the problems and then change your technique slightly. Think of the small adjustments that a hitter makes when facing a new pitcher in the world's best sport, baseball. If you're not (gasp) a baseball fan, think of the way you subtly change your argument when you see the parental face turn towards "No, you can't have the car tonight." In this section I explain how to tweak your writing techniques.

Rising from the fog of details

You're writing a poignant essay about your uncle's adoption of a homeless tarantula, waxing poetic about Spidey's first minutes in his new home. Suddenly, you stop. Spidey's initial ascent up the orange-striped wall . . . was the wallpaper really orange? You search your memory bank, but nothing pops up. Hmm, maybe the wallpaper was purple? Or chartreuse? (Uncle Eggbert was colorblind, in case you're wondering.) The essay languishes, a victim of your quest for an accurate wallpaper description. By the time you remember that Eggbert's living room in fact featured bare brick walls, it's too late. You've lost your train of thought and can't finish the essay.

Don't get me wrong. Details are great. I have placed whole chapters about details in this very book. I love details! But if you allow yourself to agonize over one particular fact, you're in trouble. Think of the issue this way: Your brain has room for only one job at a time: wallpaper remembering or essay writing. I think everyone out there can identify the right choice.

Here's what to do when you hit a detail-snag: Insert a blank line and a note to yourself. Then *keep going.* Returning to the tarantula example, you'd type:

> Smoothly sliding each of his legs over the _______ wallpaper, Spidey immediately made himself at home. [FIND OUT ABOUT THE WALL PAPER]

Remember to fill in the blanks and delete the note before you print a final copy of the essay!

Editing while writing

In Chapter 5 I explain why editing while writing or preparing to write is a bad idea. (Briefly, the two tasks rely on different mental processes, which clash.) Unfortunately, lots of people do attempt to combine these two functions while working on the rough draft. Some, for example, stare at a sentence for ten minutes trying to find the perfect verb. That's editing, not writing. So by the time the Platonic Ideal of Verb-Land shows up, the essay is on life support, because the editing has overshadowed the writing.

In Chapter 6 I go into detail on how to send your inner editor away while you're preparing to write. The techniques I describe in Chapter 6 depend on one basic principle: Don't stop to analyze when you're creating. Just keep going and leave the critical judgment for later. So in the "which verb is best" dilemma I described in the preceding paragraph, the solution is simple: Put a verb in — any reasonably sensible verb — and move on. And that's the answer to all the blocks you may encounter while working on the rough draft:

Just pour it out onto the page. Later you can punch it into shape. And later you *should* punch it into shape. (Part IV provides editing tips.)

Stopping and starting with ease

It's 3 a.m. and you're on a roll. The rough draft is zipping along smoothly. The only problem is that you have a Spanish test at 8:30 a.m. You'll have less than six hours of sleep if you can get to school by StarTrek transporter beam, and even less sleep if you go to school by twenty-first century transportation. You're afraid to stop because you'll lose the thread of logic, and you know from experience that starting again is really tough. However, Señora Woods has been sending increasingly cranky notes about "lackadaisical preparation for tests." What to do?

Short-term answer: Go to sleep *now.* Long-term answer: Stop writing at a reasonable hour and give your body the eight hours of rest that it needs to function. But when you stop work, use these tricks to make the re-start much simpler:

- Before you turn the computer off or put the paper away, jot down all the ideas floating around in your head for the next paragraph or section. Don't try to put those ideas in order, and don't worry about spelling or syntax. Just write enough to remind you of what you would write had you had time to continue.
- The normal human tendency is to keep going until you hit the end of a section. Bad idea. Stop in the middle of the section, preferably in the middle of a paragraph. If restarting is a problem for you (and it is for most people), you'll find it easier to start with something you were already working on than to approach a completely new task.
- As you approach quitting time, look over your outline. (You have an outline, right? No? You still have time to make one. Chapter 8 shows you how to construct a sturdy outline for your work.) Identify the least difficult section of the essay. Stop before you get to that section. When you take the essay out again, you should be able to convince yourself that restarting is a cinch because you know you're facing an easy part.

In case you're wondering whether this book is totally theoretical, I should mention that I myself use the tricks I just described. I have to pause in the writing of *College Admission Essays For Dummies* because other chores have been piling up. (My refrigerator contains two brownish lettuce leaves and a couple of onions. I really have to go shopping!) I plan to pause in the middle of Chapter 14, the grammar chapter, because grammar is my forte. (I wrote *English Grammar For Dummies,* as you may know. Just a little plug for the other book. Sorry.) After I fill up the refrigerator and take care of all the other undone and long overdue tasks, I can sit down at the computer again knowing that "all I have to do" that day is grammar.

Part IV

I'd Like to Finish before Retirement Age: The Final Draft

In this part . . .

With one complete draft of the admission essay resting on your desk, it's time to party, right? Wrong. It's time to rub the rough edges off your prose — to correct the grammar and spelling (Chapter 14), smooth the style (Chapter 15), run one last check on the tone and content (Chapter 16), and insert the finished product into the application (Chapter 17). In this part I tackle those last small but crucial steps to a great essay.

Don't forget to invite me to the party when you're done.

Chapter 14

Making a List and Checking It Twice: Grammar and Spelling

In This Chapter

- Checking your draft for grammar errors
- Ensuring correct spelling
- Deciding to break a rule or two

I am a grammarian. People don't call me to request my views on the Big Bang theory or the prospects of a certain dot.com startup. Instead they ask, "Should I use "who" or "whom" in this sentence?" Sigh. I'm not hugely proud of this specialized bit of knowledge, but I do have it. And you need it.

So in this chapter I hit the grammar rules — not all of them (pause for a dance of joy), but the ones you're likely to need as you check your draft. I also show you when (gasp of astonishment) you're allowed to break the rules without getting sent up the river for a stretch in the grammar penitentiary. For a complete look at grammar and its rules, check out *English Grammar For Dummies* by yours truly (published by Wiley Publishing, Inc.).

Getting the Grammar Right the Second Time Around

No one writes a perfectly grammatical first draft. Not even me . . . er, I. See what I mean? While you're creating the rough draft, you're concentrating on content and, to a lesser extent, style. The picky stuff — commas, spelling, the selection of "is" or "are" — doesn't flow from anyone's pen in an uninterrupted stream of correctness. Not in this universe, anyway.

Nevertheless, you can't leave those errors in your admission essay. The admissions committee (or the scholarship committee, if you're begging for bucks) is judging your level of education. Rightly or wrongly, they will see the quality of your grammar as an indication of academic accomplishment. And if you're writing an essay as part of a job application and your grammar is faulty . . . well, as we say in New York City, the job "ain't gonna happen." Employers generally hold applicants for professional positions to strict standards of written and verbal expression.

Memorizing grammar rules is a waste of time. If you're normal (that is, *not* an English teacher), all you want to do is to correct any errors in your essay as quickly as possible and then move on to bigger and better things. This section is divided into four parts, each tackling a different category of grammar error and correction: verbs, pronouns, sentence completeness, and punctuation. A good strategy is to go over your essay four times. With each rereading, check for one type of problem, consulting the rules and examples as necessary. After four check-ups, take up the issue of spelling. (A section later in this chapter, "Spelling It ~~Rihgt~~ Right," provides tips.)

Verbs

Every grammar check should start with verbs, because they're "where the action is," as we used to say in the sixties. Here's the definition, so you know what you're checking: A *verb* is a word that expresses action or state of being. In a sentence, the verb may be one word or a couple of words. Note the verbs, which are in italics, in these sentences:

> I *would like* to attend Silly Nutty University because of my interest in humor. (*would like* = verb expressing action)
>
> For the past two years I *have been* an active member of my school's Class Clown Appreciation Society. (*have been* = verb expressing being)
>
> Your major in Farcical Face Painting *attracts* me because I *love* disguises. (*attracts, love* = verbs expressing action)
>
> I *will be* the Picasso of farcical face painting one day. (*will be* = verb expressing being)

Verbs have three characteristics that may cause problems: tense, number, and voice.

Tense

No, I'm not talking about the sort of mood that calls for scented candles and a massage. I'm talking about *time.* The past, present, and future are indicated in an English sentence by the *tense* of the verb. Even if you don't know one iota of fancy grammar terminology, you use verb tenses with every statement you make, and most of the time you're probably correct. If you hang out with reasonably fluent speakers of English or if you watch a moderate amount of television, the proper tenses seep into your brain without any conscious effort at all. Unfortunately, even the best students of English sometimes trip over a small number of tense rules — but *you* won't, if you follow these guidelines. (***Note:*** In the following examples I've placed all verbs in italics so you can zero in on them easily. Don't italicize anything in your essay unless you're emphasizing a particular word or idea or indicating a title.)

- **Don't change tenses without a reason for doing so.** If you're discussing the effect on your worldview of your Uncle Elmer's invention of a special toupee glue, you probably want past tense:

  Elmer *spent* the rest of his life attached to the living room couch, but his discovery *eased* the life of millions. . . .

  Or, if you love drama, you may choose present tense:

  Elmer *stares* into the pot of sticky white liquid. "This *revolutionizes* the world of baldness,' he *thinks.* 'Now I *have* no fear of the wind whipping off my toupee!"

  What you can't do is hop frivolously from one to the other. Surprisingly, this practice is quite common, especially over the course of a three-page essay. Here's an example of an invalid switch from present to past:

  Elmer *patents* his discovery, but he never *used* it. He *died* in 1983.

  Just to show you the difference, here is a paragraph with valid tense switches:

  I *think* about Elmer every time I *count* the few remaining hairs on my head. I *will* never *forget* what he *said* the last time I *saw* him. "My boy," he *declared,* '*Forget* the toupee tape and *dump* the implants. Glue *will be* our family's choice forever." Because of my uncle's experience, I want to major in chemistry. (*think, count, forget, dump, want* = present; *will forget, will be* = future; *said, saw, declared* = past)

- **Add "had" to a verb to indicate that one event in the past took place before another past event.** Suppose that you're writing about the experiences that prompted you to apply to the Institute for Advanced Jailhouse Studies. You're describing the profound impression made by your childhood visits to Aunt Cleo's cell. Check out this excerpt, noting the verbs that I've placed in italics:

  I will use my degree from the Institute for Advanced Jailhouse Studies for the betterment of the human race. My determination to do so stems from my visits to Aunt Cleo's cell. Every Saturday we *visited* her, often toting a cake I *had baked* the night before. Aunt Cleo was not particularly fond of cake, but she always *thanked* me politely before asking if I *had inserted* a file.

  Notice that in the third sentence, the cake baking precedes the visiting, so the proper verb is *had baked,* not *baked.* In the fourth sentence, the insertion takes place before the thanking, as indicated by the verb *had inserted.*

The most common mistake with "had" is to place it everywhere, as in this paragraph:

When she had asked me about the file, I had replied that I didn't believe in jail breaks. I had told her that she had done the crime and must now do the time.

Too many *had's.* Here's the correct version:

When she asked me about the file, I replied that I didn't believe in jail breaks. I told her that she had done the crime and must now do the time.

Now you've got one *had,* to show that the crime took place before the conversation.

- **Add "has" or "have" to a verb to show a link between past and present.** If you're writing about your most bizarre hobby, this sentence is correct:

  I *have devoted* the past five summers to collecting cat hats.

  The *have,* added to the verb *devoted,* shows that you are still a collector. Contrast the preceding example with this one:

  I *devoted* five summers to collecting cat hats. Since 2002, my cousin Aphra *has been studying* dog earmuffs, and I plan to join her next expedition.

  The plain verb, *devoted,* indicates that the cat-hat hobby is over. (What a relief!) In the second sentence, *has been studying* shows that the dog hobby is on-going.

- **If you're writing about a work of literature, use present tense.** Some colleges ask you to discuss "a poem or novel that affected you." Because events in literature never took place, they can't be in the past. They begin again every time a reader opens the book. Hence, present tense is appropriate when you talk about events in a literary work, and past tense is best when you talk about the experience of reading it. (***Note:*** The verbs are italicized here to make them easier to find. A play title is also italicized. Don't italicize anything in your essay unless you want to add special emphasis or indicate the title of a full-length creative work.)

  My junior English class *studied* Shakespeare's *Macbeth.* I *was* profoundly impressed by Lady Macbeth's manipulation of her husband. She *tells* him that he *is* not manly, and he immediately *gives* in to her requests.

  Notice that the first two sentences have past-tense verbs because they describe the act of reading, which took place in the past. The last sentence has present-tense verbs because it discusses Shakespeare's play.

Number

Number is the English-teachers' term for singular (one) or plural (more than one). To choose the number of the verb, check out the *subject* — generally who or what is doing the action or is in the state of being expressed by the verb. (Don't worry about the small number of sentences in which the subject receives the action. They're unlikely to cause number problems.) Singular subjects are paired with singular verbs, and plural subjects with plural verbs. Most English verbs (thank goodness!) have the same form for both singular and plural, with one important exception. If you're talking *about* someone or something, the present-tense form changes, as in these examples:

> Cousin Hyperbia *eats* all day and *sleeps* all night.
>
> They *eat* two entire goat herds before sundown and then *sleep* until dawn.

In the first example I'm talking about Hyperbia (fortunately, there's only one), so she's singular. The two verbs associated with her, *eats* and *sleeps,* are also singular. In the second example, *they* is plural and so are the verbs (*eat, sleep*).

Sometimes a verb form contains *has* or *have. Has* is singular and *have* is plural. Similarly, some verb forms include *does* or *do. Does* is singular and *do* is plural.

I bet that you automatically choose the correct number for 99 percent of the verbs in your essay. However, a couple of tricky situations may trip you up:

- **Two singular subjects connected by "and" create a plural.** If you are answering a question about your dream job ("Identify an individual whose job you would like to have for a day" — a real question), you may say the following (the verb is italicized for easy identification):

  The staple and the paperclip *intrigue* me, so I want to be Herman Gooberblue, the CEO of Office Stuff Inc. for a day. (*staple and paperclip* = plural subject, *intrigue* = plural verb)

  A couple of expressions — *as well as, in addition to, along with* — appear to add to the subject and create a plural. Appearances are deceiving! These words don't affect the singular/plural issue at all. Ignore these expressions and check the subject. If it is singular, you need a singular verb. If it is plural, you need a plural verb.

- ***Either/or*** **and** ***neither/nor*** **join two subjects. Match the verb to the nearest subject.** Check out this example, drawn from a (fictional) essay answering a real question about "working for a year with unlimited resources":

If I had a year with unlimited resources, I would build amusement parks for the needy. Either skydives or a parachute jump *is* first on my agenda. The poor need hobbies as well as housing and food, but too few public agencies recognize this fact.

The *either/or* pair joins two subjects, *skydives* (plural) and *parachute jump* (singular). The singular subject is closer to the verb, so the verb is singular. If you reverse the sentence, you need a plural verb:

Either a parachute jump or skydives *are* first on my agenda.

- ***Each* and *every* always take a singular verb, no matter what these words precede.** The logic (yes, grammar has some logic, but not much) is that when you write *each* and *every,* you're talking about the members of the group one by one. Note the singular verb in this sentence:

  Each ride and attraction in the amusement park *is* free.

Voice

Verbs may be in *active* voice, when the subject is doing the action:

> I *beg* you to accept me to your school.

Verbs may also be in *passive* voice, when the subject is receiving the action:

> The gym *was demolished* by my graduating class.

The rule on voice is extremely simple: Whenever possible, use active voice. Passive is awkward and, well, passive . . . not qualities you want to communicate to the admissions committee. If you don't know who did the action in the sentence or you don't want to admit that you did it (though I advise honesty above all in your application), then passive is okay. Switching from passive to active is easy. Just figure out who is doing the action or is in the state of being discussed in the sentence and insert him or her (or them) into the sentence:

> **Original, passive version:** Many books were read and papers written for that course.
>
> **What you must insert:** Who's reading and writing? The students, of course. They always get stuck with the work, right?
>
> **Revised, active version:** In that course students read many books and wrote several papers.

One more verb rule

Last one, I promise. This oft-broken rule involves "condition contrary to fact" — an idea that isn't true or an event that didn't happen, as in "If I were a rich man" (I'm a poor woman) and other such expressions. Here's how to express these concepts correctly:

- **Place *had* or *were* in the "if" portion of the sentence.** Check out these examples:

  If I had known about your stamp-collecting major . . . (but I didn't know)

  If I were happy at the University of Hard Knocks . . . (but I'm so miserable I could scream)

- **Place *would* in the other portion of the sentence, never in the "if" section.** Check out these additions attached to the preceding examples:

  If I had known about your stamp-collecting major, I would have accepted your first offer of admission. (I didn't know, and I didn't accept.)

  If I were happy at the University of Hard Knocks, I would not seek a transfer. (I'm not happy and I am seeking a way out of this awful place.)

The most common mistake, by the way, is to place "would" in the "if" section of the sentence. Penalty box! *Would* and *if* don't get along (something about an affair, jealousy, a stolen necklace . . . I forget. Just keep them separate).

Pronouns

You've got to love pronouns, but they sure are annoying little guys. *Pronouns* take the place of nouns (the names of people, places, things, and ideas) and save you from sentences like "Albert took Albert's little sister to the pool, and Albert's little sister swam in the pool." How much simpler to say, "Albert took his little sister to the pool, and she swam in it." The pronouns in that sentence are *his, she,* and *it.* Other pronouns include *I, me, our, you, your, they, him, their,* and *us* (the easiest pronouns to spot), as well as *everyone, someone, anyone, no one, everybody, somebody, anybody, nobody, everything, something, anything, nothing, each, every, most, more, some, who, which, that, whose, others,* and lots of other words.

Pronouns have two qualities that may make you stub your toe on the path to correct English: *case* (the difference between, for example, *who, whom,* and *whose*) and *number* (the singular/plural quality, as in *he* and *they*).

Case

Fortunately, your "ear" for grammar recognizes case errors most of the time. Not many Tarzans write admission essays stating, "Me want to attend college." But a couple of situations pose problems:

- **Compounds.** In sentences with long strings of nouns and pronouns, all jumbled up, you may find it hard to choose the correct pronoun. Even if only one pronoun and noun are grouped together, you may become confused. The solution is simple. Isolate the pronoun and check the sentence. If the pronoun sounds okay alone, chances are it is okay. If it sounds strange, adjust the singular/plural form of the verb. Now does the pronoun sound better? If so, go with it. If not, try another. Here are some examples of this technique in action, all from imaginary sentences answering a real college-essay question, "Describe an expressive silence":

Sentence with dilemma unsolved: As Mom plucked shards of glass from the baseball, the living room rug, and the window frame, she glared silently at the culprits — Jessup, Millie, and (I, me).

Untangled version: . . . she glared at I . . . or she glared at me

Answer: . . . she glared at me.

Another sentence with dilemma unsolved: The completely innocent baseball players — Jessup, Millie, and (I, me) are now glaring at each other as we spackle in a new pane of glass.

Untangled version: I are glaring . . . or me are glaring

Answer: Here you have to adjust the verb number because isolating the subject in this sentence changes the subject from plural to singular. So check the pronouns with *am,* the singular verb. *I* am glaring? *Me* am glaring? *I* is clearly the correct choice. Go back to the original sentence and insert *I.*

Bottom line: Isolate the pronoun you're worried about, and chances are you'll immediately identify the correct choice.

- **Possessive pronouns with "ing" words.** Lots of "ing" words for actions — *swimming, sailing, sighing,* for example — may be used as nouns, as in these sentences:

  I just adore *applying* to college! *Filling* out hundreds of forms is so much fun!

  The "ing" words — *applying, filling* — are derived from verbs (*apply, fill*), but they are being used as nouns. For those of you who love terminology (time to say hello to the future English majors), these "ing" words are called *gerunds.* When you place a pronoun before a gerund, use the possessive form, as in this example:

  Incorrect: My parents are thrilled about *me* applying to college.

  Correct: My parents are thrilled about *my* applying to college.

  Why it's correct: Possessive pronouns are the 98-pound weaklings on Grammar Beach; they don't have much clout. In the correct sentence, the focus is on *applying,* where it should be, because the possessive pronoun *my* doesn't carry much weight. In the incorrect version, *me* is an "I can bench-press my body weight" pronoun. *Me* takes the attention away from *applying* and stresses that my parents are thrilled about *me* — possibly true but not the intended meaning of the sentence.

- **Who/Whom.** *Who* is for subjects, and *whom* is for objects. Sorry to hit you with two more grammar terms, but I'll try to keep it simple. In most sentences, a *subject* identifies who or what is performing the action or who or what is in the state of being you're talking about. (The exception? Sentences in passive voice. Check out the "Voice" section earlier in this chapter.) If you're deciding between *who* and *whom,* locate the verbs and make sure that each one has a subject. If you've got a verb flapping around with no subject, chances are you need *who* to act as a subject. If all the verbs have other subjects, you probably need *whom.* Very, very occasionally, you need *who* for another grammatical job in a sentence with a verb expressing being. (For grammar mavens: the predicate nominative after a linking verb.) This situation is quite rare, so my advice is not to worry about it.

Ninety percent of the time, *who* is correct, so if you're in a muddle and can't crack the sentence, play the odds and go with *who.*

Number

You can probably sort most of the pronouns into singular and plural baskets without much thought; *I* is singular and *we* is plural, *she* is singular, *they* is plural, and so on. *You,* for reasons too obscure to mention, may be either singular or plural. (Lots of English-speakers find the double nature of *you* annoying and insist on adding some extras to indicate plural, as in *you all, you guys,* and *youse.* All these add-ons are fine when you're talking with your friends, but not for your essay.) Why should you care whether a pronoun is singular or plural? Because you must match a singular pronoun with a singular verb and a plural pronoun with a plural verb. Also, sometimes you need to refer to a pronoun with another pronoun, and once again, singular and plural don't mix. Here are some guidelines for tricky pronoun-number situations:

- **The ones, the things, the bodies.** What I call "the ones," "the things," and "the bodies" — *everyone, everything, everybody, someone, something, somebody, no one, nothing, nobody, anyone, anything, anybody* — are singular. You probably use the correct verb with these pronouns, stating automatically that "everyone *is* here," not "everyone *are* here." Be sure that any pronoun referring to one of these words is also singular, as in this example:

  Incorrect: Everyone brought their bribe money to the admissions interview.

  Why it's incorrect: *Everyone* is singular, and *their* is plural. Don't mix and match!

  Correct: Everyone brought his or her bribe money to the interview.

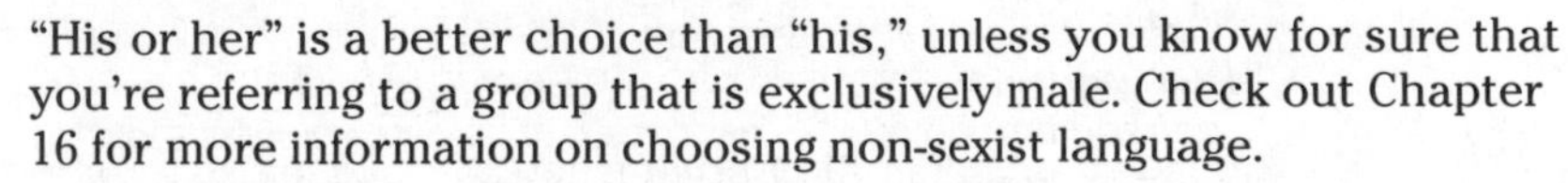

"His or her" is a better choice than "his," unless you know for sure that you're referring to a group that is exclusively male. Check out Chapter 16 for more information on choosing non-sexist language.

- **The variables.** A few pronouns used for quantity — *any, most, all, some, none* — may be either singular or plural, depending upon how you use them. If you can count whatever the pronoun refers to, the pronoun is plural. If you can't count what the pronoun refers to, the pronoun is singular. Some examples:

  Any of the competitive-eating courses at your university *are* helpful to my goal of being crowned Champion Hot-Dog Eater. (*any* = plural because you can count courses, *are* = plural verb)

  Most of the eating in my high school *is* strictly amateur. (*most* = singular because you can't count eating, *is* = singular verb)

- **Who, which, that.** These pronouns may be either singular or plural also. Identify the noun they're replacing. If the noun is singular, the pronoun is singular also. If the noun is plural, the pronoun is plural too. Some examples:

  A scholarship *that is* awarded by the Institute of Competitive Eating will allow me to realize my goal of winning the Oyster Contest. (*that* replaces *scholarship,* a singular noun, *is* = singular verb)

  The instructors at the Institute of Competitive Eating, *who are* widely recognized as the best in the world, will teach me everything I need to know about the world of food. (*who* replaces *instructors,* a plural noun, *are* = plural verb)

Two more pronoun errors

Communication is the goal of all writing, so don't make your reader guess the meaning of any pronoun, as in these sentences, written in answer to the question "Discuss a book that mattered to you":

Wrong: In *Why I Eat For Money,* it says that the annual Fourth of July hot dog-eating contest is the Olympics of competitive eating.

Why it's wrong: *It?* What does *it* refer to? Nothing.

Right: In *Why I Eat For Money,* champion eater Gus "Mustard" Bun says that the annual Fourth of July hot dog-eating contest is the Olympics of competitive eating.

Wrong: When my mother told my sister about my plans for a career in competitive eating, she cried.

Why it's wrong: Who cried? Your mom? Your sister? *She* could refer to either.

Right: When my mother said, "Your brother wants to pursue a career in competitive eating," my sister cried.

Also right: My mother cried when she told my sister about my plan to pursue a career in competitive eating.

Complete sentences

English teachers (including yours truly) emphasize complete sentences so strongly that you may think the rule is carved on Mount Rushmore. Prepare yourself for a shock. Yes, it's true that complete sentences are desirable and the basis for all written English. However, just about everyone, again including yours truly, breaks the rules from time to time. So far, life as we know it on earth hasn't crumbled from the strain, but stay tuned.

The basic ingredients of a complete sentence are as follows:

- A verb — a word or phrase expressing action or state of being
- A subject — who or what you're talking about in the sentence
- A thought that makes sense by itself, that's . . . well, complete.

Here are some examples of complete sentences and incomplete sentence fragments, all from a (non-existent) essay answering the real application question "Describe a situation in which you took a stand that was unpopular with the majority":

Incomplete fragment: Because I had the guts to defy Mr. Pickle.

Why it's incomplete: You've given a reason, but it's not attached to any context. True, the context may be clear from the information in other sentences, but this one can't stand alone.

Complete sentence: I didn't drop out of chemistry when I was assigned 149 extra laboratory reports as punishment, because I had the guts to defy Mr. Pickle.

Why it's complete: Now you have a thought that ends in a logical place. Nothing is flapping in the breeze, waiting for more words.

Another fragment: Mr. Pickle, who was overly fond of vinegar and often sang "The Brine Song" at the beginning of class, regardless of how much work we were supposed to accomplish.

Why it's incomplete: The "who" signals a description, but there's no main idea — no verb, in grammatical terms — to match with "Mr. Pickle." The reader has a description but is waiting for the central statement to conclude.

Complete sentence: Mr. Pickle was overly fond of vinegar and often sang "The Brine Song" at the beginning of class, regardless of how much work we were supposed to accomplish.

Why it's complete: When you extract the "who," the reader stays on one track. The verb "was" matches "Mr. Pickle." The meaning comes across as finished.

Another complete sentence: Mr. Pickle, who was overly fond of vinegar and often sang "The Brine Song" at the beginning of class, regardless of how much work we were supposed to accomplish, eventually drowned in a vat of cucumber salad.

Why this one's complete: Now when the "who . . . accomplish" description is extracted, a complete thought remains: "Mr. Pickle eventually drowned in a vat of cucumber salad."

One more thing about complete sentences: Don't stick two of them together without any glue. The "glue" in Grammar World is a joining word (*and, or, nor, but, for, yet, because, since, after, although,* and so on) or a semicolon (;). If you attach one complete sentence to another, be sure you've got one of those "glue" words, also known as *conjunctions.* Some examples:

Illegal joining: I told the class that Mr. Pickle's plan was immoral, the class didn't listen to me.

Why it's illegal: Check out the stuff before the comma. It's a complete thought with a subject and a verb. So is the stuff after the comma. Hence you have two complete sentences, joined only by a comma. That's a no-no.

Legal joining: I told the class that Mr. Pickle's plan was immoral, but the class didn't listen to me.

Another legal joining: I told the class that Mr. Pickle's plan was immoral; the class didn't listen to me.

Some words look like "glue," but they aren't. (Think of these words as the stick-um on very old envelopes. It doesn't attach anything; it just looks good.) Common "false glue" words include *then, also, moreover, consequently, however,* and *nevertheless.* If you want to attach one complete sentence to another with one of these words, add a semicolon, as in this example:

Mr. Pickle was forced to destroy his Purple Bomb; consequently, the world was saved, but I got extra chem homework.

Punctuation

Seeing spots before your eyes? How about wiggly lines? Don't call the eye doctor yet; you're probably just having a punctuation meltdown. Punctuation — the periods, commas, apostrophes, and other symbols in your writing — serve a valuable purpose. Punctuation indicates *how* words should be grouped, where the pauses are, and who said what. All these terrific accomplishments go hand in hand with one inescapable fact: The rules of punctuation are arbitrary (*The comma goes there because I said so!*) and annoying (*Who cares where the comma goes?*). Nevertheless, you have to follow these dumb rules in your admission essay. No doubt the admission committee wants to see whether you are capable of following dumb rules, so they'll know whether you're likely to follow *their* dumb rules after you're admitted.

Endmarks

Endmarks — periods, question marks, and exclamation points — come at the end of a sentence. (How do grammarians come up with this terminology?) Some rules:

- Don't place two endmarks at the end of a sentence.
- If the sentence is a statement ending with a quotation, place the period inside the quotation marks, as in this example:

  My guidance counselor said that I am "Hahvah material."
- For a sentence ending with a quotation, use question marks or exclamation points in this way: Place the question mark or exclamation point *inside* the quotation marks if the quoted words are a question or an exclamation. Place the question mark or exclamation point *outside* if the entire sentence, but not the quoted words, is a question or an exclamation. Some examples:

  Was the guidance counselor correct in calling me "Hahvah material"?

  I ask you, "Am I Hahvah material?"

Quotation marks

These paired lines (single in Britain, double in the United States) indicate that the words they enclose are not your own. Quotation marks tell the reader that you're repeating the exact words from a person or a text. If the quotation comes at the end of a sentence, check out the rule in the previous section (see "Endmarks"). If the quotation begins a sentence, follow this model:

> "I've always thought you were a natural fit for Hahvah University," said my mom as she tied a crimson ribbon around the old oak tree in my yard on my first birthday. (Notice that the comma goes inside the quotation mark.)

A few other rules:

- The first word of a quotation is capitalized.
- If you interrupt a quotation with a speaker tag (*he said, she complained, they bleated*, and so on), capitalize the first word of the quotation but not the first word of the continuation. An example of an interrupted quotation is as follows:

  "Because I am sure that Hahvah University is right for you," my mom explained, "you'll apply there and nowhere else when the time comes."

- Quotation marks enclose the title of short artistic works (poems, articles, stories, songs). The titles of full-length works (books, newspaper or magazine titles, plays) are italicized or underlined.
- If you insert one quotation inside another, enclose the inner quotation in single quotation marks and the outer quotation in double quotation marks. An example:

  "My college counselor told me that Pinstown is 'a better fit,' but I don't believe him," I replied as my mother began to fill out donation checks for the new library.

In Britain, quotations are enclosed in single quotation marks. Quotations inside other quotations are enclosed in double quotation marks. Thus, Britain and America are on opposite sides of the Atlantic and the Punctuation Oceans.

Commas

I hate this punctuation mark, although it is not on the top of my "Worst Grammar Rule" list. (That honor belongs to the subject of the next section, "Apostrophes.") Why do I hate commas? Because they're *everywhere* they shouldn't be in a typical essay. So before you do anything else to the punctuation of your essay, take out half the commas. (Just kidding. But be careful! Be sure you have a reason for every comma in your essay.) The rules:

- When you join two complete sentences with *and, or, but, nor,* or *for,* place a comma before the joining word. (For more information about complete sentences, check out the "Complete sentences" section of this chapter.) An example:

  I want to go to Pinstown, but my mom is set on Hahvah.
- Use a comma to separate parts of a date or an address, as in these examples:

  I won the award for best hog yell in August, 2000.

  The contest was held in Hog Heaven, Siberia.
- Use a comma to separate a word from its equivalent, when the more specific term comes first. Don't use a comma to separate a word from its equivalent when the more general term comes first. For example:

  Macbeth, Shakespeare's marvelous play, comes to mind when I think about attending the Institute of Thaneship. (*Macbeth* = Shakespeare's marvelous play, more specific term comes first — comma)

  Shakespeare's marvelous play *Macbeth* comes to mind when I think about attending the Institute of Thaneship. (now the more specific term comes second — no comma)

- Don't use a comma to separate a compound (double) verb from its subject, as in this example:

  I play the piano and sing beautifully. (no comma between the subject, *I*, and the verbs *play* and *sing*)

Apostrophes

This punctuation mark should be stricken from the language. No one in the history of the world ever needed an apostrophe; lots of languages don't even have them. But English does, and we're stuck with the rules governing apostrophe use. Sigh. Here goes:

- Insert an apostrophe to indicate that letters have been omitted, as in *don't* (short for *do not*), *shouldn't* (short for *should not*), *we're*, (short for *we are*), and so forth.
- Use an apostrophe to indicate possession, as in *John's essay* and *the students' competition.* Note that in general a singular possessive ends in *'s* and a plural possessive ends in *s'*. Here's an important exception to this rule: If the plural of a noun doesn't end in *s,* add *'s* to make the noun possessive, as in *children's, data's, women's,* and so forth.
- No possessive pronoun (*my, ours, their, hers, mine, its,* and so on) ever includes an apostrophe.

Spelling It ~~Rihgt~~ Right

I can't tell you how to spell every word in your essay because I haven't read your essay. What I can tell you in this section is how to find the correct spelling, so that you can check your own work. Here goes:

- If the essay is typed on a computer, the word-processing program will probably indicate that a word does not appear in its internal dictionary by placing a line under it. A mouse click will provide several alternatives. However, computers are not particularly smart. They won't recognize a proper name, and they won't catch every mistake. Recheck the underlined word in a good dictionary.
- How can you check for spelling in a dictionary if you don't know how to spell the word to begin with? The Catch-22 that snares all writers! Okay, try the spelling you *think* is correct. Then check a couple of variations. If you're still at sea, ask a convenient literate friend or teacher.
- Some spelling errors are really typos; you know what's supposed to be on the page, but your eye skips over the offending part. To increase the odds of catching typos, put the draft aside for a day or two, if you have time. Then read it again with a fresh perspective.

Deciding When to Break the Rules

When I'm slogging through the academic term, Friday is my favorite day of the week — specifically Friday evening, when I welcome a break in the pattern of my workdays. And to tell the truth, I enjoy breaking the daily routine even in summer. I always go out on Friday nights! The joy of pattern-breaking is fairly universal, I believe, and that's why you should *occasionally* and *carefully* break some rules when you're writing an admission essay. But which rules and when?

Here's the deal. Break a rule if you have a specific reason to do so. If you know what you're trying to accomplish and can't achieve the same result any other way, go for it! For example, I once read an essay describing a white-water rafting trip. The writer included a passage with many sentences tumbled together — in the section describing a tumbling trip through a gorge. Technically this writer was violating the rules about complete sentences. Practically, he had a very effective, fast-paced description of a raft trip.

If you break a grammar rule, be sure that the rest of your essay is perfect. You want the contrast! If you have grammar errors in every sentence, your reader will assume that you don't know the rules, not that you're ignoring them for the sake of writing style.

Chapter 15

Smoothing the Rough Edges: Polishing the Essay

In This Chapter

- Checking word choice
- Repairing awkward sentences
- Skirting monotony

Written any e-mails to friends lately? If so, you've probably chosen informal language that everyone in your crowd accepts — words that make both the sender and the receiver feel comfortable. That's your goal for the admission essay also: word choices that express who you are but also (and here's the tricky part) fall comfortably upon admissions committee ears. In this chapter I help you steer clear of jargon, slang, and sexist expressions. I show you how to make the small but important alterations that tame awkward sentences, enliven monotonous paragraphs, and put you on the path to making your rough draft a final draft.

Picking the Best Words

Suppose you're writing an essay about a leadership experience (a real question on many applications). In the rough draft you explained how you rewired an electronic door lock to release 30 tired and hungry students who were trapped in the computer lab after an artificial intelligence experiment went haywire. (Homicidal computer on the prowl, heroic rescuer — the sort of thing Hollywood loves.) Here's a paragraph from the rough draft:

> As the hours passed, everything was whack. No one had the 411 to tackle this situation. But I suddenly realized that the 5TK 3 assembly was accessible from the DP. I grabbed a handbag from this chick with too much hairspray and dumped its contents on the floor. Spying a nail file, I attacked the lock. Broken on Firsties' Day, it had a loose cover. I pried the cover off with the nail file, hooked the J-ode to the X-B Assembly, and before you could say, "Beam me up, Scotty," we were out.

What's wrong with this paragraph? Let me count the ways. It's filled with slang (*whack, 411*) and possibly obscure references (*Beam me up, Scotty, Firsties' Day*). It contains incomprehensible technical terms (*5TK3, J-ode, X-B Assembly*). And if I were the admissions counselor reading this essay, I'd be tempted to throw it in the reject pile solely on the basis of the sexist reference to a "chick."

Okay, I admit that I exaggerated the flaws so that you could pick them out easily. Also, in the interest of writing a family-friendly book, I refrained from including a tasteless sentence, though I've seen more than one bathroom reference in student essays. Your essay probably has fewer and less glaring errors in word choice. But in an admission essay, even one false note is too many. To correct those errors, read on.

Getting the 411 on slang

The expression "411," for those of you out of this particular slang loop, comes from the numbers you punch to reach the telephone information directory. Hence "411" means "information." A cute phrase, but not a harmless one. Why? The answer lies in the nature of slang, specifically, the fact that many people don't understand it. Slang is up-to-the-minute language created by an individual or a small group of people. Someone coins a phrase, and pretty soon the "in-crowd" can't get along without it. Or, in the media-savvy twenty-first century, a film-television-music person may latch onto an expression, and the public follows. But not all the public — just those who have seen the film, broadcast, concert, or whatever.

Exclusivity is essential to slang. If everyone was aware of the meaning of a phrase, it wouldn't be slang anymore. It would simply be the common language. And the purpose of slang, in my opinion, is to create an "out-crowd" — a group that doesn't understand those special, defining phrases of the "in-crowd." Also, slang that sticks around for more than a year is rare. Nobody in the in-crowd wants to be caught with one of last season's greatest hits in the word parade.

When you write an admission essay, your goal is certainly not to exclude the reader. After all, you're asking to become part of the institution (whereupon you can learn the specialized language, or slang, popular on the campus). But until you're in *their* in-crowd, take care not to use slang.

Sometimes it's tough to identify the slang popular in your area or in your particular group. Because everyone you talk to on a regular basis uses those words, you may see them simply as language, not as slang. When you examine your essay, underline any suspicious phrases. Try to step outside yourself for a moment. Are you sure that the underlined expressions will be immediately understandable to every age, in every geographic area? If you're not sure, change the underlined material. Another good tactic is to call a relative or friend who is definitely out of the loop. (Grandparents or older relatives are good for this task, as are teachers nearing retirement age.) Read the underlined material and ask the listener to tell you the meaning. If the listener is puzzled, dump the word or phrase and substitute something else.

Talking tech

Will e-tailers turn a profit this season? Did the zipper announce the election results for student government? Is the default value that you meet your friends for pizza on Fridays after class? Are you having fun yet? Techno-fun, that is?

In case some of the words from the preceding paragraph haven't reached your personal vocabulary yet, here's the deal:

> e-tailer = a play on the word "retailer" — one who sells over the Internet
>
> zipper = an electronic sign with words flowing (zipping) across it continuously
>
> default value = what usually happens, what you should assume to be true unless unusual circumstances intervene
>
> pizza = that flat round thing with cheese

Who invents tech talk? Pretty much anyone with an idea and an Internet site to publicize it. So if you hang around the Web, and especially if you're a computer geek yourself, you've probably picked up a fairly large tech vocabulary. The issue of tech talk in an admissions essay is similar to the slang dilemma: comprehension. I'm generally in favor of large vocabularies, but in the case of technical words, you can run into problems. What happens if you use a term that the admissions counselor doesn't understand? Or worse, what if the essay-readers *think* they understand but are in fact applying the wrong meaning?

Tech talk *may* have a place in your admission essay, but only under certain conditions:

- **Make sure that the term has only one specific meaning.** Just imagine your reader's reaction upon reading that "the zipper was down." You may be discussing broken electronics, but chances are your reader has jumped tracks and begun to fantasize about a whole new subject.
- **If possible, clarify the meaning of the word by providing context clues.** If your essay is about Cousin Hypatia's efforts to invent an alternative to C++, mention *computer programming language* in the sentence.
- **Consider the identity of your reader.** If you're applying for graduate work in engineering, you have more leeway. Your readers will understand technical terms that stump the average, can't-program-the-VCR

type. If your reader is likely to be someone whose highest point of technology is the television remote, substitute descriptive terms for names ("electronic message board" for "zipper," for example).

Jettisoning jargon

Jargon is any specialized language that flourishes in a limited, controlled environment — a workplace, a school, a class, or a club, perhaps. In my own controlled environment (a school), jargon includes *prog* (a shortened form of "Academic Progress Report," a parental mailing that usually reports lack of academic progress) and *F C and B* (the committee negotiating Faculty Compensation and Benefits). Jargon is truly helpful in its appropriate place; it's a kind of shorthand that saves time for both writer and reader. But in an admission essay, jargon is a problem. The essay readers are *not* in your limited, controlled environment; they're out in the big wide world, ruling over their own limited, controlled environment that you aspire to join. If you write in jargon, they probably won't understand you, and then you'll never have a chance to learn their special language.

You can probably identify jargon easily. If you're not sure about a particular expression, go with an alternative, just to be safe. Or check the phrase with someone from outside the jargon environment. (Someone from another school, perhaps, or a trusted relative who lives in another area.)

Choosing non-sexist language

Who's the chairman of the admissions committee? When you write to report your latest achievement, will you begin the letter with "Dear Sir" and explain how much you admire successful businessmen? Does your essay explain your theory that cavemen coexisted with dinosaurs? And speaking of dinosaurs, did you notice any extinct expressions in the first three sentences of this section? Here's a hint:

> The admissions committee is run by Mary Ann Gooblesdorp, who hates being called "sir."
>
> Business "men" are often female.
>
> Cavewomen didn't coexist with dinosaurs either.

See the problem? The first three sentences of this section all refer to males: "chairman," "sir," "businessmen," and "cavemen." But it is entirely possible that the group you're referring to includes females. If you refer only to males, you leave out half the human race — my half, by the way — and alienate the females (and a good number of enlightened men) who read your essay.

Somewhere in the world right now, I imagine a professor is saying, "Yes, but 'chairman,' 'sir,' 'businessmen,' and 'cavemen' are *universal* terms. They're traditional! Everyone knows that 'mankind' and other such expressions refer to both men and women." Sorry, Professor. That's what the words used to mean. They *were* traditional. But times have changed. Now these expressions simply convey the fact that the writer needs to join the twenty-first century.

Take the word "fisherpeople." This term is probably not your first choice for an essay about the inspiration you received from watching a bunch of seagoing types reel in a shark. But "fishers," "sailors," or (for those who like really big titles) "marine wildlife catchers" may substitute. Or, you can simply describe the group in detail (always a good choice), as in this passage:

> The heavy-set man grabbed a long, steel bar and leaned over the side of the boat. Two teenage girls looked on anxiously as their mother turned the reel. The great beast moved towards the boat. . . .

The point is simple: Don't choose masculine words for mixed groups. Also, don't assume that "masculine = universal," unless you're positive you're writing for an all-male audience and/or you're a time traveler from the nineteenth century.

Here's a quick guide to non-sexist substitutes for common expressions:

- **Titles:** If you have to write to the admissions office for any reason, don't address the recipient as "Sir" unless you know that you are writing to a man, in which case you may as well insert his name, as in "Mr. Aberalnick." If you don't know the name, try the title, as in "The Head of the Scholarship Committee."
- **Chair, head, leader, director, business executive:** Substitute these words for the masculine "chairman," "businessman," "headman," and so forth.
- **Human race, humanity, human beings:** These words take the place of "mankind" and "man" (referring to the whole species).
- **His or her, him or her, he or she:** A little cumbersome, but better than saying "his," "him," or "he" when you're referring to a member of a mixed group.

If you end up with a clunky sentence containing a string of "his or her" or "he or she" expressions, rewrite the whole thing, as in these examples:

Clunky sentence: Whenever I run for a student government office, I chat with each voter and ask him or her to explain his or her needs.

Sleek sentence: Whenever I run for a student government office, I chat with the voters and ask them to explain their needs.

Still more sleekness: Whenever I run for a student government office, I chat with each voter. "What do you need from the vice president of the Committee to Ban Plastic Lunchware?" I ask.

"Their" and "they" are plural words; these terms refer to a group, not to a single member of a group. If you're searching for gender-neutrality, don't choose a plural word when you need a singular. Chapter 14 goes into excruciating detail on singular and plural pronouns.

A few more rules for non-sexist language:

- **Avoid unequal treatment.** Don't call a female a "girl" unless you would call a male a "boy" in the same situation. Pair "husband" and "wife," not "man" and "wife."
- **Don't use unnecessary female suffixes.** A *suffix* is a word ending. Lots of suffixes that traditionally identify females — "esse," "ette," and the like — also indicate small size or lesser importance. Bad idea! Write "poet," not "poetess," "author," not "authoress," "suffragist," not "suffragette," and so on. The dictionary will help you choose the correct term if you're unsure.
- **When you write a description, be sure to treat both genders the same.** Descriptions often precede the word they're describing, though they can wander around the sentence at times. Wherever they are, be sure they're fair. Don't talk about "the poet" William Butler Yeats and the "female poet" Gwendolyn Brooks. Either they're both "poets" or he's "male poet" Yeats and she's "female poet" Brooks.

While you're avoiding sexism, steer clear of racial inequality as well. In the preceding example about poets, don't call Langston Hughes a great "African-American poet" if the same sentence refers to Yeats as a great "poet" without mentioning the fact that Yeats was Irish. Even-handedness is your goal.

Keeping it tasteful

Offensive language and tasteless comments have no place in your admission essay. I'm not supplying any examples here for exactly the same reasons you should bar this stuff from your essay: This is a G-rated book. But without thinking for more than three nano-seconds, you can probably come up with a fairly long list of avoid-at-all-cost words. (And if you can't, good for you! Profanity is boring and very uncreative.)

As you write your admission essay, imagine that your Great Aunt Gertrude is in the reader's chair. Follow these GAG rules, GAG being your affectionate nickname for Great Aunt Gertrude:

- Language that would shock or offend GAG should be snipped out of your admission essay.
- Dump references to parts of the body that are covered when you're in public places. If Great Aunt Gertrude can't see it when you visit, don't describe it in the essay.
- Don't discuss bodily functions that take place only in private.

Have I just ruled out everything you intended to say? Sorry. Perhaps you'd like to write about Great Aunt Gertrude's positive influence on your behavior instead?

Be especially careful with humor — a real minefield when it comes to taste. A good general rule: If you can tell the joke to GAG and to your little brother or sister, it's probably okay. If you can't, don't place it in your essay. Also, don't place any jokes in your essay unless the joke makes a point worth conveying to the admissions committee. Use the *For Dummies* books as a guide. They're funny, but all the humor relates to the material at hand. By the way, did you hear the one about the penguin and the mermaid?

Creating Stylish Sentences

See Spot run. Dick and Jane run after Spot. Spot pulls out a cell phone. Spot calls the Society for the Prevention of Cruelty to Fictional Animals. The society responds. Dick and Jane are arrested. See Dick booked. See Jane fingerprinted. See Spot celebrate. Spot is a happy dog.

Why I want to attend ~~Sadmouth~~ Jubilant Academy

Okay, you're in "no matter what, don't do this" territory here. As you check the rough draft, take extreme care to use the correct name of the institution you're actually sending the essay to. Because computer word processing programs have made it easy to cut and paste material, a fair number of applicants (who never, by the way, turn into accepted and enrolled students) forget to change the name of the college when they recycle a short answer or an essay paragraph. You may certainly reuse material, and if you're applying to five or six different places you'll probably have to do so, unless you're willing to give up sleeping and eating for a month or so. But the details, the names, the reasons why you want to attend — these should be tailored to each college. So when you write that you truly want to attend Sadmouth Academy, make sure the envelope is going to Sadmouth Academy and nowhere else.

Read the preceding sentences aloud. Not counting the dumb subject matter, don't the sentences sound awkward? Choppy, like little slaps of sound? The sentences don't flow smoothly, leading the reader from one to another. Plus, they resemble a second-grader's first efforts at telling a story — not a bad effect if you *are* a second grader relating your very first story. But if you're writing an admission essay, you're in trouble.

In this section I show you how to avoid two pitfalls of sentence construction — monotony and awkwardness. When you're done, you'll be able to write, "See the successful essay get results!"

Monotony

A couple of paragraphs ago I wrote about Spot and his attempt to foil Dick and Jane's chase. The story itself is not uninteresting (especially the part I left out, when Jane went wild in the police station and threw the fingerprint ink at Dick, who had masterminded the Spot chase). But the sentences leave a lot to be desired. Specifically, the sentence length and patterns can be improved.

Length

Sentences may be two words long (*Barney shaves.*) or run for pages and pages. (For an example of one of these verbal marathons, thumb through any Victorian novel.) I'm betting that you have few sentences of extreme length (either very long or very short) in your rough draft. Good! The ends of the sentence-length spectrum are tough to handle. However, if all your sentences are more or less the same length, you risk boring the reader by creating a monotonous sound. The solution is simple. Combine a couple of shorter sentences into one, longer sentence, taking care not to break any of the grammar rules I describe in Chapter 14. Or, chop a longer sentence into pieces (again, following grammar rules) so that you have a few short sentences tucked here and there in your essay. The key concept here is *variety.* Some examples:

Monotonous sentence length: I was inspired by Spot's campaign against leash laws. His courage to resist restrictive laws captured my imagination. Spot was willing to stand up against the Establishment. Could I live with myself if I did nothing?

Why it's monotonous: All the sentences have nine words, no more and no less.

Possible change: Inspired by Spots campaign against leash laws, I pondered his courage to resist restrictive laws. Spot was willing to stand up against the Establishment, an act that required great personal courage. My conscience spoke. I had to act.

Why it's better: Long and short sentences are mixed: 15, 16, 3, 4 words.

Monotonous sentence length: The raft drifted downstream swiftly. I hung onto the sides. Suddenly, I saw rocks ahead. The raft tipped sideways onto one boulder. I lost my left oar. The boat sped up immediately. It was clearly out of control. Rocks rushed by my frightened eyes. I struggled to hold on. Finally we reached calm waters.

Why it's monotonous: The shortest sentence is five words long, and the longest has seven words. Snooze-inducing sameness!

Possible change: The raft drifted downstream swiftly as I hung onto the sides. Suddenly, I saw rocks ahead. When the raft tipped sideways onto one boulder, I lost my left oar and the boat sped up immediately. I had no control! Rocks rushed by my frightened eyes, but I struggled to hold on. Finally we reached calm waters.

Why it's better: The sentence lengths range from 4 to 19 words. Variety is the spice of life!

Pattern

While you play around with sentence length (see the previous section), you should experiment with sentence pattern as well. We grammarians determine the pattern of a sentence by examining where the major elements of the sentence are — the subjects and verbs, the clauses and phrases. Before you have a nervous breakdown, please note that you don't have to place a grammar label on *anything* in the essay in order to fiddle with sentence patterns. Just use your ear! Read the essay, aloud or silently, and listen to the sentences. Does a certain set of sounds repeat? Do you hear the same type of word, in the same order, over and over again? If so, stir things up a little by moving a couple of things around. Some examples:

Boring pattern: I became interested in penguin habitats about a year ago. I worked in the local zoo, and I volunteered for the penguin house because I like cold weather. I read many books on penguin behavior and biology. I also discussed the birds' habitats with the chief keeper. I learned quite a bit about these animals, and I want to major in penguin biology in college.

Why it's boring: Do I really have to explain? All the sentences are "I + verb," or, in non-grammatical terms, "I + what the 'I' in the sentence is doing" (the action or state of being, in other words).

Possible change: Working in a local zoo about a year ago, I became interested in penguins. Because I like cold weather, I volunteered for the penguin house. Books on penguin behavior and biology and conversations with the chief keeper educated me about these birds, and I'd like to learn more about this subject in college.

Why it's better: The "I" shows up only three times, compared with eight in the original passage. Also, one sentence begins with a verb form ("working") and another begins with "because," a word that joins two ideas. Much more creative!

Chances are a few sentence patterns are your favorites, and unless you force yourself to become conscious of them, you'll work them to death. To find your favorites, reread a couple of your old school assignments or other written work. Check for phrases or patterns that pop up frequently. Those are your "default value" writing habits — what you'll place on the page automatically. You don't have to eliminate all your writing patterns. In fact, your default value habits may be terrific! The point is that you shouldn't overuse any pattern in your work. After you identify a pattern, reread your essay and be sure that you've included sufficient variety.

To add variety to your writing, try some of the following tricks. (Just don't overuse any of these tricks, or you'll simply create a new monotony.)

- **Place a participle at the beginning of a sentence.** A *participle* is a verb form that at times may describe someone or something in the sentence. If you begin a sentence with a participle, you'll break the subject-verb pattern that tends to dominate most people's writing. Just be sure that the participle at the beginning of the sentence refers to the subject of the sentence. Here are some "before-and-after" sentences. The "after" sentence contains a participle:

  Before: I realized that the key to the success of the experiment was the amount of salt on the cracker. I measured the salt on 1,038 crackers and came up with an average salt/cracker ratio.

  After: Realizing that the key to the success of the experiment was the amount of salt on the cracker, I measured the salt on 1,038 crackers and came up with an average salt/cracker ratio. ("Realizing" = participle, refers to "I")

  Before: My guidance counselor sent me to work at the zoo, but I stayed for three years because I liked the atmosphere.

  After: Having been sent by my guidance counselor to work at the zoo, I stayed for three years because I liked the atmosphere. ("Having been sent" = participle, refers to "I")

- **Place the subject of the sentence at the end.** Don't do this too often or you'll drive the reader crazy, but an occasional reverse-order sentence is very effective. An example in normal and reverse order:

  Normal: Betsy soared up the skateboard incline, over the rim of cement, and across the plank.

  Reverse: Up the skateboard incline, over the rim of cement, and across the plank soared Betsy.

- **Place words indicating reasons, places, or times at the beginning of a sentence.** In grammar-speak, I'm talking about phrases and dependent clauses, though you don't need to worry about those terms. Just run your eyeball over these sentences, written in normal and then reverse order.

Normal: I want to go to Hahvah University because I care about the intellectual environment of the classroom.

Reverse: Because I care about the intellectual environment of the classroom, I want to go to Hahvah University.

Normal: I went to law school after finishing medical school, and now I want to get a business degree.

Reverse: After finishing medical and law schools, I now want a business degree.

Awkwardness

An awkward sentence is easier to hear than to define. To find awkward sentences, read your rough draft aloud. (Lock yourself in the bathroom and play the radio really loud so that your family and friends won't think you're a complete dork.) The sentences you trip over are probably poorly worded, because your tongue catches awkwardness faster than your brain. After you've identified an awkward sentence, punch it around a little. If it is very long, consider breaking it into smaller segments. If the order of words sounds strange (and you didn't intend to achieve that effect), chances are you need to move a few things. Again, let your ear guide you. Here are a couple of "before-and-after" sentences to illustrate awkwardness and its remedy:

Awkward: It was at this point that I decided, based on the information that had been given to me by my guidance counselor, that I would pursue a career in penguin management.

Smoother: Based on my guidance counselor's information, I then decided to pursue a career in penguin management.

Awkward: After the votes had been counted by the secretary of the Penguin Society, I took the oath of office, which I memorized while stocking fish for the birds' daily feeding, though I did not then have access to any actual penguins and thus did not need the 50 pounds of fish in my school locker.

Smoother: After the secretary of the Penguin Society had counted the votes, I took the oath of office. I had memorized the words while stocking fish for the birds' daily feeding, though I did not then have access to any actual penguins. Thus I did not need the 50 pounds of fish in my school locker.

Saying It Once and Only Once

At this point in time I would now like to discuss an important, crucial point about how you express yourself when you are writing or speaking aloud or on paper, particularly in the college admission essay, which you write when you are applying for admission to college. No one, not one single person in the world, likes or enjoys wasting hours and minutes of precious time that is so valuable these days in our busy, event-filled lives.

Are you still awake? I just inflicted 77 words on you to say:

> Don't repeat yourself, especially in a college admission essay.

Which version do you prefer? I'm betting that the short one drew your love, and the long one your yawn. Just think how wonderful life would be if everyone said it once *and only once.* Political speeches would be five minutes long. Parents would not spend an hour explaining why you can't have the car keys for a trip to the mall. School assemblies on "The Many Ways the World Is Round" would be over in time for recess. And your little brother would stop asking, "Are we there yet?"

I could go on, but you get the point. Say it once, and then stop. Also, don't use 15 words to do a 10-word job. Some guidelines for spotting repetition:

- **Beware of double descriptions.** I call this the "tense and nervous" syndrome. "Tense" and "nervous" are similar in meaning — so similar that you probably don't need to say both when you're describing one feeling. Can you find the doubles (or sometimes triples) in these sentences?

  Robert Matses built many roads, highways, and parkways. ("Highways" and "parkways" are roads. Just say roads, or get more specific, as in "Oyster Brook Parkway," "Blue Creek Highway," and so forth.)

  We were prepared and ready for the ninth race. ("Prepared" and "ready" mean the same thing. Use one or the other.)

- **Watch out for unnecessary descriptions.** The name I've chosen for this problem is "island surrounded by water." Unless you're talking about a traffic island surrounded by cement, the water part is pretty much a no-brainer. Check out these unnecessary descriptions:

  On my tenth birthday when I reached ten years of age, I won a prize for bug collecting and identification. (On your tenth birthday, you can't reach the age of 22. Dump "when I reached ten years of age.")

  In my school the English department, which teaches literature, grammar, and writing, is wonderful. (What else would an English department teach? Toe-nail clipping? Drop everything between the commas or make another more specific statement about the curriculum.)

- **Dump unneeded declarations of opinion.** My term for this problem is the "In my opinion I think" issue. Okay, if you're citing a bunch of ideas you got from someone else and you need to draw a distinction between the opinion of others and your own thoughts, "I believe" or a similar expression is okay. But most of the time the reader knows that the statement represents your opinion. Why else would you make it? Read these examples:

  In my view, Hamlet is a tragic hero. (Just state that Hamlet is a tragic hero and then go on to make your other points.)

  Attending the School of Soft Knocks will, in my opinion, help me to face life's challenges. (Delete "in my opinion." The whole statement clearly represents your view.)

- **Be stingy with words.** Don't say, "He is a man who smirks." Just state, "He smirks." Avoid "there is" or "there are" sentences, unless you can't say what you want any other way. Check out these sentences:

  Before: There is a swan floating on the river.

  After: A swan is floating on the river.

  Before: Five students from my college are presently applying to your graduate program.

  After: Five students from my college are applying to your graduate program. ("are applying" indicates that the action is in the present)

  Before: It was here, at Sadmouth Academy, that I heard my first blues recording.

  After: I heard my first blues recording at Sadmouth Academy.

  Before: I then proceeded to learn jazz guitar.

  After: I then learned jazz guitar.

  Check out Chapter 9 for more tips on strong, specific language.

- **Don't add a string of qualifiers.** "Sort of," "kind of," "a little bit," "rather" . . . these words may be useful, but fairly often they simply take up space. Also, they make your writing sound shaky and tentative, as if you didn't have confidence in your own words or in yourself — not exactly the impression you want to give the college of your choice. Here are some examples of unnecessary qualifiers, with instructions on how to strengthen the sentence:

  I became a little bit interested in the arts. (Drop "a little bit." Either you're interested or not. And "interested" is neutral. You're not saying that you ate and slept in the studio for six months.)

My education more or less began at that moment. (Dump "more or less" and explain in what sense your education began at that moment.)

I think you might be rather intrigued by my solution to the problem. (I would delete this entire sentence and simply present the solution. You don't have to tell the university how to react if you've explained the situation well, and if you haven't, attempting to control their reaction won't work. Also, "might" and "rather" soften the meaning of your words, but if you stand behind your statement, you shouldn't need to decrease its impact.)

Chapter 16
Leaving a Good Impression

In This Chapter

- Clarifying your message
- Answering the question they asked
- Ensuring that the essay represents your true self
- Avoiding lists
- Looking over your essay one last time

Time for one last pre-flight check before lift-off . . . which in the case of your admission essay is the typing, stapling, and mailing stage. Before you put the final seal of approval on your rough draft, you need to step back a couple of steps and read it as an outsider would. Who is the person represented in this essay? What impression does the essay give of the writer's character and ability? After reading the essay, will the admissions committee be able to identify the writer's values and interests and understand more about the writer's life?

If the answers to these questions please you, you've increased the chances that your essay will do its job — to present your true self to the college or university. But achieving the distance necessary to read your work with a critical eye is a challenge. In this chapter I show you what to look for — and what to look out for — as you take the final steps necessary to turn your rough draft into a winning piece of writing.

Getting Your Point Across

What's the point of your essay? I know, I know. The point is to get the admissions committee to scream, "Yes, yes, yes we do want you, yes!" as they throw scholarship bucks in your direction. But that's the long-range goal. The immediate issue is a little different. When you first set out to write the essay, you chose a moment in your life, significant ideas, or people to describe. Now, as you polish the draft, you need to recall *why* you chose that particular topic. Then you must make sure that the reason is clear to the reader.

Getting your point across firmly and accurately is crucial. Imagine the admissions counselor closing the folder on your essay. Do you want that reader to muse, "That's nice, but why are you telling me this?" I don't think so! You have to hammer the idea home, but gently. Right about now you're probably murmuring, "'Gently' and 'hammer' don't go together." But imagine a private-eye movie, one of those old black-and-white classics, where the detective is hit from behind. Before he realizes what happened, he's on the floor and his beautiful but treacherous client is mopping his brow. That's the effect you're after: a sideswipe.

Just to show you what to avoid, here are some overly obvious point "hammers":

> I told you the story of cousin Abner and the squirrel so that you will understand my deep commitment to protecting nature in all its glory, including the acorns.
>
> I have shown that I am committed to protecting nature in all its glory, including the lowly acorns.
>
> The story of Abner and the squirrel makes it clear that I love nature and should major in environmental science.
>
> In the essay I have proved my commitment to the protection of nature.

Nothing like overkill! In each of these clunkers, the writer has talked down to the reader, treating him or her as a child who must be taught what to look for. Not a good attitude! Instead of baldly stating your point, work the main idea into the essay more subtly, in a couple of interpretive sentences. Check out these examples:

> When my cousin Abner killed the squirrel by destroying every acorn in the county, I was sad, but my grief turned to resolve. I now have a deep commitment to protecting nature in all its glory, including the acorns that supply food for our furry friends, the squirrels. (placed at the end of a story about an acorn bonfire)
>
> When my cousin Abner destroyed the squirrel's acorn supply, I knew Furrytail was doomed. As I grieved, my father confronted me. "Don't be sad," he said. "Take action. Make a commitment to protect nature in all its glory." At that moment I resolved to major in environmental science. (placed at the end of a story about an acorn bonfire)
>
> I have been committed to the protection of nature ever since I saw my cousin Abner kill a squirrel, not with a rifle but by destroying the acorn supply with a bonfire. . . . By majoring in environmental science, I'll be able to save all of Furrytails's descendents from starvation. (first sentence placed at the beginning of the essay, second sentence at the end)

For an example from a real student applicant, check out Figure 12-1 in Chapter 12. The essay presents the author's role in a fight between the author's brother and parents. The last sentence contains a statement from the author's father and makes the point of the essay clear:

> Punish you? The idea never once crossed our minds. You acted exactly as a true friend does — you stuck with your brother even though you thought there would be repercussions.

For another good example, take a look at Figure 16-1, an essay written by a student with a truly horrendous commute to school. The writer, who sat next to me on the subway each morning, was initially unsure about discussing the endless daily ride he endured for three years, even though the trip was a major part of his high school experience. But he eventually realized that his travel to school demonstrated his ability to manage time. A sentence in the paragraph emphasizes the message of his essay: "I have learned how to use my time to my advantage."

As you reread the rough draft, ask yourself what the telegram version of your essay would say. For those of you who aren't as hooked on old movies as I am, a telegram is a message sent electronically with little clicks of code. Telegrams were popular before the days of instant e-mails and messages. Because transmitting a telegram is relatively slow and cumbersome, the sender pays by the word. So the typical telegram contains only the essentials. After you've defined the "telegram" message of your essay, find the sentences that convey the idea to the reader. If you can't find those sentences, write some and insert them in the proper place.

Verifying That You've Answered the Question

Most application questions are so vague that almost any essay will do. After all, when the college asks you to "write about something that you feel is important," whatever you choose to say answers the question, at least in theory. But some application questions, such as the following, are quite specific:

- Write about a risk you've taken.
- Explain how you showed leadership in a situation and discuss what you learned from the experience.
- Describe a site within a quarter mile of your home from three different perspectives.
- Explain what you'd do with a year of unlimited funding.
- What are three personal attributes that will help you succeed in college?
- What historical event before your own lifetime has meaning to you, and why?

- Describe a situation in which you took a stand that was unpopular with the majority.
- Describe a summer service project you participated in.

When I first decided to attend my high school in tenth grade, I thought I had made the perfect choice. This school would offer me one of the best academic experiences possible, and by taking advantage of the sports and other extracurricular experiences, I would become a well-rounded student. I was aware that entering as a new student, I would have to make new friends, get accustomed to different workloads, and get a general feel for the school. However, the one thing I didn't foresee were the problems that come with having a two-hour commute to and from school.

When I first considered my commute to school, I thought that two hours merely seemed a long period of time and that it wouldn't be of any consequence. However, after serious contemplation, I realized that over the course of a week I would spend a total of 24 hours traveling to and from school. Needless to say, I began to feel a bit apprehensive about my daily commute. After my first two weeks of traveling to school, I was exhausted. I was going to sleep after midnight due to homework and would then have to wake up at 5:30 to get to school on time. I would get on the train, where I could neither find a place to sit and rest nor anywhere quiet enough to do my work. Because I had to transfer four times, I was constantly stopping whatever I was doing to change trains. I no longer thought that it would be feasible to play a sport or to be involved in any other after-school activities. Though at first my situation seemed hopeless, over time things began to improve.

As the months went by, I learned that my cursed commute was actually a blessing in disguise. Once I had learned to tune out the noise and chatter around me, I found myself with a four-hour block of time every day. I had always liked to read for enjoyment, and soon discovered that by using my train time for reading, it was quite possible for me to finished an entire book within a day or two. I was able to borrow four library books on Monday and return them all by Friday. I quickly realized that not only could I read for pleasure, but I could also finish my reading homework. I learned how to study on the train, which proved an invaluable skill. Instead of staying up until midnight studying, I could go to bed at ten and finished studying on the train the next morning, refreshed and rested. After I figured out how to write neatly on the train, I could do all my assignments on the train except those that had to be typed. When I learned how to sleep on the train either sitting down or standing up, my routine became complete. I was now able to function fully on the train, able to study, read, sleep, or complete homework.

Since I entered my high school, I have learned how to do more than just deal with my train ride. I have learned how to use my time to my advantage. By using my train ride effectively, I am able to take on more work and participate in more activities than I would have if I had lived a half hour away. Given the chance, I wouldn't change anything.

Figure 16-1: An essay example that gets the point across clearly.

These questions — and many others like them — do not accept one-size-fits-all answers. So before you check your rough draft, reread the question you're supposed to be answering. What information is the college after? What do they want to find out about you? Now go back to your essay. Have you actually provided that information? Have you answered the question they posed? If not, you have to revise.

Sometimes revising an essay to suit a particular question is a matter of changing or adding only one or two sentences. Imagine that you've written a general essay about taking your little brother to the beach. The question asked you to write about a risk. But all you've got is a couple of paragraphs about sibling bonds and the effect little Herbert's innocence has had on your worldview. Where's the risk? Well, you tell me! You chose that topic after reading the question, so you probably have a risk somewhere in your mind, on some level of consciousness. Perhaps you thought that adopting a similar attitude of innocence might make you unpopular with the "cool" group in your school. Or perhaps you were worried that you couldn't supervise a six-year-old on a crowded beach. Identify the issue and then add a few sentences clarifying the risk. Presto! Question answered.

If you're adapting one essay to several different questions (Chapter 1 tells you how), be especially careful in checking your rough draft. Be sure that the essay relates clearly to the question asked by each college.

Even when you're answering a very specific question, you still have to make the admissions committee understand *why* you wrote the essay, even if the word "why" never appears in the application question. (I know; you wrote the essay so you can get into college. But the admissions committee needs to know the personal significance of the *topic you selected* to answer their query.) Check out the preceding section, "Getting Your Point Across," for tips on explaining the significance of an issue or event in a general essay. In an essay answering a specific question, remember that even a very narrow request requires choice. For example, in order to "describe a site within a quarter mile of your home from three different perspectives," you must select a site. Well, why *did* you pick that particular place? How are you connected to it? Insert the answer in your essay, perhaps at the beginning or end. Then consider the three perspectives. *Why* did you choose those three and not another? Again, tuck the reason into the essay.

Sounding Strong and Mature

In Chapter 3 I review some of the worst errors of tone — the essay equivalent of a fingernail screeching across a chalkboard. For a complete discussion of these no-nos, turn to that chapter. Briefly, here are the guaranteed turn-offs for any admissions committee:

Presenting your true self

When a young man I know very well was applying to college years ago, he wrote an essay about an assignment he had done for AP history. He described his trip to the intimidating main branch of the New York Public Library (the one with the lions) and his search for and through difficult texts. His conclusion emphasized all he had learned about research methods. I read his rough draft, and one sentence — the first in the essay — stood out: "Having left everything to the last minute, I rushed to the library in a panic."

I was amazed, because this particular young man is conscientious to a fault and never misses a deadline. I had actually seen him leave for the library to do the assignment — at least a month before the work was due. "Why did you say that you left the work until the last minute?" I asked.

"I figured it gave the essay a more interesting beginning," he replied. Needless to say, about two seconds of additional thought showed him that he had erred. Not only was he writing something false, he was writing something that would leave a poor impression on the admissions committee! He soon rewrote the first sentence and ended up with a better — and more accurate — piece of writing.

- **"As I cogitated over my past. . . ."** Don't use every vocabulary word you ever memorized, and be especially careful not to use a word with which you're not completely comfortable.
- **"The revered elder trees lifted bark-covered arms to the welcoming dawn."** Don't aim for a self-conscious "literary" effect instead of a natural voice. You'll sound stiff and, ironically, less educated than you actually are.
- **"It was raining cats and dogs when I visited your campus."** Stay away from clichés! They're boring and uncreative. (Besides, the image of cats and dogs falling from the sky will upset animal lovers.)

In this section I show you some less glaring tone problems, which are fortunately quite easy to eliminate from your rough draft.

Projecting confidence

"I think I may be right for your school." Can you imagine a statement that is more weak-kneed than this one? Probably not. If you're right for the school, say so. If you're not, don't apply. No matter what, don't sit on the fence. Make a statement and stand behind it! Here are some tentative statements written in answer to real application questions, along with an improved, confident version of each:

Question: Write about a book that affected you.

Tentative: I enjoyed Charles Dickens' *Great Expectations,* which may be one of the best novels ever written.

Confident: When Pip receives notice that he has "great expectations," I was hooked. Dickens' novel is one of the best ever written, and certainly the best I've read.

Why version two is better: The writer describes the feelings more concretely and specifically and eliminates qualifiers. (For a more in-depth discussion of qualifiers, see Chapter 15.)

Question: Describe something you've done that you consider creative.

Tentative: I thought I might turn my campus into something that looked like a tented caterpillar, a project that was more or less inspired by the artist Christo and seemed creative to me.

Confident: My creativity was stretched to the limit when I erected a giant tent over the campus, a project inspired by the artist Christo.

Why version two is better: You must make a definitive judgment to answer that question, and you must also evaluate your own actions. Version one gives the impression that you are not up to either of those tasks.

Question: Translate a visual image into words and explain your rationale.

Tentative: Picasso's painting *Guernica* makes me think about the horrors of war, though other viewers may have a different impression. Everyone sees art in a unique way, and no one can say that one way is more correct than another.

Confident: Picasso's painting *Guernica* presents the horrors of war.

Why version two is better: You're not answering a question about everyone's views of art, and inserting a statement about others' opinions takes

The government suppository of documents

A few years ago a student, in what was undoubtedly the most embarrassing moment of his 17-year-old life, asked me whether New York City had "a government suppository of documents." As the class roared, one of his friends took him aside to explain that a *depository* is where important items are stored and a *suppository* is a way to get medicine into the body without injecting or swallowing. (You figure it out!) The student, who had been memorizing lists of words for the SAT, was seen shredding his vocabulary book shortly after class. I don't recommend that you destroy your vocabulary book, but I do recommend that you place only those words you truly understand in your admission essay.

the focus off your own ideas. And that's where the focus of your essay should be!

Question: What characteristics of our school influenced your decision to apply?

Tentative: I think I might enjoy the all-night pre-game parties, though I'm not sure whether or not I'd actually attend, depending upon the amount of work I have to do.

Confident: All work and no play is a cliché, but it is based on a true assessment of human nature. When I visited Partydown University, I attended an all-night pre-game party. The students assured me that they had already completed their course work and were now ready to relax. Such a schedule appeals to me, though of course I must concentrate primarily on my studies.

Why version two is better: Okay, version two is *not* better in that you shouldn't explain your partying plans, regardless of how responsible you intend to be. (I was just having some fun with the example.) Apart from the subject matter, version two at least expresses your views with assurance!

Sounding confident is not the same as over-simplifying a complicated situation or emotion. Suppose that you're writing about an issue that matters to you (a real question). After examining all the facts, you see that several solutions are possible, but no solution is perfect. Or, perhaps you have mixed feelings about a person who has had an impact on your life (another real question). In your essay, acknowledge all the ins and outs of the topic you're pondering. Be honest about your conflicting impulses. Chances are the admissions committee will appreciate the depth of your analysis and the degree to which you've tried to grapple with its complexity.

Most of us have learned that to brag about our accomplishments is to risk eating lunch alone for the duration of the school year, if not longer. But explaining what's good about yourself and what you've accomplished is *not* bragging. In fact, you must do so in order to write a good admission essay. Check Chapter 2 for help with this issue.

Winning without whining

"The process of applying to college is so unfair." Such a statement may be true (and in the middle of college applications, it certainly *feels* true). Nevertheless, it comes across as a whine. You'll never win the prize — an acceptance letter — if you expend essay lines crying about how horrible you feel about writing an essay. The admissions counselors are well aware of the limitations of the college application process. They understand that they're not getting a complete picture of each and every person who knocks on their college door. But until someone invents a way for the counselors to get to know a few thousand applicants intimately, the process is the only thing they've got. Besides, if you want to talk about fairness, consider the burden of *reading* thousands of pieces of paper, each carrying the hopes and dreams of an applicant. Plus, the salaries are low.

In your essay you may certainly talk about the hardships in your life, and if those hardships have had a significant impact on you, you probably should make them the topic of your essay. Just don't whine when you do so. (Also, keep your own trials and tribulations in perspective. Check out the next section, "Keeping perspective," for tips on how to do so.)

Steering away from a whine is easy. Here are a few "before-and-afters":

Whine: I've got 12 pages of history to read, a term paper to research, and 15 math problems for homework. Plus I've got to write this essay.

Non-whine: Everyone told me about the challenges of senior year in high school, but I never understood the concept of time management until I sat down to read 12 pages of history, research a term paper, solve 15 math problems, and write this essay explaining who I am.

Why version two is better: The second sentence hints at a context — time management. The essay goes on to discuss *how* the writer packs all those tasks into one day. Thus the reader sees a point, not just a complaint.

Whine: I wanted to take AP English, but the teacher chooses only her favorites, and how was I supposed to know in ninth grade that the literary magazine was going to matter?

Non-whine: I considered AP English, but in the end I enrolled in senior elective courses highlighting Chaucer and Virginia Woolf, which have introduced me to rich and satisfying literary works.

Why version two is better: The second version is positive. The first sentence tells the college that you're going to hit the ceiling every time a course you want is filled before you have time to register.

Whine: The issue that matters most to me is the environment. My generation will have to pay the price for the stupidity of the older generation, which treated our air and water as garbage dumps.

Non-whine: The issue that matters most to me is the environment. My generation will have to face the consequences of decades of mismanagement of the earth's air and water resources.

Why version two is better: The people reading your essay are probably members of "the older generation," and they won't enjoy a blanket statement condemning them for stupidity. Version two doesn't assign blame. The essay focuses on a description of the problem and possible courses of action to remedy the situation.

Keeping perspective

I once read a student paper (written by a ninth grader, not a college applicant) that referred to "that tragic day when they ran out of lobster before I had a chance to order dinner." Schoolteachers' salaries don't run to daily (or even monthly) lobster fests. And even if our salaries were suddenly increased by a factor of ten (May the school board be listening!), I like to think that my colleagues and I would recognize that millions of people around the world go to bed hungry each night.

The point I'm making here is simple. As you check your rough draft, allow your global consciousness to dominate for a moment. If you're presenting injustice, hardships, or tragedies, try to examine them in a larger context. Be conscious that whatever has gone wrong for you has probably hit some other member of the human race even harder. Or, as my mother used to say with depressing frequency, "Don't make a mountain out of a molehill."

Keep your life in perspective. An easy task, right? I don't think so. You can only understand one reality completely — your own. And the things that have hurt or challenged you are real and important *to you,* regardless of whether or not some other people would love to have your troubles instead of their own. In your essay, you should explain what has been difficult in your life, and especially, how you dealt with your problems. Just don't present the topic as if it were a matter of life and death — unless of course it *is* a matter of life and death.

To help you achieve the right tone, here are a few "before-and-after" examples:

Faulty perspective: No one has it harder than a student with a learning disability.

Better perspective: It has been a challenge to attend a competitive school and deal with my learning disability.

Why version two is better: A challenge, yes. "No one has it harder," no. The first version ignores any other potential tragedies in the school, including students whose parents are ill, those who are dealing with financial difficulties, and so on. Also, the writer of version one completely ignores some of the other little bumps in life's highway — war, famine, crime, to name a few.

Faulty perspective: My entire world crashed the day my father lost his job.

Better perspective: When my father lost his job, my family had to make a number of difficult adjustments.

Why version two is better: Okay, no one wants a ticket to the unemployment line, but "my entire world crashed" is far too strong. First of all, "entire" is an extreme. The sun still rose, the family was still there, and the polar ice caps didn't melt and flood the family house, right? Second, your essay should concentrate on what you did in response to the challenge. Let the reader make the judgments. Your job is to supply the details.

Other sand traps in the application game

As you turn a rough draft into a final draft, don't stumble into these pits:

- **Don't announce what you're writing about.** "In this essay I will show that I am the best possible applicant for Blockhead University." Don't talk about what you're going to do; just do it.
- **Don't announce what you've written about.** "In this essay I have shown that I am a complete blockhead." Subtlety rules. Check out "Getting Your Point Across," earlier in this chapter, for tips on respecting your' reader's intelligence.
- **Use good grammar.** They want to know whether you can write, and they're judging your level of education. Bad grammar tells them that you've got some catching up to do.
- **Don't lie or exaggerate.** They'll find out and then you'll be sunk. Also, if you're honest, you can face the world with a clear conscience.
- **Don't bore the reader.** Be honest, yes, but present the truth about your life as vividly and dramatically as possible.
- **Stay away from slang, profanity, and disrespect.** You're not having a burger with your pals after school; you're talking to people who have power over you. Behave!
- **Don't boast, but do present your best qualities.** Stay away from statements like "You won't find a better student anywhere!" but do include comments about your accomplishments and admirable traits.
- **Don't rely on gimmicks.** You can't disguise a bad essay by writing it in gold ink on a picture of a pot of gold. You can ruin a good essay by writing it in gold ink on . . . well, you get the point.

Faulty perspective: If I don't get into your university, I'll kill myself.

Better perspective:

Why the line above is blank: You can't renovate the first sentence into any acceptable statement. Suicide is a serious subject, and you shouldn't make such a comment even as a joke. Also, after a string of student suicides, colleges are extremely nervous. They're worried enough about the well being of their current students. Why should they admit any additional problems? Bottom line: If you mean it, seek professional help *now.* If you don't mean it, don't write it.

Complimenting without flattery

You've seen the ivy on the wall and you're speechless with admiration. Fine. You'd like to convey that admiration to the admissions committee. Also fine. So you write:

> I can't believe that someone from Famousforever University is actually reading my essay. There's no greater honor than to be considered for admission to the hallowed ground of your college.

Not fine. In fact, terrible. Admissions committees have a great deal of pride in their schools, and like all members of the human race, they don't mind a well-deserved compliment. However, if they're good at their jobs (and you should assume that they are), the admissions counselors also have a finely honed flattery detector. The preceding statement will set alarms jangling in about ten seconds, if not sooner.

Remember, you're hoping for an acceptance letter, not the Golden Shovel Award. If you admire a particular aspect of an institution, you may say so, especially in answer to the "Why did you choose our school?" question. But don't heap meaningless praise in hopes of impressing the reader. Some examples:

> **Meaningless praise:** The long, star-studded history of your institution impresses me. So many incredible people went to Famousforever!
>
> **Legitimate compliment:** When I look at the roster of alumni, I see many accomplished writers such as Felonia Handwringer, Jackson Flounder, and Philip Poeticall. The writing program that nurtured their talent has several aspects that attract me, including small seminars, peer-to-peer criticism, and intensive grammar review.
>
> **Why version two is better:** Version two is much more specific. The fact that the essay writer knows about Handwringer, Flounder, and Poeticall indicates that he or she has some knowledge of the school. The details about the writing program show that the essayist values these characteristics and also indicates genuine interest in the school's curriculum.
>
> **Meaningless praise:** Words cannot express how totally honored I will feel if I am accepted to Famousforever University.
>
> **Legitimate compliment:**
>
> **Why the preceding line is blank:** You can't fix that statement, so you should just delete it. Stay away from speculating about whether or not you'll be admitted. Just comment on the aspects of the university that appeal to you and explain (with specifics) how your talents and goals mesh with the university's programs.

For more information on answering the "Why us?" question, turn to Chapter 21.

The Top Ten Reasons Why Lists Are a Bad Idea

In a highly unscientific survey, I've determined that about 10 percent of all essay writers come up with this (very bad) idea: "Instead of an essay, I'll write a list!" Uh oh. If such a possibility occurs to you, drop it immediately. Why? To explain, I'll borrow a technique from a late-night talk show, David Letterman's "Top Ten List."

10. They remind the reader of the undone "to-do" list hanging on the refrigerator.
9. They waste a lot of space on a crowded application blank.
8. Because they contain short, cryptic statements, lists tend to be much more understandable to the writer than to the reader.
7. They make the reader think of late-night television shows, which the counselor watched instead of going to sleep at a decent hour in order to arrive at work without an intense desire for a nap, even though it's only 9:30 a.m.
6. A list gives the admissions committee the impression that you watch entirely too much television, including the late night talk shows that you should reject in favor of going to sleep at a decent hour in order to arrive at school without an intense desire for a nap, even though it's only 9:30 a.m.
5. It's hard to create the ten decent punch lines for one joke that a good list requires.
4. You can't show off your talent for description in a list.
3. Hardly anyone reads an entire list! Most people skip to the bottom, where they think the good stuff is.
2. With a list, especially one in reverse "count-down" order, you come across as a weak clone of a television personality.
1. The university wants to read your essay in order to judge your ability to write. Very few college or graduate school assignments may be fulfilled with a list.

Bottom line: Write an essay in paragraph form, not a list.

Checking the Essay One Last Time

I promise. This is it! After this section, no more checks. But before you turn it in, answer the relevant questions from this list:

- Does the essay represent aspects of your experience that you want the college to understand?
- Does the essay show the admissions committee who you truly are?
- Have you answered the question they asked?
- Is the point of the essay clear?
- Is everything in the essay true?
- Does the essay contain specific details?
- Does the essay represent your views accurately?
- Have you communicated the complexity of your thoughts?
- Have you written the essay in formal English with proper spelling and grammar?
- Does the essay sound like you — your meeting-company-on-best-behavior self?
- Have you avoided false modesty, complaints, unwarranted criticisms, blanket statements, and flattery?

Yes? Congratulations. See the next chapter for the details of presentation (how to fit your masterpiece into that little blank space, when to mail it, and so on). No? Not to worry. Tinker with the essay a bit more until you've corrected the errors.

Chapter 17

Final Answers: The Last Word on Format

In This Chapter

- Following directions
- Making sure your essay hits the target word count
- Managing paper forms
- Dealing with online applications
- Getting the application there on time

When a student in my senior English class applied to college some time ago, he faced a major problem. Tim had the grades, the scores, the extracurriculars, and the essays needed to make a good case for admission to the schools he favored. What he didn't have was a typewriter. His house had joined the computer age before Tim turned five, and the family's last typewriter hit the scrap heap when Tim started middle school. Furthermore, his handwriting ability, never great, had deteriorated over the years because he was much more comfortable with a keyboard than with a pen. Yet suddenly, paper forms arrived in the mail! After a major search, Tim and I finally located a nearly antique typewriter at my school, and this college applicant was introduced to non-computerized "word processing."

If he were applying now — as you are — he'd have more options, including separate sheets of paper (for computer word-processed essays) and online forms. But, depending upon the institution, he might still have to scare up a typewriter or (gasp) a fountain pen. In this chapter I explain how to deal with all the situations you may face in getting the essay from your brain to the admissions committee's hands. I tell you what to do when your word count is too high or too low and give you the lowdown on margins, fonts, and online submissions.

Reading the Directions

The average college application resembles a small book, and many graduate and professional school applications have nearly as many pages as the Income Tax code and just as much fine print. You may be tempted, in the pressure of application season, to skip the directions and rely on your common sense when it comes time to fill out the form. Resist the temptation! You need to follow *their* rules, and you won't be able to do so unless you know exactly what those rules are. True, most of the time your common sense will lead you to the correct format, and most of the time the institution receiving your application won't mind a minor lapse here and there. But why take a chance?

Read everything — and I do mean everything — before you fill out the application and while you still have time for emergencies, such as one more essay. I'm not kidding. In preparation for this book, I read hundreds of college and graduate school applications. About one in ten had an obscure statement (one tucked into the corner of the inner cover of the viewbook!) saying something like "All applicants for admission who wish to be considered for financial aid must submit an essay on. . . ." Imagine discovering that little fact two hours before the form is due or, worse yet, two weeks after you sent in what you thought was a complete application.

Some of the application fine print tells you how to answer the factual queries:

> *Has anyone in your family attended Woebegone University?* To answer this question, list names, relationships, dates of graduation, and likelihood that said relatives will donate large sums of money to the Annual Fund for Admissions Office salaries.

Just kidding about the last part. Also in the instructions are directions for the submission of your essays. Depending on the college, you may be told any of the following:

- **Word or page count:** The form may provide a range (250–500 words) or an upper limit (no more than two pages). Less frequently you may see a minimum (at least 250 words or one page).
- **Format:** You may be told to write the essay by hand (my sympathies, if you are). You may be given a couple of options — "neat handwriting or typing." The college may specify the size of the paper (usually no larger than the application itself, presumably for easier filing), margins, font size and type, and ink color. The instructions generally tell you whether you may attach an essay printed on separate sheets (handy for computer users) or whether you must deal with "the space provided."
- **Numbering and identification:** Most colleges tell you to place your full name and social security number at the top of each essay or short-answer page. Some ask you to identify the number and section of the question you're answering.

- **Mailing:** Some colleges provide an envelope; others send you to your own stationery stash.

Whatever they want, give it to them. Yours is not to reason why; yours is to fill in the blanks and hope they accept you. So be thorough and careful with the arbitrary, mechanical elements of your application. If you are, you give the admissions committee the impression that you're thorough and careful. Not a bad idea!

Cutting to Fit and Lengthening to Suit: Hitting the Word Count Target

I once took a job writing captions for a set of sticker books. Each caption was supposed to contain between 99 and 109 words. I did this work before the age of word processing, so I spent a great deal of time counting on my fingers, crossing out, inserting, and retyping. (This process was exactly as boring as it sounds, but I had to pay the rent.)

You're luckier than I am, even if the application calls for a word or page limit. Your reader is not going to bother to count your words and hold you to a ten-word range. However, you don't have a completely free hand either. The admissions counselors are skilled at estimating the length of your essay. If they specify "an essay of no fewer than 250 words," they expect at least one typewritten, double-spaced page with normal fonts and margins. And if they ask for no more than two typewritten pages, they will be annoyed to receive ten. They *know* how to count. They *do* have fingers.

If you wrote the essay on a word processor, you can find out the number of words quickly. In Microsoft Word, for example, click on "Tools," "Language," and "word count" for a total. If you used a typewriter, assume that one page, single-spaced, with normal fonts and margins, contains about 500 words (if double-spaced, 250 words).

If no word or page count is specified, aim for 250–500 words — long enough to show depth and short enough to hold their interest.

A normal font, such as Times New Roman or Arial, looks like the print in a book or magazine. Don't shrink or expand the type size abnormally; the best choice is probably 12 point. A normal margin is about an inch. If you're writing the essay on a computer, the default style of fonts and margins for your word processor is a good bet.

If the word count of your essay is off by just a few words, you're probably okay. But if the essay is significantly longer or shorter than it should be, you'll have to adjust. Here's how to cut to fit and lengthen to suit.

Chopping excess words

Chapter 16 provides several guidelines for concise writing. If you're over budget on words, check out that chapter and see what you can trim. After you've dumped repetitive or wordy material, try these tactics:

- **Check the introduction and the conclusion of the essay especially carefully.** A lot of repetition and unnecessary detail show up in these two spots, and many people ho and hum a bit before they get to the point. Can you pull the reader into your subject more quickly or sum up the point in fewer words?
- **Look for boring details that the reader can do without.** For example, if you're writing about the fund-raising campaign that you organized to assist retired professional athletes (the people least likely to need such a campaign, by the way), you don't need to explain exactly how you created mailing list labels. Dump that detail, but keep the part describing the celebrity auction.
- **If your essay is a general survey or a "mosaic" of your experiences (Chapter 7 describes these structures in detail), trim the essay by eliminating one element.** For example, if you've surveyed the development of your interest in grasshoppers over the course of three summers, you may want to limit yourself to two summers, with a half-sentence reference to the third summer in the introduction or conclusion.
- **Hunt for any material in the essay that duplicates information available elsewhere in your application.** Suppose you wrote an essay about your work on the school newspaper. Besides describing some of your big stories and the challenge of dealing with the editorial board, you included a paragraph listing all the positions you held on the paper throughout your high school career, including coffee-maker and senior advertising editor. If those positions are included in the "list your extracurricular activities" section of the application form, you may delete that paragraph from the essay. Remember, the essay should *add* to the committee's understanding of your identity, not reiterate a bunch of facts.
- **If you have any dialogue that may be paraphrased or summarized, you may save some space.** But don't cut all the interesting stuff!
- **Consider refocusing if your essay is seriously overlong.** Remember, a narrow and deep focus is better than wide and shallow. You don't have to explain every single affect your grandmother's existence had on your life. One or two main ideas should get your point across.

If the university accepts word-processed printouts, you may be tempted to write in a teeny-tiny font or with miniscule line spacing and margins in order to keep to the page budget. Bad idea. Some of your readers may be middle-aged, and they won't take kindly to reminders that their reading glasses have to be strengthened again. And even if all your readers are young enough to go around bare-eyed, everyone recognizes a rip off. They *will* notice your tricks, and they *will* resent them. Follow the rules!

Adding to the essay

I started this section on length with the problem of excess words because that's the one that afflicts most essayists. But from time to time applicants end up with an essay that's below the recommended word or page count. One major rule applies to this situation:

Don't pad. Add.

When I say, "Don't pad," here's what I mean:

- Don't throw extra words into your sentences just to make the essay longer, as in this example:

  Original: I grew up in Brooklyn.

  Padded: Where did I grow up, you may wonder? It was in Brooklyn that I first saw the light of day and lived during my formative years.

- Don't provide meaningless details, such as those I italicized in this example:

  After I was rescued from the sinking ocean liner, *I had a lovely lunch consisting of a bacon, lettuce, and tomato sandwich.* Then the president gave me a medal for heroism.

- Don't repeat material listed elsewhere in the application. A review of all your courses or extracurriculars will *not* enhance an essay on the meaning of your high school experience.

How do you lengthen a too-short piece? Try these tactics:

- **Add a level of thoughtfulness.** Suppose that you're writing an essay about an exchange program you participated in. Besides being exposed to new cultural experiences and a foreign language, what else happened to you? Did your world view alter? Did you appreciate your home country more upon your return? Did your career plan or life goal change? Chances are you addressed at least one of these issues in your essay, but perhaps another is also relevant.
- **Add detail.** If you wrote about your summer as a storyteller for the local public library, you may want to include a longer description of a typical session, including interactions with parents, discussions with the librarian about appropriate books, the children's reactions, and so forth.

- **Change a summary to a description.** If your essay includes a general statement, consider changing it to specifics, as in these examples:

  Summary: The children were often mischievous but always delightful.

  Specifics: At one session a little girl nestled into my lap and stroked my hair. Only later did I find out that she had just eaten a peanut butter sandwich, most of which she left entwined in my braid. But her joy at hearing *Curious George* made the stickiness worthwhile.

- **Expand the introduction or conclusion.** Either of these two spots may contain the main idea of your essay. Are you certain you've given the issue the appropriate explanation? Read these sections to an impartial audience and add as needed. (***But remember:*** Don't repeat and don't pad.)

- **Touch upon another example.** If your essay is a survey (see Chapter 7 for a full definition), you may want to include an additional example. Suppose that you've written about the affect your dad's career has had on your character. You've mentioned the family's stint in Antarctica, but you neglected to describe that awful winter at the North Pole. Bingo! You've got plenty of new material, all relevant to the topic of the essay.

Dealing with Paper Forms

It's the right length, the perfect topic, and the best writing you can possibly produce. So how do you get your college admission essay on the form? Very carefully! Read on.

On separate sheets of paper

Bowing to the reality of a computerized world, a lot of colleges simply ask that you enclose the essay, *on separate sheets of paper,* with the rest of the application. Smile gratefully at those colleges because they've just made your life a lot easier. If the essay is separate from the application blank, you can do it over and over again (either by hand or by machine) until you've got it right. You don't have to worry about messing up their form.

By far the easiest way to create a great-looking, polished-to-perfection essay is with a computer word-processing program. If you don't have a computer, check your local library or school's computer department. Also, many photocopy shops rent computer time.

Some guidelines for separate-sheet submissions:

- If you've composed the essay on a computer, simply print it out.

- If the essay is typed, be sure that the ink is dark enough to be read easily. (Replace worn out typewriter ribbons before you start. Black ink only.)
- If the essay is handwritten, be extremely careful to write legibly. (Don't forget, your reader has ploughed through a huge pile of essays and will *not* enjoy that special extra hour spent deciphering your handwriting.) Blue or black ink only. Also, ballpoint is better than marker or fountain pen ink. If the admissions counselor spills coffee on the essay, ballpoint ink is less likely to run.
- Some applications specify double or single spacing. If nothing is specified, single space is fine for typewritten work. For handwritten essays, skip lines between each line of text. That format is much easier to read!
- Include your full name and social security number at the top of every page of the essay. Don't create any other sort of heading. In general, you don't need a title for your college essay, though you may label it "Personal Statement" if you wish.

If you're like most people, your name has several variations — with or without middle name or initial, with or without add-ons such as "Jr." or "Esq." When you're applying to college, pick one format and stick with it throughout. You don't want the college to place your magnum opus in someone else's file by mistake. The social security number helps, but human nature draws us to names rather than to numbers. Don't take a chance that the admissions committee will realize that James Fuddled is the same person as James M. Fuddled, Jr.

- If you were given a choice between several questions, indicate the number and letter (if applicable) of the choice you're responding to. If you like, at the top of the page retype the question in boldface or italics.
- The paper should be normal 8½-x-11-inch letter size, white in color and of normal weight. Don't use erasable bond. Yes, you can erase more easily, but the ink smudges with the slightest touch of a finger.
- Don't enclose the essay in a folder, binder, or plastic cover.
- Place the essay in the application envelope they've given you.
- If the college hasn't supplied an envelope, a 9-x-12-inch envelope is a good choice because you won't have to fold the application or the essay.

On their form

Universities that require you to answer directly on the form are a real pain. I often wonder what they hope to accomplish. True, they'll see your handwriting or typing, not your word-processing, but what's the point? If they think such a requirement weeds out the cheats who contract out for essay writing, they're wrong. Anyone willing to take a dishonest shortcut is not likely to be deterred by the need to recopy someone else's work. Or perhaps they employ a handwriting analyst? It's a mystery to me. Plus, this requirement sometimes makes great students decide that applying to such a school is more trouble than it's worth. Surely the college doesn't want to discourage applicants.

Anyway, if you're stuck with a form, these tips will help.

Typing

First, find a typewriter. If this book goes into extra editions — I should be so lucky — and the colleges are still requiring typed-on-the-form essays, I'll probably be able to suggest that you check your local museum for a working machine. Typewriters appear to be endangered species! After you've located a machine, follow these guidelines:

- On a separate sheet of paper, take the typewriter out for a test run. Check the darkness of the print, and if it's light, change the ribbon. If the keys need cleaning, get out the brush and the cleaning fluid. (A straight pin or a sewing needle will help you clean out the "e" and "o" keys.)
- Type *very* slowly to decrease the number of mistakes.
- When you do hit the wrong key, backspace and hit it again with correction tape. Erasing with a rubber typewriter eraser makes a mess — smudges, even paper tears — and those little bottles of white fluid can cake and smear. Correction tape covers the offending letter neatly and effectively.
- You don't need a title for the essay, but if you've been given a selection of topics, indicate the number and letter (if applicable) of your choice. Don't waste space rewriting the question.
- Set side margins of ½ to 1 inch. Feel free to fill the entire space, top to bottom, as long as you don't impinge on the question lines above and below the essay slot.
- Opinion is divided on the issue of glued-on essays. Some people believe that it is perfectly fine to print out the essay on a computer and then paste or tape it onto the form. (If you do reach for the glue bottle or tape dispenser, print in normal font and follow the margin guidelines in the preceding paragraph.) Others think that an attached essay looks as lumpy as wallpaper in a damp climate. My advice? Ask your college counselor about the preferences of a particular college, or call the admissions office and chat with a friendly secretary. (They're all friendly in the admissions office because their job is to attract applicants to the college. Nasty staffers end up in the bursar's office, where they inquire icily why your tuition check is late.)
- Unless otherwise directed, single-space your essay.

Handwriting

Oh dear! You've got to write it by hand? Are you sure you want to attend the Institute of Tortured Penmanship? You do? Yes, some schools (including some medical schools) require you to ink in your essay. If you're stuck with this situation, these tips may help:

- Practice on scrap paper first until your best, most legible penmanship surfaces. Don't write in extremely tiny or overly large script.
- Blue or black ink only. Ballpoint is best because it doesn't smudge or run, even when doused by coffee spills.
- The key is readability. Remember that you're writing for a tired reader. If your script is messy, consider printing.
- If the form has lines, use them. If not, place a ruler or a piece of scrap paper on the form and use it to keep your lines horizontal. You don't want lines that resemble a graph of the stock market's recent performance.
- Ask for an extra copy of the application (or photocopy it before you start, if the college allows a photocopied submission). Then if you make a mistake, you've got another shot.
- Correction fluid doesn't really hide your errors, but it does show that you care enough to try. Rather than leave crossed-out words or eraser stains, paint over the error — *neatly* — and write in the correct version. Don't overdo the correction fluid. Lay down a thin layer, let it dry, and repeat only as much as necessary to hide the erroneous letters. Large lumps of white gunk are very unattractive!

Applying Online

Welcome to the third millennium! Many major undergraduate institutions, as well as most graduate programs and medical, law, and business schools, have made provisions for electronic applications. If you apply online, you save paper, a trip to the post office, and all the headaches addressed by the preceding pages of this chapter, such as locating a typewriter and dealing with margins.

To find out whether online application is possible, check the Web site of the college or university you favor. If you don't know the URL — the Web address — try the name or initials of the institution, followed by "edu," the educational suffix (`www.harvard.edu` or `www.ucla.edu`, for example). Or, conduct a search with one of the Internet's search engines, such as Google (`www.google.com`) or Altavista (`www.altavista.com`). Still can't find the site? Call the school's admissions office.

About 230 colleges and universities, including members of the exclusive "Ivy League," accept a "common application" for undergraduate admission. The application, found at www.commonapp.org, may be downloaded and printed or submitted electronically. Participating schools pledge to consider the common app (its affectionate nickname) as if it were their own, exclusive application. However, some institutions also require a supplemental, just-for-them addendum to the common app. Read the directions on the school's Web site or call the admissions office for guidance.

More than 100 medical schools have devised their own "common app," which is administered by the American Medical College Application Service (AMCAS). The common-application essays — "practice vision" and "personal comments" — are in Part III. You may submit an AMCAS application online at www.aamc.org. AMCAS charges a fee for its service.

Lawyers have also gotten into the common application game — and, not surprisingly, they also charge for online applications. Go to the Web site of the Law School Admission Council (www.lsac.org) for the legal "common app." If you wish to apply online, fill in the form and designate all the schools you'd like to receive your application. Factual information — name, address, and so forth — will automatically be entered into the proper spot on each school's application blank. However, you'll have to upload your law school admission essays separately to each of your chosen schools. (You can do so at the Law School Admission Council Web site; you just need a few clicks for each school.)

Most business schools allow electronic applications. Go to the Web site of each school or check out the Princeton Review Web site (www.princetonreview.com). This site, formerly known as Embark, allows you to fill in factual information on one form and then it uploads your information to every school you've selected, automatically slotting the data into the appropriate place. You'll need to send the longer stuff, including your essays and the four- or five-sentence "short answers," to each school separately. (You can take care of these tasks at the Princeton Review site.) These applications are also accepted for many other types of graduate school applications as well as some law schools, medical schools, and undergraduate programs. You don't pay Princeton Review for this application service, though you still have to shell out an application fee for each school you've selected, and some add a surcharge for Princeton Review applications.

When you fill in the essay blanks online, use the "copy and paste" commands of your word-processing program to upload the essay into the proper spot. In Microsoft Word, for example, click on the "Edit" button at the top of the screen. Then choose "select all" and "copy." The material is now saved and ready for the "paste" command. (Some online applications include an "upload" button that replaces the "paste" command.)

Faxing, Express-Mailing, and Other Panic Options

The deadline is — gulp — approaching with the speed of a runaway train. You're done, but that lovely application is still sitting on your desk. How can you get it to them on time?

The easiest option is electronic (see the preceding section, "Applying Online," for details). But if you're not on the Web, *they're* not on the Web, your modem is broken, or you simply don't trust the Internet, you need other options. By and large, faxing is not a great way to submit your essay or any other part of your application. Why? Have you read any faxes lately? The print is often blurry and the quality uneven. Remember, your essay will be read by very tired eyes. Don't place any unnecessary obstacles in the path to acceptance!

Express-mail companies (the private ones and the postal service's own version) are a better bet. You'll probably pay upwards of $10, but at least you'll know that your own (legible) version will arrive. Of course if the school is local, you can trek over there and hand-deliver your masterpiece. Just don't expect to stay and chat. Deadline time for you is also crunch time for the admissions office.

The best solution to the time problem is not to let time *become* a problem. Start your application early, finish with a week or more to spare, and let the letter carrier do the job! I've always found the US Postal service to be reliable, but if you're mailing from abroad or if you've had a different experience, you may want to invest in express mail anyway.

Part V
Analyzing Questions from Real Applications

"Oh this? I was reading some student admission essays and I didn't see the the run-on sentences coming."

In this part . . .

Got a hot tip for the fifth race at Santa Anita? No? Don't feel bad, because in this part you'll find something better — tips to help you answer specific questions frequently found on college and graduate school applications. Each chapter covers a specific type of question: the "tell us about yourself" essay in Chapter 18 and the "person who influenced you" query in Chapter 19. Chapter 20 takes you through the "subject-oriented" questions: great books (English), current or historical events (social studies), meaning of life (philosophy), and so forth. Finally, Chapter 21 explains how to squeeze the maximum amount of information into the short answers.

Chapter 18

Composing Essays Starring You

In This Chapter

- Writing about your personal experiences
- Drawing an academic portrait
- Imagining your future
- Describing and interpreting your character

When you send an application to a school, everything in it reveals something about you, from the "date and place of birth" line to the list of your extracurricular activities and awards. The ultimate in self-revelation is the essay, no matter how abstract or obscure the topic. After all, the admissions committee is trudging through all that paper because they want to get to know you. (Check out Chapter 2 for a complete explanation of the way in which all admission essays should communicate something about the writer.)

But some questions directly ask you to write about the topic at hand — yourself — including "What three adjectives describe you?" "What experience has shaped your personality?" "Where do you see yourself in 20 years?" and so forth. In this chapter I provide special tips for answering the "tell us about yourself" essay questions, so you can take maximum advantage of the opportunity they provide for self-revelation.

And Then I Took the Oath of Office: Relating a Personal Experience

Somewhere in that pile of blank applications — each a doorway to a school you love — may be a question resembling one of these:

- What experience had an impact on your goals, plans, or ideals?
- Describe a significant community service experience.
- Explain a situation in which you used creativity to solve a problem.
- Discuss a challenge you faced.

- What was your most significant success or failure?
- Tell us about an accomplishment you're proud of that has never been publicly recognized.
- Write about an important experience in your life.

To answer these questions you need two elements: (1) a story and (2) the reason you told the story. Right about now you may be saying, "Story? I thought I was writing an essay." True. You're certainly *not* creating a short story or a scene from a novel, albeit one in which all the facts are accurate. An essay is an interpretative piece of writing with a personal point of view. A good response to an admission essay question often contains elements of a story, if — and only if — you include an evaluation of the events for the reader.

If you're facing one of these questions, your first task is to scan your memory bank for possible topics. The personal inventory in the appendix, as well as the guidelines in Chapter 2, will help. After you've narrowed the field, start collecting details and ideas, perhaps with some of the techniques described in Chapter 5. Then it's time to write, guided by the wisdom (she said with a blush) in Part III of *College Admission Essays For Dummies.*

Now for some specific tips to help you navigate the personal-experience essay.

Choosing relevant material

You're not writing a complete autobiography; you're writing an essay. Don't try to narrate the entire incident you've chosen as a topic. Just concentrate on the parts that are relevant to the point you want to make. (What point should an essay make? Check out Chapter 16 for an explanation.)

Suppose that you're writing about the time you rescued a fellow skydiver whose chute failed to open. The main idea you wish to communicate is that you faced your fears before deciding to act. If this incident were an episode in the reality-TV series about your life or a chapter in your autobiography, it would probably include everything on this list:

first moment you glimpsed the pamphlet advertising sky-diving lessons

trip to the airport

take-off

pre-jump conversation with your buddy in the plane

last moment in the doorway

first step into thin air (Why is air always thin? Diet secrets?)

initial fall

understanding that your buddy was in trouble

doubts about your ability to save him without risk to yourself

decision to act

maneuvering to his side

attaching yourself to his belt

successful descent

search for a new, land-based hobby

filing of a lawsuit against the parachute-maker, pilot, and sky-diving school

In an essay, especially one limited to a few pages, recounting all those events is a bad idea. You'd end up with no room for interpretation! Worse, the main point would get lost in the crowd. Instead, zero in on the important stuff — the realization that your buddy's chute wouldn't open and your battle to overcome your fear. You may mention *very briefly* some other aspects of the incident — certainly the successful outcome — but the focus should remain on the part of the event that makes your point: You can face the scary stuff in life and succeed.

After you've narrowed the scope of your story, choose the details — the zingers, not the boring parts — that bring the reader into your reality. (Check out Chapter 9 for help with this task.) Suggest more than you say, and don't feel obliged to provide every single fact you know. The reader won't care about the type of insulation in your jumpsuit or the lucky ring you forgot to wear that day. However, the admissions committee will appreciate understanding exactly how difficult and dangerous a stunt you had to pull off. As you choose details, remember that the narrative portion of your essay is *not* the whole thing. Leave room — at least half — for interpretation. ("Interpreting the story for the reader," later in this section, explains this critically important part of your essay.)

Ranging over a long period of time

The skydiving example I described in the preceding section (product of my imagination and far too many hours watching reality shows on television) occurs in a limited amount of time. But what if you want to explain an event — actually, a series of events — that took place over a few weeks, months, or even longer? How do you focus the essay in such a case?

Easy. Think of the whole period of time as a videotape. Choose one or two (okay, maybe three, but not more) freeze-frame moments from the tape that you think the reader should see — moments that represent important points in the arc of the whole experience. Go into greater detail about those selected moments.

Greater detail, yes. Complete, no. Remember to leave room for an evaluation of the experience.

For an example of an essay that discusses events taking place over time, take a look at Figure 18-1, a student essay about a Little League baseball experience. (Everything in the essay is true except for the names, which I changed to protect the author's privacy.) The events described took place during three consecutive summers (1991–1993). The author chose three representative moments from the sum total of those years of baseball. In paragraph three he zeroes in on the help he received from his coach. Paragraph five goes into detail about the author's reaction to the break-up of his team. The references to the "family reunion" in the second-to-last paragraph bring the reader into the story one more time.

Taking the story inward

A key part of the story you're recounting is internal. The incident you chose, out of all the millions of events in your life, mattered to you. Maybe the incident changed you in some way, or perhaps your actions illustrate an aspect of your personality or character. In either case you need to lead the reader into your personal reality. You can do so by simply telling the reader about what was going on. However, three techniques borrowed from fiction (but in the essay applied strictly to the facts and used *very* sparingly) create a path to the inside. Those techniques are thoughts, dialogue, and action.

Thoughts

What was going through your head at the crucial moment? Okay, I know that you didn't have some sort of psychic tape recorder running, but chances are you remember enough of your thought process to recreate it for the reader. In the fictional skydive example I employed earlier in this section, you might have been assessing your chances for survival and a successful rescue, as in this excerpt:

> A hundred feet away. Can I get that far? And if I do, will I just take both of us down? A fall from this height without a parachute means death for Bill. No question. But if I can't get my parachute open and I grab him, we'll both die. But how can I live with myself if I don't try?

Don't overdo this technique. Thoughts are the equivalent of the slow-motion photography used in sports broadcasts. On sports shows, "slo-mo" is for the winning hit, the disputed call, or the season-ending injury — not for a routine double play! In your story, thoughts should be for moments of similar significance.

My town, geographically just northwest of Manhattan; demographically, a population of all colors, races, and religions; all the minorities, and for that matter, majorities imaginable. Movie stars, recording artists, professionals, business executives, and welfare recipients all living in close proximity. It can be no surprise that recreational activities in this heterogeneous city were organized differently from those in the predominately white, neighboring towns. For example, the baseball teams were supposed to be composed with a balance of Whites, Blacks, Latinos, Asians, and even Orthodox Jews.

In 1991, my first year of Little League baseball, I was assigned to the Orioles. As it turned out, the Orioles were the only team with all Black and Latino players and coaches. I was "the token white." I later found out that my parents were anxious about placing me in this setting, but they felt it would be an important experience for me. In retrospect, when I was introduced to my coaches and teammates, it was not a black and white experience. It was people meeting people.

Although I had played baseball with my cousins and friends and even with my father, my batting skills were not on par with those of my teammates. Instead of making disparaging comments to me, they were really supportive. Jim, my coach, spent as much time with me on batting and fielding skills as he did with the other boys. We even practiced pitching so I could relief pitch for Yusuf, our team star. Jim's son was also a stellar player. Dominic came to us from Jamaica, where he had little chance to play baseball. Regardless of skill, Jim provided an equal opportunity for all of us to play. Coach Jim, who worked two jobs to support his family, was always patient and infinitely understanding. I credit him for my insight into team effort, my sportsmanship, and especially my love of baseball.

That first year we competed for the League Championship. Each time I came to bat, clammy and queasy, I would swing high or too early. I just couldn't connect. There were no jeers, no whispers, no negative comments from the Oriole dugout. Just, "It's okay, you'll do better next time." I did. We won that championship, but we lost our team.

Feeling that the Orioles were far superior to the other teams in the League, opposing coaches and parents demanded that our team be dismantled. We were disbursed amongst predominantly white teams. The cohesiveness and camaraderie were gone. I missed Jim's gentle guidance and support. Thoroughly surprising was the way my former teammates and I cheered each other as we competed against one another. It was great to see Yusuf hit a home run, even for another team. I was thrilled when Jim Jr. pitched a no hitter. My new team, the Angels, and my hot-headed coach, who was obsessed with winning, could not win my allegiance. I vowed not to play the following year.

But there was a third and final year for me in Little League. With the aid and persistence of the original Oriole parents, Jim was able to convince the League that disbanding a cohesive team had been unfair. Our first practice was like a family reunion. We hugged, cried, stomped, and cheered, "Go, Orioles!" And we did!

Although we were thrilled with the positive results of our cooperative efforts, the greatest outcome of our endeavors was the friendships that evolved. Despite differences in our color, religion, and economic position, we found commonality and gained richer perspectives. I developed greater confidence in relating to people and looked forward to working and playing in socially and culturally diverse environments.

Figure 18-1: An example of an essay that spans a long period of time.

Don't attempt to duplicate the thoughts of anyone but yourself. You can't know what someone else was thinking, and if you attempt a guess, you've entered the realm of fiction and left essay-land. Grounds for arrest by the accuracy patrol! The admissions committee will have reason to doubt your grasp of the difference between fantasy and reality and may even question the rest of the information you supplied in the application packet.

Dialogue

Words reveal quite a bit about the person who says or writes them. (That's why you're composing an essay, right?) So consider adding some — not too much! — dialogue to your essay to illuminate character or emotion. Once again I return to two separate spots in the fictional skydiving essay for examples:

> "Bill!" I screamed when I got close enough to see his face, even though I knew he couldn't hear me in the wind. "Don't give up!"
>
> "We're alive," I yelled as our feet touched the ground. "I can't believe we're alive! That's the last time I get in a plane with *you,*" I joked.

Notice what the dialogue in the first example reveals: the author's attempt to encourage her friend, despite the fact that the author herself is afraid. The second example emphasizes the author's real fears for her own safety by indicating her surprise and relief at the rescue's success.

In an essay of limited scope and length, you generally need only a few lines of dialogue — far less than you would for a scene in a novel or a short story. But placed at the right spot, dialogue displays character and enlivens the essay.

The way others speak to and about you also reveals your character and personality to the reader. Scan this example:

> "I know you hate me because I stole your watch last week," said Bill as the ambulance roared up. "I can't believe you still risked your life to save me."

Take great care not to imagine what the other person — or you, for that matter — said. In the essay you should provide the truth, the whole truth (or at least the part that fits within the word limit), and nothing but the truth. Quote what people actually said, not what you wish they'd said or what you need to make a dramatic point.

Actions

How does the old proverb go? Actions speak louder than words. But remember to include more than the big, obvious actions when you recount an event. (As another proverb says, little things mean a lot.) Back to the skydiving example from earlier in this section:

> I grabbed the hook on my belt and forced it towards Bill's vest. The wind billowed the hook away. My hand trembled as I snatched it back.

Hand trembling is a small detail, but a significant one. The author's fear comes across clearly in that tiny sentence. Of course, in an essay you should include only a very small number of action details. As long as you don't overuse it, you can get a lot of mileage out of this technique.

Not only your own actions, but those of others in reaction to you, may reveal your personality and character.

Interpreting the story for the reader

Okay, you've taken the readers into your reality for a few moments. But you also need to make them understand why the trip was necessary. A great part of the essay — up to half, perhaps — should be an evaluation of that reality. You may attach some sentences of explanation to the beginning or the end of the essay. (Chapter 11 explains introductions and Chapter 12 tackles conclusions.) Or, as the author of the essay in Figure 18-1 did, you may weave the interpretation throughout. Notice how he reaches back from the present to the past in several spots as he evaluates his Little League experience:

> . . . it was not a black and white experience. It was people meeting people. (paragraph two)
>
> I credit him for my insight into team effort, my sportsmanship, and especially my love of baseball. (paragraph three)
>
> Thoroughly surprising was the way my teammates and I cheered each other as we competed against each other. (paragraph five)

The conclusion of Figure 18-1 carries the bulk of the message:

> . . . the greatest outcome of our endeavors was the friendships that evolved. Despite differences in color, religion, and economic position, we found commonality and gained richer perspectives. I developed greater confidence in relating to people and looked forward to working and playing in socially and culturally diverse environments.

Figure 18-2, an essay written by a student who worked on a political campaign, has plenty of detail about the events of those hectic months. (To protect the student's privacy, I changed the names and a couple of small details, but the basic writing is his and the general situation is true.) The essay traces the author's growing realization that he cared deeply about the election and about his friend's reaction. Notice how much space the interpretation takes in relation to the events described.

It feels strange when I recount some of my experiences working on Arthur Black's senatorial election campaign, since, for as long as I can remember, I have been best friends with his son, Jon. Seeing things as both an insider and an outsider has always allowed me to know the candidate as more than just another politician, a name on some ballot. At the same time, though, it has left me with a distance letting, for example, my parents' dinner guests to criticize him without reservation in front of me. I no longer remember whether I had first encountered the candidate as a father, joking around with Jon and me as we passed through the living room, or if I had seen him first as a political figure, posing beside the mayor in the New York Times. So, as a result of the two contexts in which I knew him, I took on a dual role in working on his campaign.

When Jon would ask me whether I could give up a few hours to hand out literature down in Union Square, I would be doing my friend a favor to accept. If the campaign office managers sent me down to City Hall to record a press conference, I was working on a serious election. At first, despite my minimal knowledge of Arthur Black's political stance or experience, I figured that Jon's dad was a worthy cause. And so I had agreed to volunteer as an intern on the Friends of Black campaign and report each morning to a small closet-office, where my job consisted of mindlessly entering data into a computer or delivering packages. But, before I knew it, I became interested and more involved. I became an enthusiastic member of the Black team.

Once, outside a candidates' debate, Jon's older sister Jean, the volunteer coordinator, suggested that I be the one to publicize over the megaphone. I had the privilege of shouting to the whole block, "What color is that car? Is it Smith (his opponent)? No, my friends, it's black!" I was Jon's loyal, funny friend, there to help out.

There were, however, instances that forced me to abandon my particular view of Arthur Black as Jon's father and view him purely as a political figure. I was put in the position of defending and advocating my candidate, pointing out his years of experience, his attention to the average consumer, and his plans to re-build public schooling. And, although I knew in both my heart and mind that I was supporting the correct candidate, it amused me to see the shift that had taken place in my perspective over the past few years, a shift from strictly emotional to more rational judgment, without which, I am certain, I would have devoted far less of my time and energy to the campaign.

As the race intensified, I began to hear very disparate accounts of the election, first from Jon and then from local news correspondents. To each, I had a different reaction: a tacit sympathy for my friend and a relatively objective view of a candidate's political strategies. The week of the election, wearing the Black paraphernalia, the t-shirt, the stickers, and such, I was simultaneously advocating a candidate and offering support to Jon. Election Day, watching the poll results waver, I wondered, as a citizen, who would be my next state senator, and asked myself how I would console my best friend if his father were to lose. Perhaps one of the biggest challenges of being a good friend would be picking him up when things were looking down, and at that point they were; we were faced with a question I couldn't yet answer: "What if he loses?"

Figure 18-2: An essay example that interprets a story.

> I supposed, when Arthur Black lost the election, that all the volunteers were equally upset. Still, remarks that he was just another politician struck a chord that resonated against my image of the decent man and loving father I had known growing up, and I never understood how he could bear such slander. Often, discussing the issue with my father, who suggested, "That's politics," I realized that, for me, that wasn't politics. Politics meant where all our years of hard work would end up and how my friend would take the results. Politics concerned much more than just an agenda or a resume, but I accepted that voters would, and probably should, see things through different eyes; it was just a shame we didn't succeed in showing them how deserving and qualified a candidate he was, and, to them, Arthur Black became perhaps a name on some ballot after all. But whether it was, in the end, the campaign platform or the loyalty that I had to my friend that drove me to get involved, I'll always be proud of having worked on that campaign and having felt that human side of politics, to have supported a real person.

Figure 18-2: An essay example that interprets a story.

Explaining Your A+ in Recess and Other Academic Experiences

Educational institutions, not surprisingly, are interested in your academic experience — not just the numbers and letters on your transcript, but the way you relate to school and learning. Essay questions about your identity as a student include:

- Describe a class you liked.
- Does your academic record reflect your achievement or your potential? Why?
- Discuss the strengths and weaknesses of your education thus far.
- Describe a failure and what you learned from it.
- Address any low grades or failures in your background.
- What do you wish you'd known before starting high school? How would that knowledge have changed your high school experience?
- Describe a situation in which you surprised yourself and learned something about your talents and interests.

Faced with one of the preceding questions, you have some thinking to do. How *do* you learn? What subject or type of learning is difficult or easy for you? Which class or assignment awakened your passion? It may not be the class in which you got the highest grade, by the way. When I look back at my own high school experience (so far away I need a telescope just to get a glimpse), I don't remember all the A's I got (she said modestly) in history and English. I remember the sweat I poured into Experimental Physics. Nothing in that course came easily to me, but I stuck with it and gained at least enough information to become a fan of *StarTrek* (the one with the bald captain, not the other ones). You may have something similar to recount.

To describe an academic experience, consider focusing on a particular activity or assignment. The techniques I explain in the preceding section, "And Then I Took the Oath of Office: Relating a Personal Experience," may be helpful in this task. Or, take a look at Figure 9-1 in Chapter 9, a student essay that describes exactly how the author prepared a presentation for his European History class. Notice how the author makes the event come alive with specific, vivid details.

Another way to answer the academic-experience questions is to write an essay that surveys a year or more in one subject or field. "Ranging over a long period of time," a section earlier in this chapter, explains how to portray an extended experience. Figure 18-3 is an excerpt from an essay written by a fine young mathematician. The time period discussed in the essay begins in third grade and continues through senior year in high school. The author presents sample experiences from third and tenth grade in some detail. She also briefly touches upon her passion for math at other times in her life. The essay is a mixture of long and short descriptions:

> third grade math lab, playing with tangrams instead of practicing softball (long description)
>
> car rides and math olympiad (brief mention)
>
> 10th grade class (long description)
>
> 11th grade pre-calculus and 12th grade independent study in math (brief mention)

The author ends the essay with a dose of interpretation, explaining that her mathematical studies relate to other academic experiences, such as writing and art history. She closes with a punch line that delivers her main idea: "Whatever I do in life, I will always be thinking of an equation to go with it."

In general, you shouldn't dwell on your academic shortcomings in the essay portion of your application. Even if you're describing a failure (responding to a specific request to do so), concentrate on the positive aspects of the experience. Explain what you learned from the fiasco. Check out Figure 10-1 in Chapter 10, a student essay describing how the author "fried" the circuits of his robot shortly before his trimester project (the robot) was due to be graded. Although the essay clearly states that the author failed to create a functioning robot, it also shows that he has learned something about robot construction and preparation time. The overall effect is upbeat.

Envisioning the Future: When I Retire at 20, I Will . . .

Judging from the applications I've read, I'm not the only one who read H.G. Wells' *The Time Machine* as a kid and never got over it. Dozens of schools ask you to time-travel to a future college reunion or to some other indeterminate moment that has yet to occur. Still more institutions ask for an essay speculating about your future life's work and accomplishments. Check out these questions:

- Describe the medical practice you envision for yourself.
- Discuss three possible careers that you may enter after college.
- Where will you be 20 years from now, and how will the education you receive help you to get there?
- Describe your life at 15 and 25 years after graduation.
- What are three life goals and how do you plan to achieve them?
- What will you say about yourself at your 15th college reunion?

Fantasizing about the future should be easy for you, because applying to college or graduate school is a future-oriented job. You probably already spend hours daydreaming about life in the dorm, weekend social events, and, I hope, what you'll actually learn when you're in the midst of higher education. To answer one of these essay questions, simply extend the daydreaming to a point farther in the future. Don't stall on Homecoming Weekend or your triumphant graduation ceremony; keep going until you reach the time the question is inquiring about.

To write an essay about your future, be honest, even when you're fantasizing. If you're like most people, you feel sure about some elements of your future and clueless about the rest. The writer of Figure 18-3, for example, can confidently state that mathematical thinking will always be part of her life, whether she's 18 or 81. She can't say with any certainty that she'll win the Nobel Prize in Mathematics someday, though personally I wouldn't be totally shocked if she did receive that honor. The admissions committee knows that in asking a speculative question, they're going to get a speculative answer. Nevertheless, don't stray from your true self, and stick to things that have a reasonable chance of happening.

As you put your "future" essay together, keep in mind the techniques of good writing. Be specific! Use strong verbs and nouns and lively, vigorous sentences. (Chapters 9 and 10 provide help.) A survey or chronological approach may work well with this sort of essay. You may also find the "description and interpretation" structure helpful. (Chapter 7 gives you the lowdown on these structures and several others. Check out "'Desperate' and Other Descriptions," later in this chapter, for more tips.)

"You know, your choreographic work is very mathematical," my friend said to me recently. Though my passion for dance is almost as intense as my passion for math, it was not until I heard this comment that I realized how closely related they are. This connection makes perfect sense as many things in my life are closely related to math.

My love of math started in third grade. At school there was, in addition to a science lab, a math lab. While other kids played softball, my friends and I sat on the floor of the math lab playing with tangrams (small, colored, polygonal blocks). We didn't need softball; math lab was playtime. The ordinary pieces could all fit together infinite ways to make anything from a big, multicolored square to a complex symmetrical snowflake. I still have a Polaroid of my third grade tangram masterpiece of the snowflake variety. Math became only more interesting to me throughout elementary school. My parents soon caught on, and during long car rides they used to give me strings of numbers to add, subtract, multiply, and divide to keep me from getting bored and asking if we were there yet. In fourth, fifth, and sixth grades I participated in the elementary school math Olympiads, and my after-school hours were sometimes devoted to discussing a problem or idea with my teacher.

In junior high, math was put on the back burner with my discovery of nail polish and hair dryers, but not for long. When I got to my new school in tenth grade, my interest was rapidly revived by Mr. W., my geometry teacher. He taught with an unsurpassable amount of enthusiasm and love for the subject, and the inspiration he evoked in me spread to my other classes too. My essay writing improved dramatically when I learned the techniques of geometrical proofs, and my ability to visualize molecular models in chemistry also got much better when I learned rudimentary trigonometry. When the math curricula from my old and new schools did not line up, Mr. W. was the one who supported my decision to take the tenth grade math course, Algebra II and Trig, in addition to ninth grade Geometry. This arrangement was normally against school policy, and taking two honors math courses was a load, but one I was quite happy to bear. In fact, it reconfirmed my love of math.

In my pre-calculus class during my junior year, all sorts of new doorways opened up. There is so much more out there than I ever dreamed of, and I am thoroughly excited to study as much of it as possible; I am doing an independent study in math this year, in addition to taking calculus. Studying art history in my junior year gave me a whole new outlet for my love of math. Renaissance art, one of my favorite genres, is firmly based on geometry. Its philosophy, as well as its aesthetic appearance, is highly organized and deals with several versions of the dichotomy of earth and heaven, including body and soul, and, to my delight, square and circle. My favorite music is quite mathematical; I love Bach and Mozart, and the idea of repeating modified themes is infinitely pleasing to me. My fascination with the mathematical permeates my other studies.

Many of my interests trace back to my love of math, not just as a subject, but as a way of thinking. To do math, one has to have a sense of organization as well as the ability to figure out something from a set of conditions. Whatever I do in life, I will always be thinking of an equation to go with it.

Figure 18-3: An example essay that covers a long period of time.

Medical school applications generally ask you to provide a "practice vision," and some law and business schools also require you to describe your future career. The suggestions in this section are particularly relevant to these types of essays. Figure 18-4 is an excerpt from an admission essay written as part of a medical school application. The author does not shy away from some medical

I am elementally fascinated in human minds, in human relationships. Ten years from now, I can imagine practicing psychiatry, immersed in investigations of human beings and the ways in which they experience their lives. And I can imagine teaching at an urban university, sharing these investigations with medical students in a manner similar to how I currently loop my love of literature back into the dynamism of the classroom. My interest in psychiatry will, perhaps, have pulled me in two directions.

I will be one of the thinkers of science trying to navigate that vast territory between brain and mind. This will require, first, experience with patients and a constant drive to sharpen my understanding of the biological mechanism and network of effects involved in their various types of mental conditions. The goal at large, though, is ultimately synthetic in that it needs the collaboration of many minds thinking creatively about how to unify large bodies of literature: on the one hand, the microlevel research of proteins and transmitters, or second-messengers and neural networks; on the other, macrolevel research of psychologists and psychiatrists. Among other developments, this effort will involve asking whole-brain questions with techniques more penetrating than MRI or PET or TCD @md techniques which neuroscience will be well-poised to provide in the next ten years, given the determination of creative minds.

Or, I can envision exploring the brain-mind dialectic in ways that challenge the bottom-up paradigm in which biology strictly determines behavior in a one-directional cause-effect relationship. Research biologists (at a molecular level) and psychiatrists (at the level of disorder-induced brain-wide reorganizations) are already involved in this challenge. I am interested in how addictions, or eating disorders, or the psycho-biological development of sexuality and sexual orientation - how these mental phenomena affect the biology of the brain in meaningful ways. It seems crucial to note, finally, that these two coarsely outlined directions are not without resonance.

At bottom, though, I am more interested in being a focused and penetrating physician for my patients than in being a researcher. And I do not want to suggest otherwise. The intellectual questions which drive me do so only because of their ramifications for patient care. I am also excited, for example, about the vital project of particularizing the discourse of self-spection. After Wittgenstein and Heidegger, among others, we are forced to analyze the directionality of the language-thought relationship: if one's thoughts — and therefore perceptions and ideas and feelings — are outgrowths of the language one has, psychiatrists must bring language under critical inquiry. This can happen on a patient by patient, day by day level.

I am aware that medicine is a life and not simply a career. In a similar way, the churning of the intellect is part of the texture of my life; it is not a choice. Though the politics of American health care are frustrating, what I know will persist for many more years than ten is the ceaseless stimulation psychiatry will provide. I am sure the next ten years of the neuro-sciences at large will be wildly exciting. Psychiatry has the potential to be the epicenter for their synthesis and synergies. I am ravenous to learn more about the complexities of this field, and therefore the complexities of ourselves, to be a psychiatrist capable of unifying psychology with the biology of the body as a whole. And I will do this always in the service of patients, always aware of what a privilege it is.

Figure 18-4: An essay example that focuses on the future.

terminology (*PET, neural networks,* and so on), but such words are appropriate because his essay will be read by doctors. He presents a broad view of the fields that entice him and how their basic ideas may be combined, with enough details to show that he understands the profession he is attempting to join.

Law, medical, and business schools sometimes ask you why you chose a particular profession. And even if the question is vague ("Tell us something about you that we should know," perhaps), you may want to explain your reasons for choosing a particular career. Recounting an experience that motivated your decision may do the job. So may a "description and interpretation" essay, discussed in "'Desperate' and Other Descriptions," later in this chapter.

Figure 18-5 is an essay from an application to law school. The author discusses her semester in Moscow, concentrating on the elements that relate to law — the elderly women deprived of justice, the Russian Supreme Court building, and by contrast, the U.S. Supreme Court building. Those three elements serve as metaphors for the difference in the two justice systems and the author's thoughts on her chosen career.

Daydreaming Your Way into College

How many times has an Authority Figure told you to "stop daydreaming" and get with the program? Surprise, surprise: Certain essays legalize daydreaming, requiring you to imagine yourself in an alternate reality. Questions in this vein resemble the following:

- If you could have the job of any individual, living or dead, what would you choose and why?
- If you could work for a year with a non-political person who is not personally known to you, whom would you select? Why?
- If you could be anyone else for a day — a living, historical, or fictional figure — who would it be? Explain your reasons.
- Imagine that you could work for a year with unlimited resources. What would you like to accomplish?
- If you could create a new family or community tradition, what would it be?

The first three sample questions give you a chance to "walk in another person's shoes." I won't deal with those questions here, but in Chapter 19, I explain in detail how to write about other people. The last two questions — working for a year with unlimited resources and creating traditions — directly address your values. An essay responding to this sort of question may be structured in any one of several ways:

After previous travel experiences, I considered myself fairly wise to the world, but nothing in my past prepared me for Moscow. The minute Delta flight 50 touched down at Sheremetevo II, I became an honorary Muscovite, for better and for worse.

I struggled to fathom Russia's long, harsh history and grasp the suffering that elderly Muscovites endured. I searched for an answer to Nekrasov's question, "Who lives joyfully, freely, in Russia?" and ignored the suspicious looks of those who noticed me smiling to myself. I learned never to criticize the beloved poet Pushkin and realized how stupid I looked in a bright red coat among true Muscovites in dark hues. I lived, breathed, and shared with people for whom I once held so much fear.

The memories are indelible. I survived food poisoning, but only by the grace of the American Clinic in Moscow. I walked through a Communist rally without a scratch and danced in a club surrounded by members of the Russian mafia. In freezing weather, I trudged through a bog in the vast wilderness looking for a white-tailed eagle. I could not discern whether those passed out from drink on the city streets had frozen to death.

The images that haunt me most are those of the elderly women begging or selling trinkets in the metro stations, leaning against the dirty walls as their legs grew weary, the pain in their eyes indicating the depth of injustice they had known. These strong women, who worked their entire lives in the Communist system, survived World War II, lived with alcoholic men who died young, suffered political oppression, and went hungry for decades, now receive pensions that are worth pennies ravaged by inflation. All these women had possessed was the knowledge that they would be secure in retirement, that eventually their tired legs could rest. Everything they had saved, all they had worked for, is now worth nothing. Four thousand rubles used to buy a Russian-made car; today it buys a loaf of bread.

A few blocks away from Red Square and the Kremlin, a Russian friend pointed to an indistinguishable building that houses the Russian Supreme Court. It stood in sharp contrast to the U.S. Supreme Court, which stands proudly, exuding authority and commanding respect. Like a classical temple, it is our shrine to Justice. Perhaps, then, it is appropriate for Russia to have a humble, meek building hold its Court while Lenin occupies his own grand mausoleum in Red Square. There is no marble women symbolizing justice to adorn the Court's entrance, only forgotten, fatigued women symbolizing injustice on the metro and the street. The U.S. legal system is far from perfect, but it is preferable to the undesirable effects of a legal system and a government based on men, rather than on laws. I had thought about studying law before I went to Moscow, but living in Russia made me realize that a strong, independent legal system is the sine qua non of a just society.

Seeing those women daily, their hollow glances and their downtrodden bodies and spirits opened my eyes – wide this time – to a life without joy, hope, or compassion. Thus, my time in Moscow aged me far beyond the four months I spent there. Despite my fondness for Stanford, another year of college hardly seemed possible as the challenges of term papers and selecting classes were no longer as compelling. I decided to graduate a year early, ready for a new adventure. I chose to sample the "real world" for a year and work in a legal environment before committing myself to the study of law. Not only has my job at the Department of Justice proved to be a rewarding experience, but it has solidified that commitment.

The vestiges of the honorary Muscovite still animate me. Living in Moscow taught me to take nothing for granted, to be thankful for my opportunities, and to find joy wherever I can. Nothing prepared me for Moscow, but Moscow prepared me for almost anything.

Figure 18-5: An essay example that recounts an experience.

- Recount an imaginary event — what you would do in a limited period of time with unlimited money or how you would celebrate the tradition — as if it were something that had actually happened. Use present tense (*As the final brick in the Homes for the Homeless House is cemented into place, I see the smiles of the future tenants. . . .*) or past (*With a joyous peal of bells, Help Each Other Day drew to a close. . . .*). After taking the reader into a "you are there" reality, explain at length *why* the event is important — to you or to the larger community.

  TIP

  Whenever you recount an event, real or imaginary, leave room — at least half of the essay — for interpretation or evaluation.

- Create a mosaic — a series of "snapshots" of moments from the course of the time period specified in the question. Suppose you declared your desire to spend a year negotiating peace in one of the world's trouble spots. You might briefly describe a conference early in January, the progress of a community project halfway through the year, and the renewed hope of participants as your year draws to a close. Be as specific as you can about your "plans," and be sure to clarify when you depart from reality into your fantasy achievements.
- A survey approach may suit the "year with unlimited funding" question. Discuss all the reasons why action is necessary, exactly what you would do to improve the situation, and the possible results. Be sure to provide detail for the most important aspects of the project. For example, don't simply say that you would work on your community's homeless problem. Explain where and how you'd build housing.
- The "description and interpretation" technique may be applied to fantasy as well as reality. Imagine that you're creating a "Help Each Other Day" town tradition. Describe the town square before and after the day's cleanup. Be sure to evaluate the impact of your new tradition on the town and on yourself.

Chapter 7 provides a detailed explanation of various ways to structure your essay. Regardless of how you organize the essay, remember to do the following:

- Write about something you know well. If you're fairly clueless about the topic, the essay will show the admissions committee that you know very little about the topic, even though you're claiming that it is close to your heart. Not a good message!
- You're writing an admission essay, not a term paper. Skip footnotes and lengthy factual explanations. Be specific, but remember that the focus is on you and your relationship to the topic.

"Desperate" and Other Descriptions

I understand that institutions of higher learning have a legitimate need to amass information about their applicants. That said, I must confess that some application questions (sometimes placed in the short answer section and sometimes in the essay section) make me cringe in embarrassment, especially those resembling the following:

- What three adjectives describe you? Explain.
- What attributes of your character will contribute to your success in college?
- Write on any topic that reveals your best quality, and explain why you chose this topic.
- Describe something that tells us who you are (or aren't).
- What can other members of our community learn from you?
- What about yourself would be most difficult for your potential roommate to live with on a daily basis?

The only word that pops into my head when I read these questions is "desperate," as in "they must be desperate to come up with good questions" and "you must be desperate to finish this tedious self-examination." Fortunately I don't have to answer any of these zingers. I just have to tell *you* how to do so.

These questions ask you to define yourself — a real challenge for anyone, because the old saying about not being able to "see yourself as others see you" holds true. Several approaches may help.

- Turn to your friends and relatives for advice. After they pass through the giggling stage, during which answers such as "oblivious to household chores" and "most likely to break the VCR" emerge, they'll probably give you some important information about yourself.

When you ask someone close to you to comment on your personality and values, you may hear something surprising. Before you scream and throw things, ask for an explanation. If your best friend Ruby says that you are "impatient," don't stalk off until she has a chance to add that you want social justice *now,* not later. If you hear something offensive that can't be explained away, pause before blowing your top. Remember that you're in the midst of a very stressful process. Before you jettison your oldest and deepest friendship, consider whether you're overreacting because of the pressures of college admissions.

- Looking for adjectives? Many of these questions are what I call "what would I save in a burning building" queries. Go with the flow and consider what you *would* save if you had only moments to evacuate a burning building. The answer may help you uncover priorities. A small step from priorities are your character and values. For example, if you'd save your parents and day-planner (in that order), you value family ties and an orderly life. Your personal characteristics may be "loving," "loyal," "organized," and so on.
- Though these topics are abstract, each may be answered by a story or an example. Suppose you're responding to the "most difficult quality for a potential roommate" question. You recall your experiences in the dorm during a summer community service project, particularly the tension during the first week when your roomie wanted to party and you wanted to sleep. The quality you cite is a need for moderation, illustrated by the summer experience and its resolution. (The two of you decided to let loose on Friday and Saturday nights and to hit the hay at a reasonable hour during the rest of the week.)
- Regardless of your answer, remember to *interpret* your reality for the reader. Don't just describe or recount; *discuss.*

A variation of the "describe yourself with three words" essay focuses on an object (often a picture) of your choice. This sort of question may pop up in the short answers or in the essay section. For a full explanation of the "description and interpretation" structure, turn to Chapter 7. Also check out Figures 7-3 and 21-10 for additional examples.

Chapter 19

Describing Significant Strangers and Friends: Essays About Other People

In This Chapter

- Understanding how other people shape who you are
- Discussing friends and relatives
- Showing how strangers' lives affect your own
- Writing about fictional characters

I've always wanted to answer one particular college application question. Unfortunately, no one asked that question when I was writing my admission essays (not long enough ago to qualify for a slab of rock and a chisel, but close). Here goes:

> If you could have dinner with any figure, living or dead, who would it be and why?

My answer? The nineteenth-century British writer Jane Austen, hands down. She was capable of perceptive social criticism — actually, complete snottiness — but she also had good manners and common sense. How wonderful to sit in her dining room (still in existence in the village of Chawton, England) for a meal and a chance to shred the character of everyone in the neighborhood! The only drawback would be the certain knowledge that I was providing her with an opportunity to mock *me.*

You may not get the "ideal dinner companion" question either, but chances are at least one of your applications will ask about the people who have influenced you. In this chapter I tell you all the secrets of essay questions about others — which, like all admission essays, are really about the star of the show, you.

Defining Others' Influence: You Are Who You Know

If this were a book on nutrition, I'd probably tell you that "you are what you eat" (though according to that theory I should be Chinese by now, because that's my favorite cuisine). Nutrition aside, a good number of college admissions offices apparently believe that "you are who you know." Many applications, including the widely accepted common application, inquire in one way or another about a person who has had a significant influence on your life. Some want you to stay within the bounds of reality:

- Who speaks for your generation? What is he or she saying?
- What woman in your family do you most admire?
- Discuss how one particular teacher influenced your development.
- Describe a situation in which you had to work with a person who is different from yourself.

Other questions allow you to step into the realm of fantasy:

- Which person (alive or dead) would you like to interview and why?
- If you could work for a year with a non-political person who is not personally known to you, whom would you select? Why?
- If you could be anyone else for a day — a living, historical, or fictional figure — who would it be? Explain your reasons.

Before answering any of the "person who influenced you" questions, spend a few minutes thinking about the "significant others" in your life. The Personal Inventory in the appendix is a good place to start, but you may also garner some candidates from a review of the family photo albums or, in the case of historical or literary figures, from a trip to the library or a session on the Internet. When you have some possible subjects, answer these questions about each one. (If the question addresses a real person, stick to the facts. If the question allows you to daydream, send your imagination into the arena.)

- When and how did you first become aware of this person?
- What qualities or accomplishments do you associate with him or her?
- What would your life be like *without* the presence of this person? This last exercise in *subtraction* should give you a good definition of what this person has *added* to your life.

- List several significant occasions with him or her — times when you interacted in a special way. How did you feel during these interactions? What did you learn?
- List some normal activities that you shared with this person. How did you feel during these interactions? What did you learn?

By the time you've finished "auditioning" several possible subjects, someone should emerge as a nifty topic. As you make the final selection, follow one key principle:

> The essay is not really about Mr. or Ms. X; it's about *you* in relation to Mr. or Ms. X.

Remember: You're looking for a subject that gives you ample room for discussion of *your* character, development, or values. After you've chosen your subject, the hard part is over. Now all you have to do is write the essay! The next section of this chapter, "Writing about Friends and Relatives," shows you how to tackle real people who are or have been a presence in your life. "Relating Strangers' Lives to Your Own," also in this chapter, guides you through essays about current or historical figures — people you know from the media or from textbooks but have never personally met. The final section of this chapter, "Entering the Fictional Universe," tells you how to write about literary and other imaginary characters.

Writing about Friends and Relatives

When my son was about two feet tall, my husband — all six feet of him — stooped down to chat with his offspring. My son immediately bent his little body into the same position, squeezing himself into 1½ feet of space! I think of that moment whenever I ponder the power of parental influence. Little kids tend to model themselves on the big figures in their lives, in a literal sense. As children grow, peers, even if they're younger, gain importance. Your task, in writing about a friend or relative, is to define the influence of that figure in your life.

Choosing the "big figure" in your life

Who changed your life? Parents are an obvious choice, but siblings, teachers, friends, and neighbors are all possibilities. As you take inventory of the "big figures" in your life, keep in mind that the figure you choose may have had a positive *or* a negative influence. If you go with a negative, be sure to emphasize the positive aspects of the relationship. For example, I once read an essay written by a student whose father was in prison. She candidly explained what he had done wrong and went on to discuss the strength she needed to grow up in his absence. She discussed her own values — quite different from his — and her attempt to come to terms with his mistakes. Her conclusion emphasized the love she felt for her dad, despite his flaws, and her determination to create a productive life for herself. A great essay, emphasizing the good that she had extracted from a bad situation.

If you write about someone who has made your life more difficult, take care not to indulge in whining. Even though the student I described in the preceding paragraph had good reason to complain, she was quite matter-of-fact about her experiences. Her father was in prison, and her family struggled with many hardships. The same point — I made something of myself despite my relatives' behavior — would come across quite differently if her difficulties had involved only overly strict curfew-setters or a little brother who habitually peeked into her diary.

Sometimes a group, not a single person, is a good subject for your essay. Check out Figure 19-1, a student essay describing a summer construction job. (Figure 19-1 is a real essay, but I changed the names for privacy.) The author wrote about his fellow "hardhats," using two or three paragraphs of details about their working conditions to convey the reality of their daily lives. He supplemented the general description with a couple of specifics about various workers:

> Danny — shop steward with degree in sociology
>
> Mr. G. — union boss, warned against dropping out of school
>
> Jake — laborer with a wife and three children to support, worried about car payments and rent

Both elements — the general paragraphs about the construction site and working conditions as well as the thumbnail sketches of three individuals — combine to form a complete picture. Lacking either of the two elements, the essay would be much less effective.

Selecting the scene

After you've decided the *who,* you've also got to define the *how* and *when* of the essay. You can't accomplish your goal — to show the influence of Mr./Ms. X on your life and character — with a bunch of general statements such as the following:

> Mrs. Gabble inspired me to become a better person.
>
> Chick's friendship meant a lot to me.

I never understood heroism until I met Aunt Molly.

No matter what, I can rely on my mother.

On an absolute learning curve, a summer construction job paralleled in importance the fundamental learning unique to kindergarten. "Construction 101" provided an education that was not available in the high school curriculum. I had Chemistry, yet I did not understand the properties of cement. Physics did not yield a clue about proper lifting techniques. Latin, the mother of all Romance languages, did not provide the verbal insight for the communication skills I would require for this job. My baseball cap was replaced with a hard hat; Nikes gave way to steel-toed boots. As I began to learn just how much I did not know about life, my work in construction superseded book knowledge as well as most of my social experiences. Unlike tinker toys and Legos, no building took place in my comfort zone.

Educators and government officials still believe that the most effective means of education is through the study of books in the classroom. I was about to learn that some important facets of my education would come outside the classroom and from people who by no means would be identified as teachers by our society. I would be in a different world. Many of the luxuries that I took for granted were not available on the construction site. A brown bag lunch consumed in a stifling car made the high school cafeteria seem gourmet. There were alternatives, however; undercooked, rubbery hot dogs from the local vendor or a well-balanced meal of potato chips and lukewarm, bland pizza from the aluminized "roach coach." Health Department licenses were nowhere to be found. The "porto-potty" became a fact of life.

I was the youngest and the newest addition to the site, the lowest man on the totem pole. One of my assigned, daily tasks was to carry ten gallons of water up the four completed stories of the high rise we were building. Another responsibility was loading the portable receptacles onto trucks so they could be relieved of a week's worth of waste. I overcame such grueling physical demands and persevered for two months. In so doing, I began to realize that I was taking home more than a sore back, aching muscles, and a paycheck. My mother saw my battered body and urged me to quit; I saw a glimmer of new confidence with which to face the challenges of life.

My summer in construction provided a unique admixture of social interaction and sweat. The construction site with its massive, poured-concrete infrastructure represented a microcosm of the construction industry with its unionism, nepotism, and a hierarchy of trades. There were complex relationships built into the diverse interactions among shop stewards, foremen, union representatives, and tradesmen. I began to understand the concerns of the financial backers as well as the supervisory, college-educated engineers and architects. Advancement was not necessarily linked to a strong work ethic, experience, advanced training, or even intelligence. Rather it was at the behest of the steward or union boss. Although subtle, issues of race, class, and ethnicity seemed to have relevance in the hierarchy. Life was not always fair.

As the weeks passed, the nameless men with hardhats became real people. Danny, a shop steward who had a degree in sociology, was anxious for me to curtail my career as a laborer. Otherwise, he warned, I'd end up like him. Mr. G., the union boss, promised me that I was going to work so hard that dropping out of school would never be an option. Jake, a laborer, had a wife and three children to support. Most of our conversations focused upon his having to make car and rent payments. For these men, regardless of their position, life revolved around a time clock and an hourly wage.

Figure 19-1: An essay that discusses the significant role a group has played in the writer's life.

During my final week on the job, I had mixed emotions about leaving the site and my co-workers. I would no longer have to get up at five-thirty a.m. and return home too tired to socialize with my friends. However, I would have to say goodbye to the people I had grown to respect. Their tasks were physically demanding and often not personally gratifying, yet they did not complain. My co-workers reported to work every day, regardless of the sweltering heat or the pouring rain. There were no sick days. They were family men who took their responsibilities seriously. Each of them had developed a skill which did not come from book learning, but rather from careful observation, application, and practice. They took pride in their workmanship and in knowing that their particular contribution to the building project was essential for its completion.

Obviously, "Construction 101" did not have a formal curriculum. Working with men whose backgrounds, skills, training, and goals were different from mine; adapting to the physical and psychological stresses in an unfamiliar setting, and not quitting provided me with the confidence and insight that allows me to meet the unanticipated challenges and disappointments of life's curriculum.

Figure 19-1: An essay that discusses the significant role a group has played in the writer's life.

All these statements may be true, but they ask your reader to trust your judgment and accept what you say *without any proof.* Lacking specific examples, the reader has no basis on which to make a decision. A much better strategy is to present a little scene, the sort that might appear in a short story or a novel. (However, everything in *your* scene must be true.) To zero in on the best scene, play a mental videotape of memories. Watch yourself interacting with Mr./Ms. X. Choose moments in which the influence of Mr./Ms. X was readily apparent. When you write the essay, remember to include all the ingredients that make your scene come alive — action, dialogue, and description. (Check out Chapter 18 for tips on writing a vivid scene.) Also remember to leave room for interpretation. The next section of this chapter, "Interpreting the influence," shows you how to do so.

Turn back to Figure 12-1, in Chapter 12, for a fine example of a scene that presents the author's relationship with his brother. The description of the brother's behavior serves a double purpose: It illuminates the family dynamics and clarifies the author's loyalty and priorities. Figure 19-2 is another example of a scene that focuses primarily on family members. The student author, mourning his grandmother, shows us a late night session at the piano during which he plays a few tunes and reminisces about "Nona." Although the scene covers only a few minutes in "real time," the author weaves in memories of his grandmother, facts about his mother's childhood, and thoughts about his parents and brother. Like Figure 12-1, this essay also spotlights family values.

It was quite late and I still couldn't sleep. I lay in bed staring at the ceiling and watching headlights from the cars in the street below make their way across my blinds. Rather than tossing and turning any longer, I got up and felt my way through the dark hallway toward the living room. The yellow moonlight danced on the cold wooden floor and the few city night stars twinkled over my piano's soft white keys. On the dining room table a few cups and plates remained; all week visitors had come to pay their respects and finally the last couple had gone. I tried to replay my last encounter with Nona just a few days before, to remember how she spoke of meeting my grandfather in heaven and how I, with a lump in my throat, told her one last time, "Je t'adore, Nona."

My fingers lingered in the highest register of the piano singing a dreamy melody that mirrored what I was feeling. I longed to hug my frail Grandma, but I imagined my grandparents meeting again in heaven. I remembered the black and white photographs of my mother and her family growing up in Cairo. Nona used to tell me stories of how they were driven out of Egypt because they were a Jewish minority. I remembered the tears that filled her eyes as she painfully recounted the story of my grandfather's death. She explained to me that she had urged him to take a last-minute standby ticket to join the family for my Uncle Paul's birthday on a flight that never landed. My mother was only three years old and, consequently, grew up without a father; Nona always blamed herself.

I searched my memory for traces of her perfume and all the while played out into the night. It felt good to play, even stumbling on discordant chords, I felt unrestrained as though I were a little boy again, rushing with tears into my mother's arms. And as I took amused comfort in thinking that my Nona and Grandpa might be dancing to my melody, I heard a faint whimper from behind me.

"That's so beautiful," said my mother through gentle tears. She sat down on the living room sofa to listen and I remembered how she had arranged for me my first piano lesson and how she always sat behind me as I practiced, even how I occasionally got frustrated and asked her not to. But now I put everything into her favorite piece of music and let go. I wondered if my brother was also unable to sleep, and if he was lying awake in his bed, listening: saying goodbye in his own way. Maybe my dad was thinking of his own warm, loving mother and the feasts she cooks up for us every Rosh Hashanah. And it was sad, and it was beautiful, as all our emotions lingered in the hallway. Not much else mattered, not that school was about to start in just a couple days, nor that, with my brother leaving for school, we wouldn't be living as a family, that nothing would be the same. I played to keep our home warm under the lonesome moonlit night.

And when I reached the smorzando (dying away) cadenza and everything became quiet for a moment, my mother kissed me and with a smile and dried up tears told me, "Je t'adore, mon tresor."

Figure 19-2: An essay that sets the scene around family members.

If one scene won't do the job, you may want to create a "collage" of moments during which the influence of your subject is evident. One of my favorite "collages" appears in *String Too Short to Be Saved* (published by David R. Godine), an autobiography by poet Donald Hall about his boyhood summers on his grandparents' farm. In one chapter Hall describes a family friend, Washington Woodward, with several sharp verbal snapshots, including the following:

> removing rocks from fields (his hobby)
>
> eating only one type of food until his supply was exhausted and then moving on to another (ten days of canned peas followed by a week of tuna fish, for example)
>
> collecting and straightening used nails

These and other such scenes feature young Donald's interactions with Woodward, as well as the boy's reactions *to* Woodward. The piece clearly reveals the author's admiration for Woodward's strength and perseverance, but it also shows the terrible waste of Woodward's efforts. No one scene could accomplish these two tasks.

Another strategy is to focus on an object related to the person who is the subject of the essay. Figure 19-3 is a student essay about a saxophone once used by the author's grandfather. The author describes the instrument in detail, but he is really writing about his grandfather and father and their feelings about family. Needless to say, the author's great love for his family also shines through.

Interpreting the influence

Why do you want your reader to meet Mr./Ms. X? When the admissions counselor finishes reading your essay, he or she should have an answer to that question. You can make sure the reader gets the point in any one of several ways:

- In the introduction or conclusion, state the main idea in a couple of sentences. For a good illustration of this technique, sneak a peak at the essay in Figure 19-1, which brings everything together in the last paragraph.
- If you've written a scene, let the point come across in dialogue. But *don't* stray into fiction. Quote only what people actually said. Check out the ending of Figure 12-1, in Chapter 12, for an example of this technique.

- Weave the interpretive material throughout, in narrative and/or dialogue. The reader has to work a little harder to figure out what you're trying to say, but if you do a good job, the extra effort is worthwhile. In Figure 19-2, for instance, notice how the author cleverly slips in interpretive statements in several different spots, including:

  "...dreamy melody that mirrored what I was feeling." (paragraph 2)

  "unrestrained . . . amused comfort" (paragraph 3)

  "But now I put everything into her favorite piece and let go." (paragraph 4)

  "Not much else mattered." (paragraph 4)

  "We wouldn't be living as a family." (paragraph 4)

  The author doesn't say — and doesn't have to say — that he values his family and all that they've given him. The love he feels for them and from them shines through.

Relating Strangers' Lives to Your Own

Unless you hang out with people whose names regularly appear in bold type in the gossip columns, a question on your college application may require you to write about a stranger — someone whose job you'd like to have or a person whose accomplishments reflect your values. Writing about strangers may actually be easier for you than writing about someone you know. A measure of emotion is subtracted when the subject's a stranger, and you don't have to feel guilty for including a critical comment. (Nor do you have to worry about being grounded or losing car privileges because you dissed your own personal Authority Figure.)

Before you choose Mr./Ms. X as the subject of your essay, consider the goal of the question. If you're asked about a life switch ("Who would you like to be?" "Whose job would you like to have?" and the like), the admissions office is interested in your career plans and interests. Be careful to select a figure that will illustrate your future plans or current passion. (Not *that* kind of passion! I'm talking about *hobbies.*) Questions about more casual meetings ("Whom would you like to interview?" or "Whom would you like to meet?") give you more leeway. The subject's career may be an element in your choice, or you may select someone whose values match your own, even if you would never dream of following in his or her footsteps.

Where it was once shiny, it is now tarnished. In the past, it made music. Now it simply makes noise. It was once exercised daily by a professional, but now it is practiced on by an amateur. Formerly, it was used to entertain and make people happy. Now it serves as a means to remember.

My father tells me that he was a great man, a caring husband, and a wonderful musician. I never really knew him, however, as he was disabled by Parkinson's Disease when I was very young. Grandpa's life, as I understand it, revolved around his job. As the co-president of a musical entertainment company, he had many responsibilities. This meant that he was never home on weekends. From Thursday night to early Monday morning, there was always a wedding, a society gala, or a business party to play. The rest of the week was spent at the office, meeting with prospective clients, auditioning musicians, and making contacts with party planners at hotels and country clubs. With a wife, a widowed mother, and two children to support, my grandfather had to meet many economic demands. Unfortunately, his success in the music field limited his ability to be, in the conventional sense, a family man.

When he is not at work or spending time with his family, my father can often be found exercising his fingers at the piano that sits in our living room. Music and family have been and will be forever joined in his mind. As a result, my sister and I were encouraged to play an instrument from an early age. Neither of us enjoyed the piano, the instrument of choice. Practicing was a chore that prevented us from enjoying other activities. We developed an utter distaste for the piano. However, our parents urged us to continue. Much to my father's dismay, my sister quit. Having grown tired of the piano, I would have followed my older sibling had it not been for a wonderful gift.

When my grandfather passed away, I was given his Selmer Marc VI tenor saxophone. I was told many stories about his musical career and the amazing things he did with this horn. Despite the death of his dad and his career in medicine, my father has continued to perform on club dates. With this sax, he hoped that I would one day accompany him on a "gig."

Although overwhelmed by the gift and excited about the prospects of joining my father on a club date, I was never eager to practice or perform. Originally I thought my lack of interest was the result of my early experience with the piano. I simply viewed music and practicing as punishment. With considerable introspection, I now believe my reluctance stemmed from something else.

Every time I looked at the horn, I saw the tarnished brass on the bell and the trunk. My grandpa spent so much time playing that the sweat from his hands penetrated the once glistening finish. The unsettling images of my father as a boy competing with this instrument for his father's attention disturbed me. Because my father has always praised my grandfather, I was unable to allow myself to feel anything but affection for him; conflicting thoughts focused on music, and, more specifically, my grandfather's saxophone.

Perhaps it is maturation that now allows me to play every day. With persistence and focus, I will learn all the songs in his repertoire. When summer arrives, I will once again accompany my father on club dates, but my former apathy will be replaced with enthusiasm.

Music is still an important part of my family. It once served as a means to build a relationship between my father and grandfather. Now it will help to sustain and strengthen the strong bond between my father and me. I am beginning to realize just how complex relationships can be. My grandfather played his hand as best he could. My father, with a different score and a different drummer, plays on. I hopefully synthesize what went before, learn as much as I can, and compose a new score.

Figure 19-3: An essay that focuses on an object as a way of discussing a significant person.

Here are a few other guidelines for a "stranger" essay:

- Choose someone or something that you know fairly well as the topic of your essay. If you're just vaguely familiar with the figure or job you're writing about, the resulting essay will be, well, vague. For example, I personally would choose to be Jane Austen for a day, just to experience the reality of the world that I've entered only through her novels. I'd like to sit at her little round writing table and watch the village characters pass by the drawing room window. I could write the Austen essay because I've read the novels and several books about her life. I've even visited her house! (Yes, I'm a groupie for a dead writer. I admit it.) I'm also curious about the life of Bill Gates, but I know very little about him, beyond the fact that he runs a powerful company. My lame, general discussion of Gates' job would never make the grade.
- Don't hesitate to discuss both the advantages and disadvantages of the life of the subject you've selected. Continuing with my Jane Austen example, I would be reluctant to accept the restrictive female roles that were a constant in Austen's world, though I suppose I could manage for a day.
- Be honest, even though you're writing an essay that is essentially a fantasy. If I were writing about taking over Austen's life for a day, I would certainly acknowledge my limitations: I can't write comic social satire at her lofty level (actually, at any level) and I haven't a clue about village etiquette. If your essay is about the President of the United States, don't ignore the reality of Congress, the Constitution, party donors, and other factors that are part of the President's reality.
- Don't go overboard on factual background information. Assume that the reader is educated (because the reader of your essay *is* educated). Do a little research if you like — checking, for example, birth dates or other statistics. But the essay shouldn't sound like a school report. The admissions office won't appreciate an "I looked this stuff up and I'm going to use it if it kills me" attitude.
- Remember the admissions committee will expect to learn about your values from this (and every) essay. *The "why" portion of the question is crucial to the essay's success.* Don't skimp on the details. Take a look at these examples:

  TOO GENERAL STATEMENT: If I were the Prime Minister of Antarctica, I could do a lot of good.

  BETTER, MORE SPECIFIC STATEMENT: If I were Prime Minister of Antarctica, I'd protect the continent's ecosystem by pressing my fellow heads of state to sign a treaty limiting emissions that contribute to the greenhouse effect. I've worked on the global warming issue as president of my school's Ecology Club, and the Prime Minister's job would give me a wider scope and greater power to make a difference.

> ANOTHER TOO GENERAL STATEMENT: I'd like to interview Olive Oilier, the star player of the newly formed Women's Professional Football League, because her job is interesting.
>
> ANOTHER MORE SPECIFIC STATEMENT: I'd like to interview Olive Oilier, the star player of the newly formed Women's Professional Football League. Though I myself would never want to play such a rough contact sport (plus, I have little athletic talent), I am interested in people who go beyond the expectations of society. I'd ask Ms. Oilier if she felt pressure while she was growing up to conform to the traditional definition of femininity.

The essays responding to the "stranger you admire" questions may be structured as events, surveys, or descriptions. (Check out Chapter 7 for the lowdown on various structures.) Read the essay in Figure 19-4, in which the author (a real student, whose name I changed for privacy) describes a meeting with Franz Liszt, an important musical figure. The twist is that the event is totally imaginary! No lies here; the reader is tipped off to the fantasy in the first paragraph, where the author declares that he is taking the subway to meet a "19th century pianist from Hungary." Though this event never took place, the essay reveals the author's attitude towards Liszt and towards music itself. It also reveals the writer's original, creative mind. Notice the mixture of dialogue, action, thoughts, and interpretation — a real winner!

Entering the Fictional Universe

When I'm immersed in a good book, I often feel that I've stepped between the covers and entered an alternate reality. A great film also pulls me out of myself. I may not be on the screen or between the covers of the novel, but if the artwork is vivid enough, I can certainly imagine the characters' lives. That's exactly what some college applications ask you to do, in questions such as these:

- What character or characters from fiction, film, theater, or television intrigued you or taught you something?
- Describe a character in fiction or in a creative work that had an influence on you and explain that influence.

"42nd Street. Grand Central," announced a muffled speaker as the subway car screeched to a halt, its doors sliding open. "Change here for Metro North." A crowd of passengers enveloped me, their heat striking forth in one gargantuan wave. With no way to speed up the pace of this herd as it pushed its way up the grimy stairs and onto the station's main floor, I glanced nervously at my wristwatch. I couldn't believe that this 19th century pianist from Hungary would arrive before I did. Finally in the terminal, I searched the crowd for his face. My piano teacher had told me to look for a long-haired young man holding a composer's baton. If it came down to choosing between two men, he had added, "He might be wearing a cape." There he was, wearing the cape indeed…green velvet!

"Mr. Liszt?" I asked without too much risk of mistaking him for someone else.

"Jean Jacques, I presume, splendid to meet you," he replied shaking my hand.

"So, Sir, I-I mean Mr. Liszt, how was your trip?"

"Rather excellent actually, they played my 'Danse Macabre' in the terminal," he said with delight as he winked at a female passer-by. I recalled that he's said to have been the rock-star of his generation!

"Jean, why don't we stop in one of these cafés and chat, shall we?" he said, strutting into Starbucks. "Two café lattes!" he ordered as we sat out on the terrace, overlooking endless waves of hurried, flustered people, I myself emanating an air of anxiety.

"So, why so uptight, kid?" he asked. I was ready to explain that I had always been musical, having performed on guitar and bass, but never before on piano.

"Well, there's this recital tomorrow, my first ever, and, it's one of your 'Consolations,' num-"

"Number 3?" he interrupted his green eyes illuminating.

"Yes!" How did he know? "How did you know?"

"That's my favorite," he said gently. Slowly, he turned with a smile and gazed ahead. "Jean Jacques, do you know what I was feeling when I played that piece?" he asked. I shook my head. "Exactly!" he looked back at me, "Just as I don't know what Duke Ellington intended me to feel in playing one of his pieces." Duke Ellington?… nevermind. "Jean Jacques, look at these people in front of you," he continued. I listened intently. "They're not thinking about much at all right now, are they? The next few hours of their lives will most likely be all about catching planes and attending the meetings of tomorrow and the day after that and so on: meaningless. Like you, right now, concerned about the recital, about your future. There will be other planes, Jean. That's what the music's about."

Content with his explanation he sipped his drink. I nodded and pretended that everything was clear to me, disregarding the fact that there were no planes in Grand Central, and even the fact that I was drinking coffee with this legendary Romantic composer, but then shook my head in confusion.

"Jean Jacques," he raised an eyebrow at me, "Look, my boy, look again." I did look again, but now I could see only a stream of flushed faces, tired eyes, and heavy steps: all became clear.

Figure 19-4: An example of an essay that discusses an imaginary meeting with a historical figure.

Figure 19-4: An example of an essay that discusses an imaginary meeting with a historical figure.

"So what you're saying is that there is no time in music only the rhythm of your heartbeat, that music is meant to be scrutinized but its beauty should inspire and provide enchantment." I got more and more worked up. "You're saying that music isn't about hitting the right keys but rather singing that dolcissimo section from my soul. That's what'll overwhelm them with emotion; that's what will knock 'em dead. If I feel it, they'll feel it. If I see that pink sunset on the desolate beach or that longing gaze into a lover's eyes, they'll see it too." I was on my feet now and preaching to the whole café; the herd had stopped running, they put down their belongings and stood listening, mesmerized, spellbound. "That's what gives meaning to music, it's the sublime, endless, lingering, standstill of time, of fear, and when you're in the music, nothing can touch you. To treasure each moment is the most natural thing in the world and, perhaps, the most beautiful. That's what the music's about, each and every second of it…right?" I asked as I played the last few measures of the piece. He smiled a proud smile, tears in his eyes, as he listened to me sing that melody…dolcissimo! And as the crowd ripped into applause, there was nothing left to settle, except, perhaps, the check.

The techniques described in the previous section of this chapter, "Relating Strangers' Lives to Your Own," may apply to the "fictional character" essay as well. A few additional points help you tackle this sort of essay:

- If you're writing about a character who is likely to be widely known to a university audience — Shakespeare's Hamlet or Yoda from the *Star Wars* films — don't include a long list of identifying factors. Do cite the elements of the character that appeal to you. Check out these examples:

  UNNECESSARY INFORMATION: Hamlet is the Prince of Denmark, returned from his university studies to find his father dead and his mother remarried. He knows that he must kill his father's murderer, but he can't act on this belief.

  RELEVANT INFORMATION: The title character of Shakespeare's *Hamlet* intrigues me. For much of the play he ponders the issue of revenge, struggling with the morality of killing the murderer of his father. When he cannot act, he delves into his own personality and questions the meaning of his own existence. I like the fact that Hamlet is a thinker; he takes nothing lightly and perceives the complexity of human motivation.

  See the difference? The first example gives background, but the second interprets the character.

- If you're writing about an obscure creative work — perhaps a film one of your classmates made or a short story that came out last month — anchor the reader by providing a few sentences of plot summary and character description. Then go on to discuss the aspects of the character that appeal to you.

- Always use present tense when writing about literature or other creative works. Hence, "Hamlet dies," not "Hamlet died."

Chapter 20

Responding to Essay Questions in the Subject Areas

In This Chapter

- Reacting to a quotation or discussing literature
- Pondering philosophical or scientific ideas
- Explaining your views on art
- Writing about historical events or current issues

An admission essay is supposed to reveal facets of your character. But you can turn the tables on the admissions committee by examining the questions they've chosen for hints about *their* deepest desires. Some essay topics, such as "What is your favorite required reading?" and the like, tell you that the counselors are fans of the world's best subject, English. (In case you haven't figured it out by now, I'm an English teacher.) Others indicate that the committee has at least one frustrated scientist or philosopher in its ranks: "Will science or religion have more relevance in the twenty-first century?" or "What technical invention has the potential to change humanity itself?" A couple of topics display the committee's artistic ambitions, including "What reflects idiosyncratic beauty?" and "Design a play area representing the 'thrill of the unknown.'"

The subject-area questions are less common than the topics I discuss in Chapter 18 ("tell us about yourself") and Chapter 19 ("tell us about a significant person"). Nevertheless, if your application contains a subject-area essay, the tips in this chapter will help you achieve maximum success.

We Really Wanted to Teach English: Answering Literature and Writing Questions

Ah! My favorite field! I love questions that tap into literature or creative writing. These essays tend to fall into three categories: the "favorite book" or "reading list" topic, the creative writing sample, and the poem or quotation analysis. The English-oriented questions roam around a bit, depending upon the application. Some schools place them in the short answer section, and others make them full-length essay topics. The helpful hints in this section may be applied to either situation. Chapter 21 provides additional detail on squeezing everything you need to say into a brief response.

Discussing books

The "book" questions are an attempt to identify what you read and what you think about after you've read it. Questions in this vein include:

- What books have you read for pleasure?
- What is your favorite required reading? Why?
- Contribute a book to the school reading list. Tell us what you would choose and why.
- Name the five best books you ever read, in order. Tell us why you've given priority to the first book on your list.
- Name six books or articles you've read recently. Choose one, telling us why you read it and how it was significant to you.

When writing about books and reading lists, your first stop should be the bookshelves in your home and the public or school library. Browse around for a few moments, pencil or handheld computer ready. Every time you see a book you enjoyed, jot down the title and author. Flip through the chapters and read the blurb on the book jacket to remind yourself of the contents. Don't stop until you have a dozen possibilities. Later, narrow the field by circling those that have special appeal or significance to you. Before you make the final cut, take a few minutes to brainstorm about each title. (Turn to Chapter 6 for an explanation of several techniques guaranteed to unearth your best ideas.)

Don't even *think* about choosing a book that you haven't read. Admissions counselors are professional educators — perhaps former teachers and *definitely* former students. They know when someone is blowing smoke into their eyes, and they've probably read tons of book summaries online or in those little study-aid paperbacks. If they suspect that you've taken a shortcut or chosen a title that is beyond your ability in hopes of impressing them, they've learned something important about you — something that will undoubtedly hurt your chances for admission. Better to go with a title you know and love, regardless of level, than to pretend that you've read a scholarly work.

After you decide on a topic, keep these points in mind:

- Your answer should state the title and author of the work, how old you were when you read it, and why the book mattered to you. If it still has an impact today, explain its effect on you.
- If you're writing about a non-fiction book or article, briefly mention the important points, or at least the points you related to. Don't waste space recounting lots of facts. You're not taking notes for a test; you're discussing the book in relation to your own life, values, and ideas.
- Don't retell the plot of any literary work. Simply refer to the events, providing enough information so that the reader may understand your point. If the book is a well-known classic, don't bother giving background information. Explain a bit more about obscure works.
- In writing about literature, use present tense. Romeo *loves* (not *loved*) Juliet, because whenever the play is read or enacted, the drama unfolds anew.
- "Book" questions are not English literature tests. The university is interested in your writing skills, true, but more interested in how you relate to the work. If you're discussing *Of Mice and Men,* for example, don't go off on a scholarly tangent about the symbolism of the dog's death in relation to a particular school of literary criticism. Instead, concentrate on your connection to the novel, seen in this example:

  Too scholarly and impersonal: The dog dies because he is no longer productive. The lives of the ranch hands, Steinbeck implies, are similarly expendable. As critic I. Noitall commented, "The 'I-Thou' nexus of communication . . . blah blah blah blah.'"

  Better, personal version: I was particularly moved by the death of the dog. What sort of society tosses "useless" members away? I ask myself these questions as I chat with my great-grandmother. At 90 she can no longer work, but her wisdom and her love for my family is a treasure. In the world of Steinbeck's novel, she would be considered expendable, just as the dog is.

- Do be specific about the effect of the book on your worldview or actions, as in this example:

  Too general: After I read Steinbeck's novel *Of Mice and Men,* I became interested in social justice.

  Better, specific version: After I read Steinbeck's novel, I volunteered at our town's homeless shelter. Each "client" who came in became a possible Lennie or George to me.

Writing creatively

Of course, all writing is creative, as you know from reading the extremely imaginative but fact-filled (she said demurely) *For Dummies* books. But some writing is *officially* deemed "creative," including these classic questions:

- Write page 217 of your autobiography.
- Translate a visual work of art into literature.
- Describe the view from your window.
- What is an expressive silence?

For these topics, take your spirit out of its tight shoes and let your mind run barefoot in the meadow. (See? Just thinking about this sort of writing ignites my imagination.) Have some fun! The colleges that place these questions on their applications want to see your creative side.

Creativity all bottled up? The first thing you need to do is *calm down.* The imaginative part of your brain shuts down when you tense up. So go for a walk, wash the dishes, or turn to some other mindless, physical activity. Then try that essay again. (The techniques in Chapter 6 will also help you uncork your imagination.)

A few — very few — guidelines do apply to creative questions:

- Just because you're being creative doesn't mean you should ignore the question. If they've asked for a slice of your autobiography, don't send in a blank sheet of paper (as one student planned to do) because it represented his view of the meaninglessness of all individual lives. If they ask for an autobiography, they want an autobiography, not a stationery sample.
- Keep to the word limit, if stated, and follow the specified format ("on a separate sheet," "in the blank space below," and so on).

- Show the finished product to someone you trust. (Chapter 4 explains what kind of help is "legal" and what you must avoid.) Ask the reader to summarize the impressions or ideas your creative piece conveys. If the reader's comments match your intention, fine. If not, consider adjusting your work. For example, suppose your piece entitled "A sparrow falls" is, you believe, a serious statement about the nature of life and death. If the trusted reader laughs and comments that he's never seen a better parody of artistic snobbery, you may want to rewrite.
- Even in a creative work, grammar and spelling rules apply unless you have a valid *and readily understandable* reason for breaking them. In general, geniuses can get away with coining new words (Joyce's *Finnegans Wake* is a good example), but we ordinary mortals can't.
- Remember that the committee is reading *tons* of material. Be kind to their eyes and stick to legible formats and fonts. An essay about the invention of the microscope scratched into a grain of rice is clever, but your reader may sweep it away (or cook it) without reading a single word.

Bottom line: You can be as creative as you wish, within a few, sensible limits. Go for it!

Reacting to a poem or a quotation

You've probably answered the "react to a poem or quotation" question a million times during your educational career. I've asked a fair number of these questions myself on literature tests. The application blank prints a passage (usually, though not always, an excerpt from a longer work) and asks you to discuss or explain it. Some of the passages are strictly "English" oriented, and others may fall into the category of history or philosophy. Many are from famous people, at times an alumnus or professor of the institution. (They're bragging a little, hoping to impress you.) Here are a few illustrations:

> In his famous novel *Animal Farm,* George Orwell wrote that "All animals are created equal, but some are more equal than others." Do you agree? Is this statement relevant?
>
> Pearl Buck wrote, "Do right in spite of feelings." Discuss.
>
> According to Elizabeth Cady Stanton, "Women's discontent increases in exact proportion to her development." Do you agree or disagree? Relate the quotation to your own future.
>
> In response to the poem printed below, choose something worth paying attention to and describe it.

In this sort of essay, the college is attempting to elicit ideas and judge the way you think. They want to know whether you understand the question and whether you can discuss the topic in depth. As you write the essay, remember these points:

- Don't research the life of the author or speaker and tuck those facts into your essay. The question addresses the passage, not the life of the speaker. For example:

  Bad idea: Elizabeth Cady Stanton was a famous crusader for women's rights. She said that "women's discontent increases in exact proportion. . . ."

  Why it's bad: They know that Elizabeth Cady Stanton was a famous crusader for women's rights. That's why they're quoting her. Just get to the point!

- Don't discuss the literary techniques displayed in the passage. They want to know what you think about the content, not the style. Check out this example:

  Bad idea: In her poem Dickinson employs personification when she writes, "Because I could not stop for Death/He kindly stopped for me."

  Why it's bad: Sounds like you learned something in poetry class that you're desperate to show off. Dump the literary terminology and talk about the ideas of the poem.

- You may bring personal experience or narrative in your answer, as long as you tie those remarks to the passage. Don't assume that the reader will instinctively relate your sentences on the thrill of winning the badminton tournament to Orwell's comments on equality. State the connection.

- If the poem or passage is very long, you may focus on one part of it, though you should take care to select an important idea, not a detail.

No matter what, be sure to present your own ideas and/or experiences in your essay. You're not writing a school report; you're writing about yourself.

We Stare into Space a Lot: Responding to Philosophy and Science Topics

Okay, I apologize for the stereotype. I know that some philosophers are extremely practical (though I did see someone with an American Philosophical Association nametag walk right into a coffee shop wall one day). A certain speculative quality clings to people in these fields, and that speculation is evident in some application questions. Check these out:

- We are not here to worship what is known, but to question it. Comment.
- In the age of electronic media, what is the role of the printed word? What will be its role in the future?
- Will science or religion have more relevance in the twenty-first century?
- Everything should be made as simple as possible, but not simpler. Do you agree or disagree with this statement? Why?
- How has a scientific or mathematical theory affected your thinking?
- Is the study of history important to a scientist? What about the reverse?
- Design an experiment to determine whether toads can hear.
- What technical innovation has the potential to change humanity itself?

As you see, you're not going to get a technical question like "What is the atomic weight of marshmallows?" or "Explain the image of Plato's cave." College admission applications tend to be more general. Here are some tips on how to answer scientific and philosophical questions:

- Most of these questions pop up in the optional section of the application. That is, each is one of several alternatives. Don't select one of these questions unless you actually have something to say. If you haven't thought at all about the issue — or, if you've come up dry after pondering it for hours — go with a different topic.
- Don't write an encyclopedia article or a book report. If you've read something relevant to the question, you may certainly cite it, but don't go overboard on the facts/figures/experts' opinions. The admissions committee wants to know what *you* think.
- The admissions committee also wants to know that you *do* think, preferably deeply. Consider all aspects of the question before writing your essay. Imagine, for example, that you're commenting on the role of the printed word in the twenty-first century. Check out these statements:

  Bad statement with little thought: The book is over, finished, kaput. In my century, the twenty-first, everyone who is anyone is online, and everything will soon be online also. I can get anything I want with my computer, so paper is irrelevant.

  What's missing: Complexity! Not everyone has a computer. Technology changes by the minute. So what happens to data stored on out-dated machines? Will it be lost? And how will I read in the bathtub (my favorite place to immerse myself — sorry for the pun — in mystery novels)?

Beginning of a better statement: Although information technology has great advantages, its increasing use raises issues of class, economics, and personal preference. . . .

- You may support your ideas by describing personal experiences, but a simple narrative will not answer any of these questions. You need to create a reasoned, structured argument. (Check out Chapter 7 for an explanation of some useful structures for your essay.)
- Take a stand, assuming that you *have* a definite viewpoint. Of course, if you see merit in both sides of an issue, explain the pros and cons of each position.

If you're applying to a specialized school (a science institute, perhaps), your application will probably be read only by professionals in the field. You may refer to advanced concepts and use sophisticated terminology. If you're applying to a non-specialized undergraduate institution, stay away from jargon specific to one field of study and write for a general, though well-educated, reader.

We're Paint-Stained but Happy: Expounding on Artistic Topics

If you're hoping to spend a couple of years with people sporting splashes of Burnt Ochre and Titanium White — in other words, art majors — your application may well contain an essay about (this will shock you) art. Topics in this vein include:

- Choose a person, object, or site within ¼ mile of your house and interpret it from three perspectives.
- Life is short; art is long. Discuss.
- Describe how a work of art (music, dance, visual, and so forth) influenced you.
- What films do you like? Why?
- Translate a literary work into the visual medium and explain your rationale.

If you panic every time you step away from the easel or tripod, relax. The main selling point for your application to an arts program is likely to be a portfolio of your work — slides of drawings and paintings, tapes of your film or dance performance, and similar material. But the essay can help your application. An arts essay gives you a chance to show the school that you know how to create something with words and that you have the ability to be logical as well as creative. As you respond to an artistic question, keep these points in mind:

- Creativity rocks. Unlock your inner creator (see Chapter 6 to find out how) and allow your imagination to dominate.
- Spend a little extra time outlining your essay before you write. Chapter 8 explains outlining techniques to ensure that the logical links are clear to the non-Picassos out there.
- Art has a specialized vocabulary, and if you know it, you may use it. Just don't go overboard. You're not writing a library paper; you're writing an essay.
- Accent the personal, rather than the critical view. Suppose, for instance, that you're answering the first sample question in this section, which asks you to interpret a person, object, or site from three perspectives. You've picked an ancient Native American burial mound. The mound may be discussed as a work of landscape art, as a historical or cultural treasure, and as a tourist attraction. As you expound on each of these three perspectives, don't forget to include your own personal view — the deep emotion you felt upon encountering evidence of ancient life for the first time.

We Love Timelines: Discussing Historical or Current Events

Enjoy peering into the past or dissecting the daily newspaper? Then admission essays drawn from social studies topics are for you. In this section I take you through two different types — the found-everywhere "issue" essay and the less common historical event essay.

Writing an issue essay

The common application, a document accepted by more than 200 schools, includes this option:

> Discuss some issue of personal, local, national, or international concern and its importance to you.

Variations of that question appear on even more applications:

> Racial, ethnic, and religious divisions continue to trouble society. Based on your own experience, what hopes and fears do you hold for the future?

> Describe a current issue in your community or country or in the world and explain how you would resolve it.

The best answers to this "issue" essay question have two ingredients: facts about the issue and a discussion of your personal involvement or connection to the issue. The two elements do not need to be equal in length, but they must both be present.

For a great example of an issue essay, check out Figure 9-2 in Chapter 9, an essay discussing global warming. The student author gives basic information about the Kyoto Treaty limiting greenhouse gasses. He explains the positions on the treaty of the European Union and the United States. He talks about the probable effects of the treaty's enforcement and describes the campaign of a major environmental group to support the treaty. Finally, the author explains the actions of his club, the Junior Statesmen of America, regarding the issue. Another great issue essay is Figure 20-1, which discusses the plans of a major retailer to build a superstore in a small community. (For the sake of the student-author's privacy, I've changed the names of the store and community.) Notice the level of detail the writer provides:

- the effect of the development on the community (eviction of hundreds of residents, destruction of a soccer field, increased traffic and pollution)
- the actions of the protest group LIANA (lobbying) and the mayor (ignoring the lobbying and holding secret meetings)
- establishment of new student group (SANAD) to fight the development
- final result: withdrawal of support by mayor, company backing out
- change in author's thinking after this protest

Also notice the number of details that personally connect to the author:

- author has played baseball and soccer on the field
- his absence from the town because of college
- founding of student group
- writing to mayor
- ideas about corporate restraint
- political affiliation (Republican)
- changed views on government's role

When New Agriculture, Inc. claimed a large portion of downtown Holldale to build a superstore, much of the community was devastated. The developers wanted to evict hundreds of people from low-income housing, destroy two churches, and put a parking lot on a majestic green field which I had played soccer and baseball on in my youth. The implications of such a development would have been horrific: the fragile local streets would have been crushed, traffic would have increased at least threefold, pollution would have risen, and there would have been a large risk of flooding. Although I would be in college when the building would be erected, I could not sit idly by and let a heartless corporation destroy the lives of low-income households and alter the lifestyles of my family and friends.

Many of the community's adults formed LIANA, Local Inhabitants Against New Agriculture, and actively lobbied the local governments to stop the development. Unfortunately, the mayor was in charge of this type of zoning, and he frequently met with New Agriculture's lawyers privately and refused to divulge what had happened. He was adamant that the New Agriculture store be built, in spite of widespread disapproval among the citizens of New Park, Cypressmont, Hoponit, and Caryville.

After the mayor's local hearings, a poor excuse for public relations in which he scowled at elderly people who had lived in Holldale their entire lives and pleaded not to let a corporation destroy their town, I felt that there had to be some way that I could join the noble battle. Over the 2000-2001 Christmas vacation, I founded S.A.N.A.D., Students Against New Agriculture Development. As a student I wouldn't have much sway in the battle, since nobody would care about what a minor, who won't even be able to vote once he turns 18 because of his foreign citizenship, would have to say. From my prior experience on political campaigns, I knew that politicians like to have organized youthful support, since it generated sympathy and good public relations. I used that to unite students from various schools in the surrounding towns.

We frequently wrote to the mayor about our disgust with the New Agriculture development project. Our actions were feeble, but when politicians from Holldale's neighboring towns and the community at large saw that young people were adamantly opposed to the development project, they took action. This ran askew from New Agriculture's hope that the youth would embrace the project so they could have a trendy vegetable store nearby. Our existence added fuel to the fire, and as our membership rose we came to be seen as a threat.

Miraculously, within four months the mayor permanently withdrew his support for the project. LIANA had pushed back the date of the project's approval until after the local elections, and the mayor realized he wouldn't be re-elected unless he halted the development. On that glorious day, the community rejoiced, for we had triumphed over a multinational corporation.

This endeavor has changed my outlook on corporate capitalism. After direct experience with an international giant trying to tread over my small suburban neighborhood, I realized that there have to be restraints on corporate capitalism. Sadly, the primary reason for New Agriculture's failure was the wealth and prosperity in my neighborhood. If there had not been so many lawyers and businessmen who actively supported LIANA, and their children who were involved in S.A.N.A.D., the entire community would have been destroyed. There should be a stronger government to stop the New Agricultures of the world from stampeding over poorer communities, as they have been actively doing. There is no reason why they should have to tolerate large unwanted corporations. Although I have retired S.A.N.A.D., since the local battle has been won, I still want to help prevent corporations from being excessively greedy.

Figure 20-1: An example of an issue essay.

Before I had founded S.A.N.A.D. I was an ardent Republican. Almost a year later, I am still a Republican, but my views have been changed forever. I realize that economic and political questions are more complex than they appear to be. I can't just look at an economics equation to decide my stance on issues such as rent-control and property rights. These issues have intricate social facets and human concerns, which in the aftermath of New Agriculture's attempt to use local laws to carry out a malicious act, I have learned to factor into my decision-making.

Figure 20-1: An example of an issue essay.

When you choose a topic for the "issue" question, you may find it easier to write about something that connects personally to you. A purely intellectual topic is a lot tougher! If you care about gun control, for example, but you've never owned a gun, seen one (from either end), or campaigned about any aspect of gun ownership or limitation, you may not have much to say in your essay. On the other hand, your involvement doesn't have to be direct. Returning to the gun control example, suppose that you have been deeply affected by television coverage of school shootings. Because of what you've seen, you have formulated a strong opinion on the subject and have a lot to say. Go for it! Anything that arouses your passion can turn into a fine essay, even if all your experiences with the issue occur via the media.

Graduate school applicants planning to major in history or government and similar fields are often required to write issue essays. Don't expect a softball question at this level, and don't provide a general answer. Show what you know, and remember that post-graduate admissions committees will expect evidence that you actually understand something about the field. Grad school issue questions include:

- Analyze a public policy or public management problem and propose a remedy.
- Analyze a public policy problem related to international affairs and suggest a solution.

Delving into the past

Much less common than the issue essay are questions asking you to evaluate past events. Some of these questions concern people ("Which historical figure would you like to meet?" and other such questions). For help with that sort of essay, turn to Chapter 19. Other essay questions resemble this one:

> What historical event before your time has meaning to you? Why?

Before selecting a historical event to write about, consider your family history. Do any events from the past connect to your forbearers? I once read a fine admission essay about the Great Hunger, a period in Irish history that is also called the Potato Famine. The student's ancestor had left Ireland alone, at the age of 14, to seek his fortune in the United States when the family's potato crop failed. The author did a great job relating those nineteenth century events to his own family.

When you write a "historical event" essay, remember these points:

- In discussing a historical event, accuracy is essential. If you have only a little knowledge about an aspect of history (World War I had something to do with trenches and gas, but you're not sure what, for example), you won't be able to write effectively on the subject. Take the "historical" option only if you're secure about the information.
- Don't overload the reader with dates and obscure facts. You may include *some* specifics, but be sure that the details support the general points you want to make.
- Decide on one main idea, the point you want the essay to make. That point should relate to your own life and beliefs or to our society today. Imagine that you're writing about the struggle for women's suffrage. Why do you care about the vote? What form does that struggle take for a citizen of the twenty-first century? Your essay should connect the past to the present.

The historical event/person essay is always offered as one of several options. If you don't have something real to say, skip this essay and select a different application question.

Chapter 21

Getting the Most Out of Short Answers

In This Chapter

- Writing effective "short answers"
- Surveying the common short-answer questions
- Finding answers to oddball questions

To get the most *out of* the short answer section of your college application, you need to get the most information *into* the space or word limit provided. You can't ramble on philosophically about your favorite extracurricular activity or meander through a long explanation of why the college you're addressing is an absolute perfect match for your talents. You've got to make your point *fast.*

When I say, "short answer," I refer to brief statements (usually 200–300 words or less) that you write to interpret some aspect of your school record or experiences, not to the no-brainer lists and factual data that are, of course, also short and also answers. A question about your "most meaningful activity" and a "Why us?" query appear on many applications. You may also be asked to write a few sentences about your favorite books, community service experiences, and other topics. Transfer applicants are always required to write about their reasons for seeking a change. Short answer questions (sigh) don't normally take the place of the full-length essay or essays required on most applications. These little guys are an extra added attraction, guaranteed to soak up all those pesky free minutes you're stuck with after completing the rest of the application.

In this chapter I show you how to squeeze the maximum benefit from the lines allowed you in the short-answer section. I also provide helpful hints and examples of the most common brief responses.

Saying a Lot in Little Spaces

If you've ever taken a poetry class, chances are the teacher showed you some *haiku,* a poetic form that originated in Japan. Traditional haiku are only three lines long. Faced with the choice of reading and analyzing a haiku or a long poem, you may be tempted to opt for the haiku. It looks like a poetic finger snap — a second after you start reading it, you're done. But closer examination shows you that a haiku is packed with meaning. Furthermore, writing a haiku is extremely tough. In only a few words you must make your point, create a vivid image, and suggest philosophical depths. As poets and students of poetry have discovered through the years, long poems are actually easier to read and write than tiny haiku!

So too are the short-answer questions on college applications. Compared to the full-length essays, short answers appear simple at first glance. After you've sweated over a 500-word personal statement, you see a four- or five-line blank and think "piece of cake." But when you start to choose words for those lines, you realize what a tough job faces you.

Tough, but not impossible. To create an effective short answer, keep one word in mind. Which word? *One!* Here's what I mean:

- Each short answer must make *one* important point. If you're writing about your most meaningful activity, for example, you can't explain everything you learned from your stint as president of the Computer Debugging Society, describing the three new programming languages you mastered, your triumphant bake sale to raise funds for a new printer, and the club trip to Silicon Alley. If you really want to say all that, turn the Computer Debugging Society topic into a full-length essay and submit it as a personal statement. If you choose that topic for the short-answer section, limit yourself to an explanation of your new understanding of programming languages or to one of the other relevant ideas.
- The information in your short answers should appear in only *one* place in the application. Don't waste space repeating information or observations from the full-length essay or from elsewhere on the form.
- Consider letting the reader "see" *one* tiny scene in each short answer. Returning to the fictional Computer Debugging Society, you might include a sentence or two showing how tough it was to learn a new programming language, as in this example:

  I love the cooperative atmosphere of the Computer Debugging Society. At meetings members sit in front of their computers, balancing three-inch-thick C++ manuals on their laps. Fueled by extra-tall lattes, everyone shares programming tips and celebrates each other's success.

- Never use two words in a short answer if *one* will do the job. In other words, don't write, "He walked slowly into the room." Instead, say that he "ambled" or "strolled" or "edged" into a room. Check out Chapter 9 for some help with this task. Chapter 15 also offers tips on writing concisely.
- If you can, let your short answer open the door to *one* additional idea. Besides the details you give on your main point, include a few words suggesting something more. Again, I refer to the imaginary Computer Debugging Society:

  I never understood logic until I figured out a mapping program with my fellow debuggers. (main idea of the short answer = cooperative work; additional suggestion = you mastered logical thinking)

Let the power of *one* be your guide through the short answers, and you won't go wrong!

Topics that pop up in the short-answer section of one college's application may appear in the full-length essay section of another institution's form. Read the directions *early and often* to be sure you come up with the correct word count.

Answering the Most Common Short-Answer Questions

Perhaps more than any other section of the application, the short-answer questions produce a sudden desire to enroll in the army (*anyone's* army) rather than spend even one more minute writing dumb answers for people you've never met. Depending upon where you apply, you may encounter only a handful — or dozens — of different short-answer questions. Fortunately, most fall into a couple of categories. In this section I give you hints for the most common short-answer questions.

Playing favorites

The college doesn't care about your color preferences or the television rerun you're most likely to watch when you're supposed to be studying for a math test. But institutions often do ask you to write briefly about your favorites, in questions such as these:

- Which extracurricular activity was most meaningful to you? Why?
- Which academic class stands out?
- Describe one summer activity during your high school career.

Fitting it in the blanks

You've got the perfect short answer, and it *looks* like the perfect length. But when you write it on the application form, you end up with 15 words that won't fit anywhere. You consider — and reject — curving up into the margin in order to include that last crucial idea. Sound like your worst nightmare? Not to worry. Before you type or handwrite your answer, photocopy the form. Use the photocopies to practice writing or typing your answer in the space provided. If it doesn't fit, trim it and check the fit on another photocopy. When you're sure that you have room for everything, fill in the answer on the actual application blank.

- What activity from your high school career would you most like to continue during your college years?
- What teacher, class, or project was most significant to you?
- Briefly discuss a significant work experience.

Your transcript and other sections of the application have already listed *all* your clubs, honors, courses, jobs, and service projects. The preceding questions give you a chance to shine a spotlight on one element. But which one? Don't look for the club/course/job/whatever that you think is the most impressive. Instead, go for the experience that truly has extraordinary significance for you. In other words, answer the question honestly!

After you've decided on a topic, use one of the idea-gathering techniques from Chapter 6 to, well, gather ideas. Then select one point to highlight in your answer. Ask yourself *why* this particular activity/class/teacher impressed you so much. What did you learn? How did you change as a person or as a student as a result of your participation? Identify the message you want to convey (*I learned how to deal with people who are different from myself, I never before understood the horror of income tax,* whatever). Search your memory bank for a moment when that message is obvious or look for examples illustrating the main idea of your answer.

Suppose you're writing about a summer job with the town's police department. The point you want to get across is that riding around with a cop for two months made you appreciate a society governed by law. Your answer briefly describes an encounter between feuding neighbors and the officer's even-handed enforcement of the law, even though one party to the dispute was the officer's own cousin. You set the scene in two sentences and then in a couple of additional sentences go on to make your point about a just society.

Although you're working with a tight word limit, don't skimp on details. *Specific* is always preferable to vague. Also, because including every detail is not an option, look for *representative* moments or examples rather than a general summary.

Check out Figure 21-1, a "favorite activity" short answer that focuses on the author's volunteer work at a local hospital. The author's main idea is the satisfaction he gets from distracting children from their pain and illness. Notice the specifics, including:

- board games such as Chutes and Ladders, Monopoly, and Candyland
- teaching reading and math
- playing the saxophone
- name of the hospital (changed here for privacy)
- connection to high school community service projects in peer tutoring and teaching 7th graders
- mention of other work as an EMT and in the dialysis unit

Community service was a rewarding part of my high school life. Mentoring, peer tutoring, and teaching seventh graders were particularly gratifying activities. As a natural extension of these roles, I now volunteer in the Emergency Room and on the cancer ward of the Children's Hospital of Blainesville, Alabama.

As a volunteer in the Emergency Room, my greatest challenge is to divert the child's attention away from his/her illness or wound. After triage and initial treatment, the patient and I engage in activities including playing board games, reading, and simply conversing.

On the cancer ward, my responsibilities are more complex. The majority of these children are terminally ill. Removed form their homes, schools, and friends, these patients realize that they are not leading normal lives. In order to insure that their education is not compromised, the hospital provides classes. I teach reading and math to elementary-aged children. When the lessons are over, we play games including Twister, Monopoly, Chutes and Ladders, and Candyland. On occasion I have entertained them with my saxophone.

From my exposure as an EMT and as a volunteer in a dialysis unit, it is apparent that I am lucky to be healthy. Dedicating myself to helping these less fortunate children feel better about themselves brings me tremendous satisfaction.

Figure 21-1: An example of a favorite activity short-answer essay.

Another "favorite activity" answer is Figure 21-2, in which the author describes an unpaid work experience that was anything but his favorite. The annoyance factor in his summer job taught him something about life and was, in his view, ultimately positive. (Note: The names have been changed to protect the innocent!) Once again, pay attention to the number of specific details:

father's view that author should learn "the value of hard work"

father/son disagreement

duties of the job (deliveries, computer data entry)

boss's attitude

desire to quit

positive assessment of the experience

The most important activity in my high school years has been my job at Records For You, a small music company in my home town. Because life in my sheltered suburban community consisted of a string of material handouts, my father thought that I should learn "the value of hard work." I objected, for I had completed a challenging first year in high school and had spent over half of my summer studying chemistry so that I could fit AP Art History into my sophomore schedule. I insisted that as a student, I knew what it meant to work hard, and I was being deprived of a summer vacation, but he still forced me to take the job.

For the first three weeks, I delivered boxes of records and posters across the hot city. I was not paid and had to cover my transportation and meals, since they were supposedly doing me a favor by providing me with this work opportunity. My boss took no interest in me; the time we spent communicating was when he gave me orders or told me how to do things better. While I yearned to quit after the first week, I knew that my parents would have been ashamed and angry, so I labored on.

After the first three weeks, I was assigned to build a large computer database. I spent eight hours a day in front of a computer, mindlessly inputting data. I pleaded with my boss to let me carry on with deliveries, and he agreed, on the condition that I finished the database first, a task so large that after two weeks it was still incomplete.

During my five weeks working at Records For You, I had hardly any pleasure. After I left the job, I complained to my father about his making me take it, but he just smiled, for he knew he had succeeded.

In retrospect, it was a positive experience. I had adopted a better work ethic. I had worked hard in school because I was genuinely interested, but the job taught me to work for the sake of working. I learned the valuable lesson that the world did not revolve around me, and that in this time in my life I had to take orders and not question them. The discipline that my boss instilled in me has stuck. I have learned to do a good job at everything that is assigned. My father was right, those painful five weeks taught me something new, which has had a positive effect on my life.

Figure 21-2: Another example of a favorite activity short-answer essay.

One more example: Read Figure 21-3, a "favorite class" description I adapted from a student's essay. The description zeroes in on the teaching methods in an art history class. The student includes lots of specifics — names of paintings and artists, the use of stories, and the topic of a paper she wrote. Her enthusiasm shines through clearly.

Writing about favorite books and films

Psst! Read any good books lately? Been to the movies? Great, you've got college application material, specifically, these variations of the "favorite or most significant activity" short answer:

> Write about 200 words discussing a book you've read.
>
> What is your favorite film? Why?

Information in Chapter 20 helps you with the book question. You can adapt the tips in Chapter 20 to the "favorite film" topic also. Remember that the admissions counselors judge *what* you choose to write about as well as *how* you explain your interest in that particular work. Don't aim over your head, selecting something you think will make you appear more intellectual than you actually are. (And don't *ever* write about something you haven't read or seen.) But neither should you pick a book that has all its words in little balloons or a film that consists of car chases and explosions and nothing else. Go for a book or film that has aftereffects — the kind of art work that bears thinking about. If it's instantly forgettable, with no levels of meaning to explore or information to digest, it's not a good choice.

Figure 21-3: An example of a favorite class short-answer essay.

> It was the beginning of February, spring was a long way off, and I was fifteen and in a teenage slump. In the past art history classes had been something for me to try to stay awake through. I was mildly interested sometimes, but most of the time I had to struggle to keep my eyes open when the lights went out for the slides. But Dr. Elgar's ninth grade art history class was magical. Because of her teaching, two dimensional slide projections became four dimensional stories with real people in them. Her style was matter-of-fact but contained intense enthusiasm and love for the subject. It was as if she had just come in from having lunch with Carravaggio. I was no longer counting the minutes until the end of class but instead trying to get the seat closest to the front so I could find all the hidden symbolism in David's "The Death of Marat." At the end of her classes I felt invigorated and eager to learn more, and I even found myself reading more than the assigned material. For my final project in the course I wrote a comparative paper about Degas' "The Dance Class," and Homer's "Bathers" that I actually enjoyed writing. I do not remember all the stories Dr. Elgar told, but I do remember how to study and appreciate art history.

Dealing with "Why us" questions

When the romantic partner of your rosiest and most far-fetched fantasies finally calls, you may be tempted to ask, "Why me?" just so you can hear how wonderfully attractive you are. (I know, I know. In the real world the answer to "Why me?" is "because everyone else will probably turn me down," but that's not a suitable response for a college application.) The application version of the romantic "Why me?" is "Why us?" and resembles the following:

- What first made you think of our college?
- What aspects of this school influenced your decision to apply?
- What experiences in your life prompted you to apply here?
- Why are you a good match with our institution?
- Discuss your reasons for applying to our school.
- What characteristics of our school do you find most appealing?

You may imagine that the institution you're applying to has a collective ego and that this sort of question requires you to stroke that ego a little. Well, you're probably right! Institutions are made up of human beings, and human beings (you may have noticed) like to be appreciated. But rather than meaningless flattery, the admissions committee asks "Why us?" because they really want to know the answer. Keep these points in mind as you reply to the "Why us?" question:

- In any sort of writing, specifics are better than generalities, but details are absolutely crucial in a "Why us?" response. A canned, vague statement such as "I want to learn and your school will help me do so" tells the admissions committee one of two things: a) you don't know much about their college or b) you have put very little thought into your choice. Remember, admissions committees want to admit students who will stay at their college through graduation, and applicants who actually know something about the place they're applying to are a better bet. If you give the impression that you stabbed a pin randomly into a college list in order to come up with a selection, the committee will not be pleased. They may rightly assume that you're too lazy to think carefully about your future and to check up on the place where you want to spend the next chunk of your life.
- If you've actually visited the campus, refer to that experience, citing buildings and activities by name. If you sat in on a class, explain why the teacher or students impressed you. Once again, *be specific.*
- If relatives or friends attended the university you're applying to or the university representative visited your high school for an information session, you may cite their comments, explaining what impressed you.
- Mention your own educational or career plans in relation to the college. (*I'd like to study Egyptian pyramids with Professor Tomb of your archeology department and then excavate in conjunction with the Ministry of Antiquities,* for example.) At the risk of annoying you I'll say it again: Be specific!

Time for some examples. Turn to Figure 21-4, a short-answer response for an application to an institution I'm calling "Freedom University," which is not the college's real name. The student who wrote the "Freedom U" selection had visited the college and interacted with current students, as the essay makes quite evident. The student's response shows that she understands the college's self image and its pride in an "anything goes" attitude.

On my first visit to Freedom University, I sat in on an information session where an admissions officer told us, "If your essay is going well and you want to go on for a little longer, go ahead. This is Freedom U! We want you to calm down a little." This statement is an accurate reflection of the relief that overcame me when I visited Freedom University. At first I was excited that I wouldn't have to count the words of my essay and whittle them down to under a precise 500. As the college hysteria progresses, this statement provides more substantial relief. I feel as though Freedom U is a place that understands the purpose of its actions. I am encouraged by the fact that the quality of applicants as people as well as students is examined, and that diversity exists not only in the form of racial and cultural diversity but in diversity of opinion as well. In determining where I prefer to spend the next four years of my life, the most important factor is my fellow students. The individuality, intellect, and sincerity that I found in Freedom U. students each time I visited is one of the main reasons I am drawn there.

Figure 21-4: A short answer to the "Why us" question from a student who visited the university.

Now run your eyeballs over Figure 21-5. The student author was not able to visit the school personally, but she did attend an information session held at her high school and speak with alumni and current students. Her answer focuses on the college's location and her perception of its quality of life. (***Note:*** The name of the university and its representative have been altered.)

When Alex Miller came to Horace Mann and described student life at Vandelay, I found myself imagining a lifestyle completely different from the one I am used to. Among other things, he described long and leisurely dinner discussions that stretch late into the evening as a normal occurrence at Vandelay, with students finishing work late into the night. I became completely enchanted with Vandelay largely because the overall quality of life sounded excellent. I ran into the cafeteria right after the information session with a huge smile on my face and excitedly told my friends why "Vandelay rules!"

Although I have found my niche in the fast paced and high stress feel of my school and home city, I think that the next four years are a perfect time to try something new. What appeals to me about Vandelay is its integration of slower paced Southern lifestyle and tradition with excellent and rigorous academics. I have always wanted to experience Southern culture and way of life (and held a soft spot for southern accents.) My conversations with Vandelay alumni and students have given me the overwhelmingly solid consensus that it is a friendly and fun place with challenging academics and great opportunities.

Figure 21-5: A short answer to the "Why us" question from a student who met with current students and alumni.

One last example: The writer who composed Figure 21-6 also relates to campus atmosphere (once again I've changed the name of the school) and includes information about specific areas of study in which the college is particularly strong.

My high school has provided four challenging years in which my mind has been expanded and I have learned copious amounts. I want to attend an intellectually stimulating college community, where I will reap the benefits of working vigorously. Agonia College offers the most demanding courses of study, and consequently the student body is self-selected, filled with student-scholars who are genuinely interested in academics. I plan to major in economics with a political international relations background, and Agonia has an excellent economics department, if not the best in the world. I prefer Agonia's practice of teaching the pure sciences and humanities at an intellectual level, rather than teaching courses related to careers, which are for graduate school. Going to school in New York City, I have been exposed to a dynamic urban environment, and feel that the campus of Agonia has a similar vibrant metropolitan vibe to it and many opportunities to attend cultural events. The city of Chicago would complement my education at the university well.

Figure 21-6: A short answer to the "Why us" question.

The answer to "Why us?" may be placed in more than one spot in the application. Check out Figure 21-7, a student's answer to a question inquiring about a book that had a significant effect on his thinking. The student chose a book written by a professor at the college and indicated his desire to take a course with that individual. ***Note:*** This student was sincere and honest in his reply; he really did like the book. Don't choose a book you haven't read just to impress the admissions committee. What will you do if the admissions interviewer wants to discuss the book with you?

During my A.P. European History course, I picked up the habit of browsing through The New York Review of Books to find new interesting historical works. One jewel I encountered was Anthony Grafton's *Leon Battista Alberti: Master Builder of the Italian Renaissance*. Through a historical lens, I marvel at both Leon Battista Alberti and Anthony Grafton.

Before learning about Alberti, I had never grasped the depth of the accomplishments of a true Renaissance man. A cryptographer, mathematician, scientist, architect, painter, sculptor, and philosopher — it is difficult to contemplate how a single man mastered such a wide range of disciplines in just one lifetime. When learning about Alberti, I realized that our society is moving away from the ideal of a multitalented Renaissance man, and more towards job specialization. While I know I will always remain a speck next to this giant, I aspire to become like Alberti and to master everything I pursue.

Professor Grafton has both depth and breadth to his historical knowledge. After reading Cardano's *Cosmos: The Worlds and Works of a Renaissance Astrologer, The Foundations of Early Modern Europe 1460-1559*, along with his work on Alberti, I am awed by his ability to explain topics in history thoroughly in a captivating manner. It would be a pleasure to learn from professor Grafton, through his lectures and his course on the Renaissance and Reformation.

Figure 21-7: An example of a short-answer essay with the "Why us" question included in another question.

Moving on: The transfer question

A variation of the "Why us?" question is aimed at applicants who already attend a university or graduate school and want to pull up stakes and transfer to another. This sort of "Why us?" question may call for a full-length essay or a shorter response. Either way, the content is the same:

- Discuss what is lacking in your current school. Don't trash the place; simply state what you need that your current college cannot provide — a larger student body, more activities, smaller classes, whatever.
- Explain how the college you want to transfer to can fill the gaps in your educational experience. For example, if you've expressed a desire for a career in international diplomacy, mention the Foreign Affairs major of the school you're applying to.

  Do your homework and be sure that the school you want to transfer to actually offers what you say you want. In other words, don't tell a college with an average class size of 3,498 that you're seeking intimate seminar-style learning with plenty of professorial attention. You'll look like a fool and, more importantly, you'll end up dissatisfied even if they do admit you.

- Discuss the primary attractions of the new school, including as many specific details as possible: *I want to attend Anhedonia State because of its scholarly collection of depressive literature and its campus-wide ban on keg parties,* for example.

Figure 21-8 is a full-length transfer essay adapted from one written by a student dissatisfied with his freshman year at a major university, whose name I changed for privacy. Figure 21-9 shows you how this response may be shortened for a school that places this question in the short-answer section. In both versions, the author states what's good about his current school, which I've called "Central State," and what is lacking. He identifies factors that will be different in his hoped-for new school, the name-changed-for-privacy "Northern State."

No, I am not homesick. I have friends. The work is not overwhelming. Nor has it interfered with my involvement in extracurricular activities. My first semester has been a time of transition as it is for most college freshmen. Making decisions regarding course selection, seeking advice from advisors, and utilizing time efficiently have all been part of the process, accomplished at a distance from the familiar support structures and cues of both home and high school. As a result, I have developed a greater sense of myself and my abilities, both academic and social. The experience has been satisfying. However, with all due introspection and now retrospection, I feel a change is necessary.

Sociologist Lev Vygotsky believed that peers play a major role in an individual's development and learning. The students and friends with whom I grew up were extraordinarily bright, competitive, and creative. In high school, discussions and opinions on almost any subject were spontaneous and interesting. At Central State, the small class size and the seminar formats have presented a great setting in which to learn. The highly motivated professors, who encourage participation, have been the highlight of my experience thus far. However, the level of student interaction has not been gratifying. Conversations concerning classroom topics and related materials have been limited. I have not been sufficiently challenged or stimulated by my peers.

During my first semester, I have come to realize the influence a community has on my learning and growth. At Central State, the campus is active from around eleven in the morning until three in the afternoon, Monday through Friday. One Saturday in October, while walking to the dining hall, I realized that I was one of five people on campus. With the majority of undergraduates living in on-campus dorms, the campus of Northern State fosters a unique intimacy. The campus is lively throughout the day. Such activity creates a comfortable environment that promotes interaction and the formation of strong bonds between members of the community. Having experienced a year of college and dorm life, I am more aware of what is best for me. As a transfer student, I would appreciate this style of living even more.

Based on conversations with current students, it is my understanding that members of the Northern State community make it a unique place to live and learn. Many renowned professors choose to teach at the undergraduate level. Having the chance to interact with an instructor such as Avery Marks, whose passion and mastery of botany are unrivaled, would be quite an experience. The most defining aspect of Northern State's faculty, however, is the manner in which they approach their role in influencing a student's life. Professors, instructors, and advisors guide the student so that he/she can make independent decisions.

Furthermore, the structure and aspects of Northern State's residential colleges foster the formation of relationships. For the remainder of my undergraduate years I want to return "home" to a very close group of friends for nightly dinners and conversations concerning daily activities. The strong bonds that are formed within a diverse group of people who make up these individual communities create an optimal atmosphere in which to grow, socially and intellectually.

All aspects of Northern State seem to enhance learning. Guidance from faculty members and challenges from peers within Northern's close-knit community create a setting in which I can pursue current interests and discover new one while simultaneously discovering my future direction. This is the purpose of the undergraduate experience.

Figure 21-8: A full-length essay in response to a "Why transfer" question.

No, I am not homesick. I have friends. The work is not overwhelming. Nor has it interfered with my involvement in extracurricular activities. I have developed a greater sense of myself and my abilities, both academic and social. However, with all due introspection and now retrospection, I feel a change is necessary.

The students and friends with whom I grew up were extraordinarily bright, competitive, and creative. In high school, discussions on almost any subject were spontaneous and interesting. At Central State, the small class size and the seminar formats have presented a great setting in which to learn. However, I have not been sufficiently challenged or stimulated by my peers. At Central State, the campus is active from around eleven in the morning until three in the afternoon, Monday through Friday. One Saturday in October, I realized that I was one of five people on campus. With the majority of undergraduates living in on-campus dorms, the campus of Northern State fosters a unique intimacy. The campus is lively throughout the day.

Having the chance to interact with an instructor such as Avery Marks, whose passion and mastery of botany are unrivaled, would be quite an experience. The most defining aspect of Northern State's faculty, however, is that professors, instructors, and advisors guide the student so that he/she can make independent decisions. Furthermore, the structure and aspects of Northern State's residential colleges foster the formation of relationships.

Figure 21-9: A shortened version of Figure 21-8 to fulfill the short-answer "Why transfer" question.

Lassoing the Mavericks: Responding to Unusual Short-Answer Questions

Having combed through 250 college applications, I've picked up some terrific creative writing ideas for my English classes. I've also become convinced that more than a few admissions committees were up *really late* when they wrote some of those questions. In this section I show you how to deal with the mavericks of the application world — the oddball short answers that pop up only occasionally — such as the following:

- If you went into your closet and your clothes could talk, what would they say about you?
- What is your definition of success?
- Jot a note to your future college roommate relating a personal experience that reveals something about you.
- Describe something that reveals who you are (or aren't).
- How do you plan to manage your time while in college?
- Submit a photo or drawing and briefly explain its significance.

All these questions, by the way, are variations of more common topics. When you consider the definition of success or discuss your plans for time management, for instance, you're defining priorities and values, an offshoot of the "tell us about yourself" essay. Similarly, interpreting a photo, a drawing, or a closet full of Armani knockoffs reveals much about the way you think. Depending upon the photo or drawing (or wardrobe), you may also have the chance to disclose more about your life and experiences.

A good approach to the oddball question is to list every idea you may possibly want to explore in your answer. Then take each idea in turn, composing four or five sentences about the topic. Gradually, one idea will take hold of you, and you'll find yourself writing more and more, on your way to an acceptable answer.

The "oddball" questions are partly designed to take you off the beaten track, to see how creative you are when challenged by the unexpected. (Not a bad test for potential applicants, when you think about it.) So as you answer an unusual question, let your playful side emerge. Don't blow off the question or present yourself as incurably silly. Do let your creativity rule!

Check out Figure 21-10, a delightful foray into a teenager's closet written in answer to the "if your clothes could talk" question. The author chose to write a fairly long response, but I've adapted it here to show how it might serve for a briefer answer. The author uses several items of clothing — an apron, a ragged pair of sweatpants, and a formal suit — to illustrate her memories. The author's strong sense of family, her loyalty to friends, and even her career plans become clear after this quick trip through her closet.

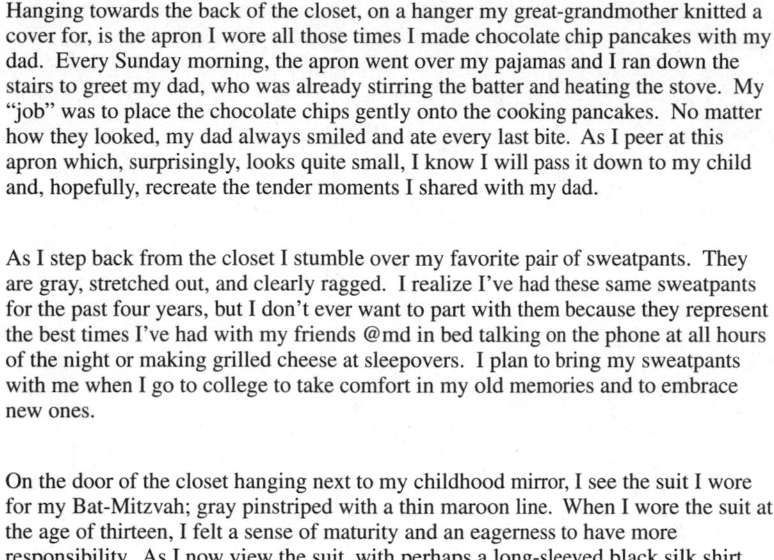

Hanging towards the back of the closet, on a hanger my great-grandmother knitted a cover for, is the apron I wore all those times I made chocolate chip pancakes with my dad. Every Sunday morning, the apron went over my pajamas and I ran down the stairs to greet my dad, who was already stirring the batter and heating the stove. My "job" was to place the chocolate chips gently onto the cooking pancakes. No matter how they looked, my dad always smiled and ate every last bite. As I peer at this apron which, surprisingly, looks quite small, I know I will pass it down to my child and, hopefully, recreate the tender moments I shared with my dad.

As I step back from the closet I stumble over my favorite pair of sweatpants. They are gray, stretched out, and clearly ragged. I realize I've had these same sweatpants for the past four years, but I don't ever want to part with them because they represent the best times I've had with my friends @md in bed talking on the phone at all hours of the night or making grilled cheese at sleepovers. I plan to bring my sweatpants with me when I go to college to take comfort in my old memories and to embrace new ones.

On the door of the closet hanging next to my childhood mirror, I see the suit I wore for my Bat-Mitzvah; gray pinstriped with a thin maroon line. When I wore the suit at the age of thirteen, I felt a sense of maturity and an eagerness to have more responsibility. As I now view the suit, with perhaps a long-sleeved black silk shirt replacing the original pink cotton one, I can see myself seven years from now, wearing this suit as a lawyer.

Figure 21-10: A short answer to an oddball question.

Part VI
The Part of Tens

"Your essay looks fine, I just don't think you're merry enough."

In this part . . .

The famous *Dummies* Part of Tens gives you a ton of information *fast.* In this part I explode ten myths about the admission essay, provide a list of ten great essays by masters of the genre, and tell you ten things that you absolutely *must* do when you write your own essay.

Chapter 22

Ten Myths About the College Essay

In This Chapter

- Debunking common myths about the essay

With the same fervor that people exhibit while explaining their most recent Elvis sighting, college applicants tend to tell each other the truth (the whole truth and nothing but the truth) about the admission essay. The only problem is that lots of what "everyone knows" to be true about the essay is pure myth. In this chapter I puncture ten myths about the college admission essay.

Writing Style Doesn't Matter

"It's what you say, not how you say it." Heard that one before? This concept is a close relative of the also untrue "It's the thought that counts." (Right, like I don't care that you gave me an almost dead bouquet of flowers for my birthday instead of the CD player you purchased for your other best friend.) Of course the admissions committee is interested in what you have to say, and you should expend plenty of time and care choosing a topic for your essay. (The appendix helps, if you're stuck.) But *how* you express yourself is also important. You'll have to write tons of papers in college and graduate school, and the institution wants to know that your skill level is up to par. So don't skimp on the writing effort. Draft and redraft until you've got a logical, focused, creative piece. And (she said in her sternest English-teacher tone) check your grammar and spelling. They *do* matter.

Finding the Right Topic Is No Big Deal

The flip side of the preceding myth is that the topic of your essay is not important. "You can write about anything as long as you write well." Not exactly. True, zillions of topics are possible winners, depending upon how you handle them. But the admissions committee wants to see something of significance *to you.* If your essay leaves them scratching their heads, asking,

"Why did this applicant tell me all this stuff?" you're in trouble. And if *you* can't figure out why you told them all that stuff, you're in bigger trouble. Bottom line: Spend more than a couple of nano-seconds selecting a topic that reveals an important aspect of your experience or personality.

Focusing on a Certain Topic Guarantees Admission

This myth is more persistent than the aforementioned "Elvis is still alive" theory and just as silly: *Write about your mother and they'll definitely take you. Hahvah wants something with a lot of book titles in it. Agonia accepts only people who mention current events . . . especially wars . . . they love wars.* Nope! No shortcuts here! You have to discover and develop your own topic and write it well. Accomplish that task, and you've taken your best shot. Then you'll either get in or you won't. The application process has no guarantees at all, ever, for anyone, and people who tell you something different are indulging in wishful thinking.

Discussing Any Topic Is Okay

Okay, this is a myth that comes close to the truth. But only close. If you handle a topic properly, nothing is an automatic rejection. However, warning flags may go up if the admissions committee reads about *unresolved* problems that are likely to cause trouble for you — and for the college — as you move on to the next level of study. So if you haven't managed to finish even one homework assignment all year, if you have a persistent desire to cut class, or if something even more serious impedes your academic or personal life, seek help from a guidance counselor or trusted adult. And until you've got the situation under control, write about something else.

Following Instructions Isn't Important

Tempted to show your creativity by ignoring the word limit or specified format? Bad idea. No matter how many friends tell you that "they don't really mean it when they say 500 words or less," follow the instructions. Yes, your ten-page essay may land on the desk of an indulgent reader who has a couple of hours to kill before the mall opens, but it's more likely to be perused by a tired, over-burdened reader who has to plow through a couple of hundred submissions before the mall closes. Also, ignoring their requests tells the admissions committee that you have a tough time obeying rules — not a good message to send to people who may want to ask you to attend class, keep the dorm clean, and do the assigned reading.

Talking about Ordinary Lives Is a No-no

Spreading faster than a computer virus is the myth that near-death experiences and starvation-level poverty are prerequisites for the college essay. Uh uh. A regular, happy life with non-psychotic parents and an average trip through high school also make the grade, at least in terms of essay material. The secret is that most applicants, generally young adults or late teens, haven't had very many newsworthy experiences. But if you write about your own life honestly and thoughtfully, with the details only you can provide, you'll stand out from the crowd.

Using Scholarly Language Is Impressive

When the admissions committee reads the essay, they want to meet *a real person,* not some souped-up version of a dictionary/encyclopedia merger. Nor do they want to see your latest research paper (unless of course they specifically request it) or a book report. So don't plug in every word tested on the last SAT and ACT. Don't twist normal verbal expression into some tortured pattern that appears intellectual. Sound like yourself (the "company's here" version, not the "food-fight" version of your personality) in your application essay.

Writing One Essay Is Enough

You can — and should, in the interest of maintaining sanity — adapt one essay for several different applications. Chapter 1 tells you how to do so. But if you try to squeeze an essay about a current issue into a slot the college has earmarked for a description of your views on art, you may be in trouble. I say "may" because censorship/funding of the arts is always in the news, and an essay about that current issue works well for the artistic-viewpoint question. However, if you wrote about soybean tariffs, you can't make that essay relate to art. Bottom line: Don't take shortcuts. Adapt where logic decrees you may do so, but write something new when nothing else will do.

Seeking Help from Lots of People Is a Good Idea

Many applicants, nails bitten to blood level and anxiety risen to stratospheric heights, look for help with their admission essays. (Thanks for buying this book, by the way, which I hope you'll find *extremely* helpful.) But don't go overboard on the help aspect. First of all, some "help" crosses the line into academic dishonesty. (Chapter 4 tells you how to tell the difference between legitimate assistance and "Do not pass go; proceed directly to jail" over involvement.) Secondly, if too many people read and comment on your essay, you'll go crazy sorting through conflicting advice. Choose one helper — a teacher, college advisor, or parent — and ignore everyone else.

Formatting Your Essay into the Standard Five Paragraphs Does the Trick

The standard five-paragraph composition is the workhorse of high school academics; it gets you through history essays, English reports, and a host of other assignments. However, it does *not* serve you well for an admission essay. Why? Because an admission essay is not homework. It's an attempt to show the admissions committee that you're ready for higher level work. Also, your life won't fit neatly into the five-paragraph pattern. A bit more creativity is necessary! Check out Chapter 7 for better formats.

Chapter 23

Ten Great Essays to Inspire You

In This Chapter

- Reviewing well written and inspiring essays

This is a highly personal list of my favorite essays, a mixed bunch in terms of style, subject matter, and length. If you need a spark plug to get your essay-writing engine going, browse through a few of these gems. None were written as college admission essays, but all display fine writing from a personal point of view — the goal of your admission essay.

Because they're so good, these essays are anthologized in many collections. If you can't find them in a general book of essays, check with the librarian in your school or public library for alternate publications.

In no particular order, here are ten great essays.

"Letter from Birmingham Jail" by the Reverend Martin Luther King, Jr.

One of the most eloquent essays of the modern civil rights movement, King's "Letter from Birmingham Jail" was written in 1963 during King's incarceration for a non-violent protest. The essay is an answer to a plea from several white ministers in Birmingham, Alabama. The ministers asked the black community to call off protests against Birmingham's segregated bus system, contending that the protests did more harm than good and that the black community should patiently seek justice through the courts. King explains clearly why patience, nearly a century after the end of the Civil War and emancipation of the slaves, is not the answer. As you read this essay, notice how King builds his argument, fact by fact, to an inescapable conclusion.

"Of Studies" by Francis Bacon

Okay, I admit that Francis Bacon is an old timer; he was born in 1561. And yes, he sounds old. But if you can pick your way through some strange spelling and punctuation, you'll find a gem. Bacon's technique is compression. He makes his points with a minimum of words; you almost feel as though you are reading a series of machine-gun bursts, each bearing a short but deep message. In fact, Bacon's style is so concise that every sentence could be the topic of another essay. "Of Studies" discusses education — a topic close to the heart of all college applicants who are not completely fixated on keg parties.

"Mother Tongue" by Amy Tan

Novelist Amy Tan (*The Joy Luck Club*) reflects upon the nature of language in this essay. Tan's mother immigrated to the United States from China, and her English always reflected the grammar and usage of her first language, Chinese. Tan relates several incidents in which people respond differently to the same message delivered in her mother's imperfect English and in Tan's own college-educated speech. Tan's weaving together of anecdotes and interpretation may serve as a model for your admission essay.

"The Search for Marvin Gardens" by John McPhee

This essay is one of my all-time favorites because of its strange but extremely effective structure. McPhee bases this piece on the fact that the properties in the original Monopoly game were named after places in Atlantic City, New Jersey. In the essay he constantly cuts between two separate stories — two players zooming through a series of Monopoly games and descriptions of the actual places that are bought or landed on during the games. The title comes from the one spot that McPhee can't locate in Atlantic City. McPhee's structure may stir your creativity; also notice the sparse but vivid details he chooses to create word pictures of each street.

"The Solace of Open Spaces" by Gretel Erhlich

Erhlich lives in Wyoming, a sparsely populated state. Her lyrical descriptions of the landscape are interspersed with short anecdotes about life in the "open spaces" of that state. Erhlich manages to show the reader how a physical setting can shape one's personality and worldview. If you intend to write an admission essay focused on a place, check out this essay for a fine model.

"The Lives of a Cell" by Lewis Thomas

The scientifically-inclined may learn a lot from reading this essay by Lewis Thomas, a medical doctor and author. Thomas considers the basic unit of life, the cell, and wonders whether the cell serves as a model for the organization of human society, the universe, and other little things like that. Thomas builds his case by way of examples, which he labels "items." The essay is a good model for students who want to write about highly technical subjects in a readable way.

"Eastern Middle School" by Thomas Friedman

Thomas Friedman, an award-winning columnist for my hometown paper, *The New York Times,* gained much respect after the September 11th attacks for his analysis of the United States' relations with the Arab world. In this essay he describes an assembly at Eastern Middle School in Washington, D.C., in which children of many different racial, ethnic, and religious backgrounds work together. Friedman uses the assembly description to respond to the perception, often stated by anti-American extremists, that American society has no values. Friedman concludes that our society values diversity and mutual respect and that those values are "hiding in plain sight." As a New Yorker and an American, I was moved to tears by this essay. As an English teacher and a writer, I was impressed by his technique of describing an event and interpreting its meaning.

"The Negro Artist and the Racial Mountain" by Langston Hughes

One of the most important writers of the Harlem Renaissance, Langston Hughes is primarily known for his poetry. He also wrote essays, and this one, dating from the early 1920s, is terrific. Hughes focuses on the role and identity of an African American artist in an unjust, segregated society. He discusses the power of stereotypes and considers the obligations of an artist to counteract (or to ignore) those images. He concludes that an artist must be true to an interior, personal vision without worrying about how his work might be interpreted. The essay is a fine model for many reasons, but I'll just point out one quality I admire and that you may want to adopt. Hughes knows who will object to his ideas and what the counter arguments will be. He acknowledges those points and provides a response. Great technique!

"On Lying in Bed" by G.K. Chesterton

How can you not love an essay that begins this way: "Lying in bed would be an altogether perfect and supreme experience if only one had a coloured pencil long enough to draw on the ceiling." Dynamite beginning, don't you think? As you may have guessed from the spelling of "coloured," Chesterton was British. Written in the early twentieth century, the essay points out that lying in bed is one of life's pleasures. According to Chesterton, the simple things in life — such as lying in bed — should take precedence over other goals usually deemed more important. Agree with him or argue until your tongue dries up. Either way, Chesterton draws you into the subject with a great first sentence.

"On Keeping a Notebook" by Joan Didion

What do writers write in their notebooks? Author Joan Didion provides a ton of examples in her essay, "On Keeping a Notebook." Then she goes on to interpret the significance of the items she jotted down. Her examples are not long-winded explanations but rather super-quick snapshots. Taken as a whole, they reveal the purpose of a writer's notebook. To understand how to create a vivid scene in just a couple of lines, read this essay.

Chapter 24

Ten Absolute Musts for College Essays

In This Chapter

- Understanding what you must do to create a successful essay

The college essay is a variable creature. One writer's effort may be totally different in form and content from another applicant's work, even though both essays achieve their purpose — an acceptance letter from the college. However, a few hard and fast rules do apply to the college essay. Which rules? Read on.

Keeping It Real

They want to meet *you* — not what you imagine a prime candidate for admission to be. The essay should sound like a real person, not someone who swallowed a vocabulary book or memorized an encyclopedia. Present your best self, but be authentic.

Answering the Question

If they ask you to write about a person who influenced your choice of career, don't send them an essay describing every stain on your childhood baseball mitt. True, lots of application questions are so vague that almost any answer will do the job. But that one little word — "almost" — is crucial. Read the question before, during, and after you write the essay. Then read the question again! Be sure that you've answered it!

Following Directions

They want it "in the blank below." Or, they want it "on a separate sheet of paper." They like staples. They hate staples. The essay should be "500 words" or "no more than two pages" or "brief."

Whatever they ask for, give it to them! (Chapter 17 provides tips on format.) Remember, the admissions committee placed the directions in the application for a reason. Maybe for even more than one reason. Your task is not to figure out why they're requiring a specific format; your task is to follow directions.

Being Specific

Unless your spaceship crashed on the moon and you were rescued by extraterrestrials, it's unlikely that your life — in its *general* outline — is dramatically different from the lives of hordes of other college applicants. Whatever topic you choose has probably also been chosen by someone else. Fortunately, the *details* of your experience are always unique. If you write with specifics, you will emerge as a distinct, one-of-a-kind person. Plus, your essay will be more interesting to read!

Getting Personal

The essay is about *you,* no matter what the topic. A detached, scholarly assessment of the chances for nuclear disarmament may attract a publisher or impress the instructor of your Contemporary History course. But an impersonal college essay will not achieve its primary goal — to present *you* to the admissions committee. (For a complete explanation of your role in the essay, check out Chapter 2.)

Expanding the Basics

When you fill in all those blanks, you give the admissions committee basic information about your life both in and out of school. The essay is not the spot to repeat long lists of courses or clubs or jobs that appear elsewhere in your application. Instead, the essay should *expand* the admissions committee's understanding of your experiences and ideas. Of course, the main idea of your essay may be stated somewhere else. If you're writing about your stint editing the school paper, for example, the fact that you held such a position is on the list of extracurricular activities. But if the reader finds out nothing new, you've wasted a golden opportunity.

Holding Their Interest

Even if your essay rises to the entertainment level of the instructions on an income tax booklet, the admissions counselors will read it. They have to, because reading admission essays is part of the job. But they won't read your essay happily unless it's interesting. To attract and keep the reader's attention, you don't need shocking events or strange sentences. You need good writing!

Meeting the Deadline

If the application is due on November 15 (or January 1 or whatever), don't assume that the deadline is only a starting point for negotiations. Instead, see the deadline as a brick wall that you can't smash through. Get it done and get it in *on time.* (For tips on time management, read Chapter 1.)

Going Easy on the Eyes

If they can't read your essay, they can't appreciate your wisdom or gasp in awe at your accomplishments. Regardless of format — handwriting, typing, or word processing — be sure that the essay is legible. Don't make the admissions committee squint at microscopic letters. Don't send them into guessing mode because they can't figure out whether you wrote "shad," "shed," or "shod."

Using Good Grammar

Okay, I admit as an English teacher I'm a bit biased. I tend to obsess about the difference between "who" and "whom" and whether or not a comma is in the correct spot. But even people who are not nuts about grammar care about spelling, punctuation, verb tense, and all those other things that English teachers scream into your ear on a regular basis. The college you're applying to wants to know whether you can write correctly. So dig out the rule book (and check out Chapter 14) and polish your prose.

Appendix

Personal Inventory

"Deciding what to write. That's what got me," said Jordyn as he showed me his college essays. He's not alone. For years students have told me that the toughest part of writing a college admission essay is finding a topic. The subject, of course, is already clear — your life, your ideas, your personality. But the topic! Who knows.

Not me, certainly. But somewhere inside you lies *the* topic, in fact, tons of topics, each just waiting to be explored and turned into a great essay. This personal inventory is designed to unearth those topics from your memory bank. (And if you decide to skip college, you can always send it to a dating service.)

Don't be discouraged by the number of questions listed here. You don't have to answer all of them, and you don't have to answer any of them in detail. Work your way through the categories that seem most appealing, jotting down a phrase or two — just enough to remind you of the answer. If you're inspired by any particular question, grab a sheet of scrap paper or turn on the computer and write everything that occurs to you.

When you're finished filling out the inventory, turn to Chapter 2 for instructions on turning memories into essay topics.

Some of these questions dig fairly deeply into your personal life. Don't feel obliged to share the most private parts of your life in your admission essay. The admissions committee wants to get to know you, but they should be treated as strangers to whom you've just been introduced, not friends in whom you confide. So if secrets surface as you fill out this questionnaire, keep them!

Family Ties

Applications frequently ask you to describe an important person, someone who has influenced you. Or you may be faced with a question about your identity — how you define yourself. Family stories may be useful for these essays.

This part of the inventory makes you think about your family background and interactions. I've even thrown in a couple of questions about your most distant ancestors, people who lived long before you were born, because sometimes thinking about your family's heritage helps you understand its current reality. (Still another great essay topic!) Don't worry if your family falls firmly into the non-traditional category. Plug your own definition of family into these questions and answer away. If you wish, answer the same questions about your stepparents or other parental figures in your life.

Parents

What are your parents' backgrounds? Think about their upbringing (economic, social, ethnicity, schooling, and so on). Have any of those factors influenced you?

Have your parents told you any stories about their lives that struck you as important in some way? If so, what was the best story?

Does your upbringing differ from your parents'? Do you feel fortunate because of those differences? Do you feel deprived because of those differences?

What is the best lesson your parent(s) taught you? What were you doing when you learned this lesson?

What's your favorite memory of your parent(s)? Why is this memory important?

Have you and your parents struggled over any issues? Which ones? Why? What was the outcome of the struggle? How did you grow from that struggle?

If you become a parent someday, which traits of your parents do you hope to show to your offspring? Which traits do you hope to avoid? Why?

Siblings

Have your brothers and/or sisters affected your life? Can you define their influence? Describe a situation in which that influence can be seen.

What is your favorite memory of your sibling(s)? Least favorite memory? Why?

What have you learned from your siblings? Describe the situation you were in when you learned this lesson. What were you all doing? What did they say? How did you react?

What have your siblings learned from you? Describe the situation in which they learned this lesson. What were you all doing? What did you say? How did they react?

Has the size of your family or your birth order (oldest, youngest) had any effect on you?

Grandparents and extended family

Do your grandparents see you often? Have your grandparents passed down any special traditions to you? What are those traditions? What do those traditions mean to you now, in the twenty-first century?

Have your grandparents had very different lives, in comparison with your own life? How? Have they made any decisions or sacrifices that shaped your life?

Do you have any family heirlooms? What are they? Describe the objects. Why are the objects important? What traditions do these heirlooms represent? What will you pass along to your heirs someday?

What family legends have you heard (about any family member, including ancestors)? What do those legends mean to you?

Are any special places associated with your family? Think about homelands, vacation spots, the site of historic events, the family house, and so forth.

General family questions

When was your family most proud of you? Why? How did they show their pride? How did you react?

When was your family disappointed in you? What did you learn from that event?

What qualities do you appreciate most about your family? Why? How does your family show those qualities?

What would you change about your family, if you could? Why?

Have you ever helped your family? When? What did you do? How did they react?

Have you ever wanted to help your family but were unable to do so? How did you feel? Why couldn't you help? What did you do instead?

What is your earliest memory of your family? What does that memory show about your childhood?

Describe a typical holiday celebration of your family. What do your customs reveal about your family and your place in it?

Describe a typical Saturday morning, Friday night, weekday evening, and/or weekday morning in your house. What does your routine reveal about your family and your place in it?

How are you different from your family? What does that difference reveal about your own identity?

School days

Because you're applying for admission to a school, it's not surprising that the institution is interested in your life as a student. The questions in this section of the inventory are designed to draw forth your thoughts on your school days — what you learned in your classes and about yourself. The memories you retrieve here may be useful for application questions about important experiences, such as "Describe an event that shaped your personality." You may also find material here for questions about your successes and failures in school, your most challenging or interesting academic experience, books or fictional characters that you admire, favorite teachers (for the "person who influenced you" question), and so on.

Strengths

What is your favorite subject? Why do you like it? Describe a typical day in this class. What sort of activity in this class do you most enjoy? Describe yourself taking part in that activity.

What skills or talents do you have that you must apply in your favorite class or classes? In what activities (lab reports, term or research papers, tests, discussions, projects, and so on) do you excel?

Describe a project you're proud of. How long did you work on it? How did you go about your work? Why was this project special?

Weaknesses

What subject is hard for you? How did you meet that challenge? Were you successful? What did you learn from your success or failure?

Describe a project or assignment that you wish you could do over. Why were you dissatisfied with the initial result? What would you do differently now? What did this project teach you about your own strengths and weaknesses as a student?

Who has helped you through tough times in school? What did they do? How did you react? What changed because of their help?

Teachers

Who is your favorite teacher? Describe a typical experience with that teacher. Describe a special, out-of-the-ordinary experience with that teacher. What did you learn about yourself from this teacher? What message would you like to give this teacher?

Have you had a teacher who was tough on you? How did you react to the challenge? What did you learn about yourself from this teacher?

Learning styles

Think about silent study, discussion, notes, creative projects, writing, and other academic tasks. Which ones are hard and which ones are easy?

How do you budget your time? Can you describe a long-term project and how you scheduled the work?

How do you handle pressure? Describe one time when you felt nervous or stressed out about an assignment. What did you do? What did you learn from that situation?

Are you the same student you were ten years ago? Five years ago? Two years ago? What have you learned about yourself *as a student*?

Group experiences

Describe a group project that went well. Why was the group successful? Did everyone participate? Did anyone goof off? How did the group handle the goof-off? Were you a leader? What did you do? What would you do differently?

Describe a group project that did not go well. Why did it fail? What would you do differently if you were assigned that project again? What did you learn from that project?

General school issues

What would you like your teachers to say about you at graduation? What do you think they *will* say about you at graduation?

When you return for your reunion (pick a year), how do you think you will feel? What reaction will you want from your former classmates? What qualities will stand out in their minds when they think about you? Why?

Did any special or significant events occur during your years at your current school? Describe the most important event. How did you react? How did that event shape your ideas?

Community

"No man is an island," wrote poet John Donne. (No woman is either, I might add, feminist that I am.) You live in a community, a country, and increasingly, in a global village. These questions are designed to clarify your thoughts about your role in those three contexts. Answers here might apply to essays asking about (surprise, surprise) your community, but they are also relevant to questions about your values. The "write about an issue you care about" question is a natural for this section.

The locals

Describe your local community. What makes it unique? When you think about the community, how do you fit in? How does the community see you?

Have you contributed to your community? In what way? How did that experience affect you?

If you could change one thing about your community, what would it be? Why? Realistically, can you change your community?

Which values of your community do you share? What makes you different from others in your community?

What issues face your community? Think about the environment, social interactions, government, the economy, and so forth. Which issue is most important to you? Why?

Do you still live in the community of your birth? If not, why did you move? What was the experience of moving like for you and for your family? What does your community of origin mean to you, now that you no longer live there?

Your country

Think about your country. What does it mean to you? What do you appreciate about your country?

What aspect of your country would you like to change? Why? What would you substitute? How would you go about making a change?

What sort of contribution do you see yourself making to your country now or in the future?

Which values of your country do you share? Which do you reject? Why?

Do you still live in the country of your birth? If not, why did you move? What was the experience of moving like for you and for your family? What does your country of origin mean to you, now that you no longer live there?

Global village

How connected do you feel to events happening in other countries? Which events concern you the most? The least? Why?

When you think about your future, do you see yourself as participating in diplomatic or governmental relations? What will be or could be your role?

What responsibility do citizens of your country have towards citizens of other countries? How should those responsibilities be met?

What draws people from many countries together? What separates people? What should be changed about the way people relate to their own nations and to other nations?

Which issues are of global importance? Think about the environment, diplomacy, the economy, health, nutrition, war, terrorism, and so on. Which issue is most important to you? Why? What can you do about the issue?

The Future

The application era of your life is future-oriented. You're thinking about the next few years at the institution you're applying to, and the institution is considering the next few years with you. But you're also pondering your long-range plans: career or personal goals. Similarly, the institution wants to know what contribution you will make to the world. These matters are sometimes addressed directly by questions such as "What are your career plans?" and "How would you be involved in campus life?" Material from this section may also be useful for a general "Write about yourself and your goals" question or the "issue important to you question."

Personal

Describe your life as you imagine it 5, 10, 15, and 50 years from now. Where will you be living? What will your day be like? With whom will you live? What will you be proud of?

What will your town paper say as they report on your 100th birthday?

Professional

What are your career plans? Why did you choose this particular career? Where will you work?

How do you hope to contribute to the field? How will you go about making that contribution?

What branch of the field most attracts you? Why?

What current trends in your field will shape the future of the profession? Which trends will fade away? Explain your reasons.

The world

What current trends will shape the future? What trends will fade away? Explain your reasons.

What will your generation contribute to the world? How will your generation be different from those that preceded it?

What is the greatest danger to the future of the world? What is the world's greatest hope?

Think about any element of modern society (computers, books, the media, cars, and so on). How will that element change in the future? Why? How will society be different because of that change?

Identity

Your identity is made up of a set of descriptions that you apply to yourself or that others apply to you. Some factors that create your identity are your race, ethnic background, nationality, religion, gender, sexual orientation, and age. In this section you may come up with material for the general "personal statement" or "tell us about yourself" questions.

Think about your race, ethnic background, religion, gender, and other aspects of your identity. Do any of those factors affect how you see the world? Do any of those factors affect how others see you? Explain. Also, describe a situation in which one or more of those factors mattered.

Think about physical appearance and ability, mental ability, and emotions. How would you describe yourself in terms of these qualities? Have any of these factors mattered in terms of how you see yourself or how others see you?

Should any of the factors cited in the preceding two questions matter? Why or why not?

Describe a situation in which you were a minority because of some aspect of your identity. (Perhaps the people around you were of a different age, religion, or race.) How did you feel? What did you learn from that experience?

What adjectives (descriptive words) apply to you? Why? Think of situations in which you displayed those qualities.

What's the first thing about yourself that you would tell a new friend? Why?

What does your best friend know about you that no one else knows?

If you had to transfer to a new school, how would you choose a lunch table? What would you look for? What would the people at that lunch table see when you sat down? What would you talk about?

Describe your ideal roommate. Why have you chosen these characteristics?

What has been most important in shaping your personality? Name one person. Describe one event.

People

"People who need people are the luckiest people in the world," sang Barbra Streisand. So everybody's lucky, except perhaps for a hermit or two in a far-off desert. *You* certainly need people, and not just the admissions counselors who will read you essay. The questions in this section should help you pinpoint figures that have been important in shaping your life — material that will help you answer the question about "figures that have been important in shaping your life." (Am I clever, or what?)

Scan the family section of the appendix and pick out people who have been important to you. Describe their influence on you. Think of situations in which that influence was obvious.

Think about world figures, both present day and historical. Whom do you admire? Why? What contributions do you attribute to those people? Would you like to contribute in the same way or in a different way? If you could sit down to chat with any of those people, what would you say?

Review the books you read for school or for pleasure. Which characters made a strong impression on you? Why? If you could chat with one of those characters, what would you say? How do you imagine the character would answer you? Why?

The No-Category Category

I call this section "no category" because "general" is too boring. Here are the questions that don't fit anywhere else!

What books have you read recently? Which was best? Why?

What media do you consult regularly (television, Internet, radio, newspapers, magazines, and so forth)? What are the advantages and disadvantages of those media? How would you change the medium if you could?

What is the most creative element of modern life? (Think film, computers, art, whatever.) Why? How do you create?

Where have you traveled? What made a strong impression on you? Why?

What was the best summer of your life? Why?

Have you participated in any volunteer programs? What did you learn? What did others learn from you?

What is art? Beauty? The meaning of life? The price of tomatoes? (Sorry. Big philosophical terms make me yearn for the concrete details of life.)

Index

• Symbols •

• A •

• B •

• C •

• F •

• G •

• H •

• I •

• J •

• K •

• L •

• M •

• N •

• O •

• P •

• T •

• U •

• V •

• W •

• Y •